# Postmodern Suburban Spaces

Joseph George

# Postmodern Suburban Spaces

Philosophy, Ethics, and Community in Post-War
American Fiction

Joseph George
University of North Carolina at Greensboro
Greensboro, North Carolina, USA

ISBN 978-3-319-41005-0      ISBN 978-3-319-41006-7   (eBook)
DOI 10.1007/978-3-319-41006-7

Library of Congress Control Number: 2016954924

Cover design by Samantha Johnson

Printed on acid-free paper

This Palgrave Macmillan imprint is published by Springer Nature
The registered company is Springer International Publishing AG Switzerland

*To my Dad, still the smartest guy I know.*

# ACKNOWLEDGMENTS

Like all projects, this book owes its existence to contributions from my various communities, beginning with my fellow graduate students at the University of North Carolina at Greensboro. In particular, I owe thanks to Matt Mullins, Dan Burns, Zach Laminack, Andrew Pisano, and Cindy Webb, for the thoughtful conversation, well-timed comments, and, of course, the many suggestions for further reading.

I would also like to give special thanks to those who helped guide this project in its form as a dissertation, starting with my readers Tony Cuda, for reminding me to act like a literary critic and for offering boundless reassurance, and Scott Romine, for exposing me to some of the most important texts in my academic development and for supplying infallibly precise and essential critiques. I am most indebted to my adviser Christian Moraru, for introducing me to thinkers who still shape my understanding of what literature is and does, for the intellectual hospitality he has extended, and for the encouragement and guidance he has given as the project evolved from dissertation to book. I hope to become a scholar worthy of their example.

Finally, I need to offer special thanks to my children: Dylan, Alyse, and Kierstyn. I thank the older two for being patient as I kept my nose in books and fingers on keyboards to finish this up, and the youngest for listening to me read through drafts as I took her for walks or tried to rock her to sleep. It would take a book ten times this length to tell you how much I love you.

# Contents

Introduction: Nowhere to Now Here     1

1   Against Fence Thinking: Welcoming the Racial Enemy     43

2   My Home Is Your Home: Property,
Propriety, and Neighbors     81

3   Domesticated Strangers: Fissures Within
the Nuclear Family     121

4   Assimilation and Appropriation: Contest
and Collaboration in Global Suburbia     163

Conclusion: Changing the Suburban Myth     183

Work Cited     191

Index     203

# Introduction: Nowhere to Now Here

At the end of Richard Yates' 1961 novel *Revolutionary Road*, protagonist Frank Wheeler finally proves that he does not belong in the suburbs. He and his wife April claimed as much throughout the story, envisioning themselves as the lone intellectuals in a place where "[n]obody thinks or feels or cares any more; nobody gets excited or believes in anything except their own comfortable little God damn mediocrity" (60). This disposition prompted a plan to abandon their neighborhood for a faux-Bohemian lifestyle in the French countryside, the failure of which occupies much of the novel's plot. When a despairing April dies from complications caused by a self-administered abortion, the shock destroys Frank's sense of propriety and drives him to behavior unbecoming of a middle-class suburbanite. The narration of the scene highlights Frank's difference from his neighbors:

> The Revolutionary Hill Estates had not been designed to accommodate a tragedy. Even at night, as if on purpose, the development held no looming shadows and no gaunt silhouettes. It was invincibly cheerful, a toyland of white and pastel houses whose bright, uncurtained windows winked blandly through a dappling of green and yellow leaves. Proud floodlights were trained on some of the lawns, on some of the neat front doors and on the hips of some of the berthed, ice-cream colored automobiles. (323)

Where Frank believed that his intelligence and temperament separated him from other suburbanites, the narrator makes a distinction between the depth of his sadness and the neighborhood's original design; it is Frank's

© The Author(s) 2016
J. George, *Postmodern Suburban Spaces*,
DOI 10.1007/978-3-319-41006-7_1

"desperate grief" that makes him "indecently out of place" because his neighbors are too inoculated by their televisions and mod cons to respond to his calls for help (323). The emphasis on design or intention found in this passage, and in fact throughout *Revolutionary Road*, foregrounds one of the central facts about postwar American suburbs: more than just a residential model, they are imagined to be a specific type of place for a specific type of person. The phrases often used to describe them, "common interest development" (CID) or "planned community," reveal the intentionality associated with the phenomenon, a fact Yates addresses with the Mrs. Givings character, a realtor constantly searching for "*really* congenial people...*Our* kind of people" (336). For the private contractors, Federal regulators, and affluent homeowners who hastened the suburban boom, the "right type of people" were those who best fit a certain American ideal, following a Cold War imperative to separate the capitalist West from godless Soviets. The marketing, and legal contracts, that defined the postwar American suburbs, in all their variety, was motivated by an ideal of the American Dream for the "right" people.

Yates' novel roundly rejects the victory narratives, to use Tom Engelhardt's phrase, on which the model was founded. Along with contemporaneous novels *The Man in the Grey Flannel Suit* by Sloan Wilson (1955) and *Rabbit, Run* by John Updike (1960), *Revolutionary Road* has become a classic of American suburban fiction, among the first to chronicle the middle-class malaise that has become as integral to the phenomenon as its well-manicured lawns.[1] For William Whyte, John Keats, and other anti-suburban crusaders, Yates' Frank Wheeler, Wilson's Tom Rath, and Updike's Harry Angstrom serve as literary representations of larger social and cultural problems, evidence that the space is best suited to materialist sellouts who are ultimately undone by their own privilege. According to critic Catherine Jurca, author of the most important study of suburban fiction *White Diaspora*, these characters embody "sentimental dispossession"—"the affective dislocation by which white middle-class suburbanites begin to see themselves as spiritually and culturally impoverished by prosperity" (7). What was intended to be an American utopia has become instead an empty dystopia, where conformist fakes are daily confronted with empty doppelgängers across the yard and down the street.

Although Yates and his contemporaries certainly mock these middle-class values, their works are not solely satirical. As they decry the consumerism, conformity, and conservatism on which the residential model was founded, these novels also perform a critical reconceiving of the phenomenon by thinking about neighborhoods, first and foremost, as a place where people live. They take the communal aspect of suburbia seriously and imagine what happens when a group of people share a space designed to accommodate one particular identity. If, as I will demonstrate throughout this introduction, the American suburb is an imaginary space, then the portrayal of Revolutionary Hills Estates and similar neighborhoods directly addresses the use of this quintessential modern American residential landscape.

It is fitting, then, that Yates opens his novel with a smaller type of planned community: The Laurel Players, an amateur theater troupe in which April Wheeler is the main attraction. With his characteristic acerbity, Yates' narrator describes the quick establishment and dissolution of a group devoted to a single ethos, providing a study of suburban associations in miniature. Over the course of a few pages, the players shift from a team unified in a common pursuit—in which they "disarm each other...with peals of forgiving laughter" and exchange "apologetic nods" when a partner flubs a line—to an affiliation of backbiters perpetually disappointed with one another. The narration repeatedly draws attention to the high ideals the players took to their performance, noting that they may be "an amateur production," but they are a "costly and very serious one." The director of the performance puts it more bluntly: "Remember this. We're not just putting on a play here. We're establishing a community theater, and that's a pretty important thing to be doing" (4, 5). And yet, the individuals who belong to the troupe could not embody that ideal, a point Yates makes via a telling social metaphor: the "*virus* of calamity, dormant and threatening all these weeks, had erupted and now spread from the helplessly vomiting [lead actor] until it infected everyone in the cast but April Wheeler" (8–9, emphasis mine). The phrasing here not only describes the unsuccessful staging, but also a shared guilt that cannot be isolated to one source. Yates underscores the communicable nature of the failure by expanding his gaze to locate the Players' ambition within the larger social milieu, drawing attention to the audience—who, "[a]nyone could see...were a better than average crowd, in terms of education and employment and good health" and who "considered this a significant evening"—watching with great expectations for "the brave idea" of the endeavor, "the healthy, hopeful sound of it: the birth of a really good community theater right here, among themselves" (6–7). Yates ironically twists the audience's presumptions, as the same social conventions that led them to judge and ultimately disregard the Players have now become binding, forcing them to behave in a manner contrary to their desires, as decency required them to greet the finale not with disgust or even relief, but with applause that was "conscientiously long enough to permit two curtain calls" (10).

At first glance, the downfall of the Laurel Players reinforces the stereotype of the "socially hyperactive" suburbanite, who is too shallow, too caught up in competitiveness or material goods to appreciate depth of feeling or authenticity (Gans 154). The suburbs, these critics suggest, are simply and unavoidably filled with the wrong type of people. But as savage as his portrayal may be, Yates refuses to stop at such easy answers. "Blame for the failure of the Laurel Players could hardly be fobbed off on Conformity or The Suburbs or American Society Today," the narrator explains, "How could new jokes be told about their neighbors when these very neighbors had sat and sweated in their audience? Donaldsons, Cramers, Wingates, and all, they had come to [the Players' production of] *The Petrified Forest* with a surprisingly generous openness of mind, and had been let down" (60). The juxtaposition here between the common critiques of suburbia, complaints that Frank himself levels in his most condescending moments, and generous neighbors underscores the utilitarian nature of the theater project: everyone had gathered in pursuit of a particular goal, and that pursuit corrupted their community. The neighborhood formed its bonds of association on unreal, impossible goals and ignored the needs of one another. But, as I will explain throughout this introduction, *Revolutionary Road* uses this judgment not as an end to itself, but as a means to envision a different type of suburban interaction, one based on care for the other people with whom one lives.

*Postmodern Suburban Spaces* argues that the critique and reimagining of suburbia found in *Revolutionary Road* is far more common than commentators have recognized. The received wisdom insists that, regardless of the way neighborhood designs and populations have evolved over the past 70 years, American suburbia is nothing but a materialistic wonderland reserved for conformists and fakes; but works ranging from *Revolutionary Road* to Gloria Naylor's *Linden Hills* to Gish Jen's *Mona in the Promised Land* repeatedly portray neighborhoods as fundamentally residential, places where people live together. This attention does not exempt real-world suburbs from the reputation they have earned, but the fiction does ask us to think of them not as places that advance a single identity, but as spaces for face-to-face interpersonal relations. *Postmodern Suburban Spaces* argues that the usual distinctions between suburban insider and outsider are too reductive, insufficient for describing the depth of pathos Yates gives his seemingly shallow Wheelers, the heroic quality Cheever imbues in Neddy

Merrill and Johnny Rake, or the something "quite intricate and fierce occur[ing] in homes" that fascinated Updike (Howard 11). Rather than celebrate the nationalist and materialist conformity of pro-suburban stories or endorse the antagonistic stance of anti-suburban propaganda, I contend that most fictions instead highlight the messy and contingent results of infinite individuals sharing space with one another, making fractured and non-determining communities together. Where planned suburban communities are built around an ethos of middle-class values—for example, homeownership, materialism, the nuclear family, the safety of children above all other values—the fictional communities treat shared space, proximity, as the only binding aspect that the members have in common.

These stories require a nuanced interpretative approach that understands literary fiction as a creative response to larger social forces and philosophical desires, which often combines sympathy with satire and refuses to cohere into a fully totalizing comprehension of the text. I provide that approach by tracing instances of what I call "critical hospitality" in suburban fiction: moments when others—in the phenomenological sense of the word—share space, resulting in face-to-face relations that defy the limiting and contractual forms of community imposed by an intended design and forces individuals to construct their identities in relation to those in proximity. By aesthetically expressing the complexity of these interactions, literary fiction depicts singular modes of association that allow for plurality and difference, simultaneously advancing and critiquing suburbia's potential as a relational matrix. A range of authors—including white male realists Richard Ford and John Irving, playful postmodernists Don DeLillo and Joyce Carol Oates, satirists Tom Perrotta and T.C. Boyle, and chroniclers of the immigrant experience Gish Jen and Chang-rae Lee—reject the traditional imperatives of exclusion and authenticity and focus instead on the explosive relationships that occur when people dwell together. This refocusing of imaginary suburbia can open possibilities for the real-world suburbs, better connecting the stories to real moments of interaction.

## OUR SUBURBAN CENTURY

When the 2012 census revealed that "in 27 of the nation's 51 largest metropolitan areas, city centers grew faster than suburbs between July 2010 and July 2011," the fact highlighted not a resurgence in urban living populations, but the dominance of the suburbs, which had previously "grown faster than city centers in every decade since the 1920s"

(Doughtery). Suburbs have always been a part of American life, often in the form of more natural areas surrounding metropolises in the Midwest and Northeast. However, the model's rise to prominence truly began with the Long Island Levittown neighborhood—followed by two more Levittowns, in Pennsylvania and New Jersey—which established the style that most Americans associate with the term "suburbia": rows and rows of single-family houses, with the same floor plan, governed by fairly strict guidelines. Traditional suburban sprawl stems from a ring style development, in which wealthier land owners, dissatisfied with the quality of newcomers to the area or desiring more "rustic" landscapes, abandon the inner-ring neighborhoods near the city for expanding outer-ring suburbs. Likewise, penurbs—a type of neighborhood that "looks like the city thinks the country should look"—have built up in Maryland (Goddard 2). Other increasingly common suburban models eschew the hub–spoke relationship of city and suburb by enticing phenomena most often associated with urban areas, including big box stores, business and medical centers, and even sports arenas to create more self-sufficient "edge cities." Finally, gated communities and "lifestyle suburbs," designed for everything from gay families to the elderly to Disney employees, embrace the exclusivity that suburbia has always implied. More than just changes in layout, these neighborhoods also accommodate a wide variety of housing structures, from traditional track homes to McMansions, apartments to town homes to duplexes.

Unsurprisingly, in the same way the postwar American suburb has changed in structure, it has also changed in make-up over the past 70 years. Where early American suburbs were relegated to those with money to afford transportation to the city and not reliant on the services offered by urban areas, the Levittown suburb emphasized a new middle class, populated by "new money" veterans returning from the front. While cost of living prices have always prevented those with certain incomes from buying property in these areas, a number of initiatives—including the housing stipend in the 1944 Serviceman's Readjustment Act, the 1956 Federal Highway Act, and the Housing and Community Development Acts of 1974 and 1985, and the more recent 2009 Making Home Affordable program (MHA)—have made it possible for those of different classes to move to suburban neighborhoods. At the same time, the Great Recession has struck suburbia particularly hard and, as a result, "the number of poor individuals living in the suburbs of the nation's largest metropolitan areas rose by more than half (53 percent), or 5.3 million...more than twice the rate of increase in cities, where the poor population grew by 23 percent, or 2.4 million" (Kneebone and Berube 17). More importantly, the racial make-up of the modern suburb has changed. As I will discuss in greater detail in the next chapter, suburbia has been a contested space, where, as David Roediger's *Working Toward Whiteness* explains, ethnic Europeans such as Jews, Poles, and Irish staked their part of the white mainstream, in part by distinguishing themselves from those of African or Mexican descent. And yet, despite the rhetorical and legal standards that aided these maneuvers, the past 70 years have seen growing suburban diversification, not only in the form of non-white Americans moving into neighborhoods, but also the influx of immigrants into the areas.

Even with all of these changes, Americans still think of suburbia as a fairly stagnant and monolithic space. They see, more or less, the opening of the television series *Weeds*: rows of identical houses, populated by families of identical white people, showing off their identical material goods, a presentation scored with a condescending song about "little boxes made of ticky-tacky [that] all look the same" (Reynolds). Undeterred by this unfavorable picture, Americans still also think of it as a homeowner's utopia, which combines urban sophistication with rural simplicity, giving most Americans their best opportunity to have a house and a yard, which, as I will discuss in a later chapter, has always held a privileged position in the American mind. As opposed to cramped city dwellings, the suburban home supplies citizens with their own space and (at least the pretense of) autonomy to exercise one's individual will. To that end, homeownership also signifies success and individual achievement, as found in the rhetoric of real estate advertisements that proclaim the peace and tranquility once enjoyed by those in the country. The correlation between suburban homeownership and success is so strong that even when specific neighborhoods were poorly designed and constructed, residents believed that "these new houses and raw neighborhoods could always be upgraded" (Hayden 152). Suburbia also offers a tranquil community; against the commotion and difference that marked the urban milieu, suburbanites live among other suburbanites—those who have also earned the right to own their house, who send their children to the same school, and who shop at the same grocery stores. Inevitably, suburbanites encounter their neighbors, but the decorum codified in neighborhood covenants and contracts calls for limited interaction, claiming a middle ground between interest and intrusiveness, solitude and isolation.

But, as commentators have often observed, these are luxuries reserved for those who live inside these neighborhoods; outsiders have considerably less. Suburbs exemplify what Robert A. Beauregard calls "parasitic urbanization," which produced "the trauma that devastated older, industrial cities, created a crisis of national consequences, and undermined the way of life that had defined achievement in the United States for hundreds of years"; because of this shift, the "dominance of the center—the industrial cities had been the nuclei of the emerging metropolitan areas—was replaced by a fragmentation of the periphery brought about by suburban development" (4). Concentrating wealth in neighborhoods adjacent to cities harms schools, which are funded by local property values, relegating underprivileged students, who often need more attention and aid to compete, to the schools with the fewest resources. Defenders of such practices regularly invoke principles of liberty, claiming that suburbanites have no financial responsibility for places where they do not live and for schools where their children do not attend, but this view downplays the inextricable link between the two spaces. The majority of suburbanites still work in the city, and often rely on it for cultural and commercial enrichment, a connection made possible by municipal infrastructure and services, such as access via roads and police protection. The reliance on automobiles to commute from home and work creates a greater pollution problem and exacerbates the country's continued reliance on natural gas. Furthermore, the nature of suburban sprawl necessarily requires the abandonment of old abodes and building new ones, resulting in a ring effect. As the affluent move further out, the ring encroaches further into forests and natural resources, diminishing wildlife preserves and leaving behind shells of steel and concrete to be occupied only by the indigent trapped in failing cities.

Moreover, the emphasis on "like-minded neighbors" has led to the twin problems of conformity and exclusion. Long before the establishment of the modern suburb, government-endorsed mortgage lenders worked to ensure homogeneity in neighborhoods. The worst early offender was the Federal Housing Administration, which "allowed personal and agency bias to affect the kinds of loans it guaranteed—or, equally important, refused to guarantee" (Jackson 207). On a more immediate level, communities wrote their own racial covenants to bar members of certain ethnicities, setting forth standards that remained influential even after they were deemed illegal by the 1948 Supreme Court decision Shelly v. Kraemer. Perhaps the most famous examples of suburban racism are the incidents of "white flight," in which the middle-class Caucasians abandon urban areas when they become too racially diverse. As will be discussed in Chap. 1, the escapees rarely couched their objections in explicitly racial terms, but instead referred to either property values or safety. According to Catherine Jurca, the concern for safety leads to "victimization narratives," stories about urban crime that allow "Babbitts begin to think of themselves as Biggers"; these narratives provided justification for well-to-do citizens who wanted to avoid difference by leaving the city (8). This affinity for similarity also gives rise to another notorious element of suburban life: the Home Owners' Associations (HOAs) and their covenants, conditions, and restrictions (CC&Rs). These phenomena have become paradigmatic in suburbia, contributing to cultural and economic gentrification that has diminished all involved.

These myriad problems are particularly troubling because, despite what some supporters insist, the suburbs did not "just happen." Rather, their proliferation is largely the result of a number of political, commercial, and social forces all working to expand the US dominance initiated in the years following World War II, a fact captured by the term "planned community." As I will discuss in greater detail in Chap. 2, the first Levittown subdivision came into existence to alleviate a mid-1940s housing crisis, but even this was not just a natural occurrence; it was partly influenced by Herbert Hoover's valorization of private ownership as a key aspect of the American ethos before the Great Depression and exacerbated by the prevalence of young soldiers returning from the Great War with young families waiting and a housing stipend from the GI Bill in their pockets. Levittown was not the only solution posed by government officials, but it beat out other options—such as the publicly funded Greenville housing project—because of its connotations of individualism and capitalism. Thus, Levittown and the various modern American suburbs that followed resulted from "enormous" federal influence, from the Federal Highway Act of 1916 and the Interstate Highway Act of 1956, which "moved the government toward a transportation policy emphasizing and benefitting the road, the truck, and the private motorcar" to an "incentive to detached-home living provided by the deduction of mortgage interest and real-estate taxes from their gross income" to even "the reimbursement formulas for water-line and sewer construction" (Jackson 191). Furthermore, explicitly partisan government actions, such as Johnson's "War on Poverty" and Nixon's suburban strategies, continued to shepherd middle-class whites out of the city while trapping African Americans in urban project housing. As these divisions crystallized, politicians learned to build constituencies along these lines, most famously by conservatives Richard Nixon in 1969 and Ronald Reagan in 1980, but also by Barack Obama in 2012. These forces harnessed the power of middle-class wealth to advance their interests, and therefore had a stake in protecting suburbanization.

The political and economic forces at work here remind us once again of the ideological stakes of postwar American suburbs. More than just a residential landscape, writes Dolores Hayden, suburbia has become "the site of promises, dreams, and fantasies...a landscape of imagination where Americans situate ambitions for upward mobility and economic security, ideals about freedom and private property, and longings for social harmony and spiritual uplift" (3). The decisions that shape suburban communities—those concerning the inclusion or exclusion of certain peoples, or the behavior valorized by group standards—are made in response to real-world concerns, particularly during the Cold War period in which the suburbs thrived. In fact, the modern American suburb is a product of war, and the Levittown subdivisions were very much built using production techniques streamlined in the industrial war effort, as indicated by the housing stipend included in the GI Bill that gave "official endorsement and support to the view that the 16 million GI's of World War II should return to civilian life with a home of their own" (Jackson 233). As an example of what Alan Nadel has called "containment culture," the postwar suburb was part of a "privileged American narrative during the cold war" devoted to the "containment of communism" in which conformity "became a form of public knowledge through the pervasive performances of and allusions to [these] containment narratives" (2, 4). To examine the tactics by which suburban fiction refigures these tightly designed associations, then, we must first step back and trace the motivations behind suburbia to their roots in Western social contract theory. By looking at the connections between early democratic philosophy and modern suburban construction, we can see the ideal communities that planners desire and the assumptions that authors such as Yates complicate.

## Toward a Philosophy of the Suburb

I believe the clearest manifestation of suburbia's social philosophy is in the use of HOAs and CC&Rs. Of course, not all suburbs have such regulations; however, they are central to the sitcom-style tract housing that dominates the American imagination and, therefore, inextricable from the symbolic suburbs engaged by the fiction I examine. Nominally, CC&Rs

exist to maintain property values for all residents; they "allow owners to tailor their control over neighboring uses, and because these restrictions are ostensibly private and consensual, they can do so in considerably greater detail than would be possible through publicly imposed constraints in zoning" (Brooks and Rose 48). By looking closely at philosophy motivating even the ideological constructions of suburbia, we see a clear picture of the assumptions about selfhood made by its designers and the contractual nature of the communities they plan.

Most importantly, CC&Rs reveal the contractualism associated with suburban communities. For many neighborhoods, CC&Rs provide the most immediate form of governance. According to urbanist Jon C. Teaford, the limited involvement of state and federal governments is part of suburbia's allure as homeowners believe that CC&Rs reflect the interests of actual residents better than laws developed by a bureaucratic legislature. "[T]o millions of Americans who wished to stake out their own spheres," Teaford argues, suburbia provides "diverse ways of life away from the restrictive authority of big-city assessors, health authorities, and police, and removed from the corruption, congestion, and stressful hubbub of the central city" (41). Similarly, Robert Jay Dilger describes HOAs as "private governments" that "generally meet the expectations of [its] members, real estate developers, and local government officials" (158). Even communitarian Daniel A. Bell, who recognizes the very real threat HOAs pose to the public sphere, acknowledges that a liberal democratic society gives people "a right to freely associate in communities not governed by such virtues as fraternity and social equality," and therefore, "[i]f people want to form hierarchical and exclusivist communities...they have a right to do so" (168). As each of these examples indicate, contractual thinking emphasizes individual rights and carries that into the social realm; to "stake out their own spheres," suburbanites view one another as fellow signatories first.

Despite this language of individual freedom, HOA "horror stories" have only increased in recent years, including incidents in which an 8-year-old girl was prohibited from using sidewalk chalk in her driveway or homeowner sued for displaying a flag with a football team logo.[2] A number of anti-HOA activists, such as Ward Lucas, have cropped up in revolt, decrying HOAs as a violation of liberty tantamount to totalitarian rule.[3] Political scientist Evan MacKenzie has made the most thorough argument against HOAs, contending that the practice has transformed communal living spaces into "privatopias." In the absence of larger government regulation, McKenzie argues, "[p]rivate developers and businessmen... have long been the dominant force in American urban planning," and as a result, "American real estate development corporations, with government as a silent partner, have chosen to build a new kind of community that serves as a monument to privatism" (7–8). The potential for self-determination offered by limited government and local rule, McKenzie claims, is undermined by commercial interests and binding contracts created by developers and realtors—many of whom no longer actually live in the neighborhood.[4] To McKenzie, these contracts pervert the ideals of classical social contract theory as they create "a state of nature devoid of people except for the developer-creator, who begets the 'community' and its social order to his liking and makes it unchangeable" (146). But Michael Monohan, who shares McKenzie's distrust of CC&Rs, believes that they reveal the competitive individualism inherent in Thomas Hobbes' vision of the commonwealth. This debate has been furthered by several critics who find a correlation between suburban governance and the theories of Hobbes, John Locke, and Jean-Jacques Rousseau—or their American followers Jefferson, Emerson, and Thoreau—even if they disagree about the accuracy of the theory's application to the suburbs.[5]

Of these thinkers, I find Rousseau particularly relevant as the connections between his social theories and his vision of selfhood reveal some of the key assumptions motivating suburban associations. The right to choose one's associates is paramount in Rousseau's philosophy as people only form communities with those who will benefit them; because this requirement necessarily limits the diversity and size of societies, Rousseau prefers smaller civil units, such as the village or the city-state, which anticipates the suburb's position on the periphery of the city or country.[6] Rousseau insists on these smaller units because he wishes to defend the right of autonomy. As in the suburbs, Rousseau's contract only allows for a restricted autonomy, but both arrangements justify these restrictions by claiming that individuals can only achieve their wishes through associations and therefore must accept the burdens required to maintain them. Furthermore, Rousseau believes that self-interest or self-love (*amour de soi*) benefits a society because a self-interested individual will do what is necessary to reinforce the community that secures his or her advantages. CC&Rs operate under the same logic, claiming that a homeowner who takes care of his or her own property, for example, will raise the value of all the properties in a neighborhood. Finally, self-esteem (*amour-propre*) can only come from associations as isolated individuals have no others to acknowledge and respect their rights. And while Rousseau fears that *amour-propre* might distract from the more beneficial *amour de soi*, a certain aspiration for the rights conferred by social interactions initially motivates community formation. Again, the CC&Rs are the key here—they provide a model of interaction and expectation that allows individuals to achieve these three goals.

Rousseau's notion of the "general will" helps explain why property owners would accept HOA restrictions. According to Rousseau, the pre-social savage man may be perfectly self-sufficient, but natural calamities and the desire for rights drives him or her into societies. In the same way homeowners accept certain restraints on the use of their property to gain admission into a neighborhood, Rousseau argues that "[w]hat man loses through the social contract is his natural liberty and an unlimited right to everything that tempts him and that he can acquire. What he gains is civil liberty and the proprietary ownership of all he possesses" (151). Despite assent to these restrictions, most people are vigilant to avoid unnecessary and harmful burdens. Rousseau insists that each member of a society ensures the necessity of regulations by submitting to the "general will." The general will is the manifestation of the people's decision—not located in a particular individual, such as Hobbes' all-powerful sovereign, or even in the will of a representative body, but rather in the collective opinion of a society's members. And while Rousseau does concede that private interest might initially contradict the general will, he claims that the very fact that most accept these burdens proves their benefit. The society Rousseau envisions "is one of a limited number of solutions to the problem of collective action: citizens who evaluate alternatives from the vantage point of their common interests and are prepared to act upon this judgment can avoid the unwanted outcomes awaiting rational egoists whose wills are fixed upon a narrower object" (Hill 39). In short, Rousseau's social contract secures the rights and protection craved by the modern citizen while preserving the inalienable autonomy he or she needs.[7]

Rousseau's vision of selfhood and the individual's relation to society is central to his theory of government. Although Rousseau never actually used the word "authenticity," Charles Guignon notes, "it seems obvious that all of the core assumptions built into the concept of authenticity are fully worked out in his writings" (59). Indeed, a concern for the authentic identity informs all of his discourses, including his political thought. The pre-social savage, Rousseau writes in his "Discourse on the Origins of Inequality," can be completely happy and sufficient without community: "as long as they applied themselves exclusively to tasks that a single individual could do and to the arts that did not require the cooperation of several hands, they lived as free, healthy, good and happy as they could in accordance with their nature: and they continued to enjoy among themselves the sweet rewards of independent intercourse" (65). In the same way *Emile* formulates a pedagogy that mitigates society's tendency to "denature" its members, Rousseau's political theories advance a social structure that protects the authentic self from the contamination of others. As indicated by his praise of Geneva as a state where "all private individuals" are "known to one another," and his claim that the group best suited for his social contract is one "where each member can be known to all, and where there is no need to impose a greater burden on a man than a man can bear," the society that best defends authenticity is one where members can recognize one another (26, 170). However, what they recognize is not the authentic neighbor—not the pre-social identity social contract theorists wish to defend—but a person who meets the requirements of a contract. These bonds then distinguish between a false external self, who performs the contract's terms, and a true, authentic internal self that is not affected by the community's demands. The notion of authenticity advanced by Rousseau motivates much of the suburban emphasis on conformity and gestures. According to Monohan, CC&Rs reconfigure the neighbor from a proximal figure—the result of a "shared social context which generates and conditions our interests in the same way that it conditions and renders our ability to individuate ourselves"—to an "isolated individual unit which happens to share loose, and purely formal, bonds with other similar units" (125, 123).

We see examples of Rousseauist thinking in the actions of modern HOAs. The articles published on the trade website HOAPulse.com repeatedly turn to rhetoric of reasoned individualism to help mitigate conflicts between the board and residents. Articles by Chuck Miller compare a "Community Association" to "a small government" because it has "a Board of Directors (the leaders), and a group of homeowners (the populace) governed by the Board of Directors" ("Dealing With Difficult People"). Accordingly, Miller valorizes difference, but warns against the self-interested board member who "generally wants to get on the board to further his or her own agenda" and is "not concerned about the democratic process nor the interest of their fellow board members" ("Going Rogue"). Each of these cases recall Rousseau's *amour-propre*—after all, the rich life envisioned by Miller can only come through association—while still assuming the presence of rational individualist actors who work together for personal self-interest. It is no wonder that David R.W. Brooks and Carol M. Rose find a theoretical model to examine neighborhood covenants in Rousseau's image of a Stag Hunt, a game in which "two (or more) persons, or, we might say, players, can do best by cooperating on a large task and sharing the proceeds (hunting a stag)," the success of which requires "assurance that the other is going to cooperate to take the larger prize" (14–15). So central are these concepts that they even appear in boilerplate CC&R disclaimers, such as the following from Washington's Canterwood subdivision near Puget Sound: "Keep in mind that the Covenants, Conditions & Restrictions (CC&Rs) are meant to protect the rights of each individual while maintaining an agreeable limit of decorum to ensure that a neighbor's property values and way of life are not adversely affected" (http://www.canterwood.org/). Good neighborliness, according to these examples, comes from adhering to the standards of the community, by heeding the terms of the contract, and showing one's self to be in agreement with them.

As these instances demonstrate, the intended suburban community is that of independent agents abiding by predetermined agreements. They have come together in pursuit of a set of articulated objectives—to claim a middle-class identity, safety, investment in property, and so on—and expect all members to work toward those goals. As they seek them out, participants accept certain restrictions and conform to certain standards to make themselves legible as such. Those who cannot, or are perceived to not, aid these efforts will be barred from entry or punished. These contracts assume the existence of a fully formed, autonomous self, for whom others are ultimately unnecessary for one's subjectivity.

## SUBURBAN ANXIETY TO SUBURBAN AUTHENTICITY

The concepts of independent selfhood and contractualism are repeatedly called into question in suburban fictions, including *Revolutionary Road*. Yates directs his full satirical ire at the rational individualism applied to a communal setting, as evidenced in the Laurel Players scene. When the players turn on one another, they do so because their collaborators have failed to live up to the goal and validate the contract. But where these failures result in little more than embarrassment for bull-headed members, the tone shifts dramatically in a later scene that both anticipates Frank's desperate run and references the Laurel Players debacle. Recovering from a long, bitter argument that culminates with Frank delivering a pompous lecture on his wife's inability to love, April spends her twilight hours penning a letter to repudiate his "*cowardly self-delusions*" (302). But after destroying her letters for being "weak with hate," April gives up and resigns herself to her existence. Frank awakes to find a sitcom-esque vision of marital happiness: a rich breakfast, an attentive wife, and a kiss to send him on his way to work. April stands smiling in the doorway until he leaves, then cleans up the house and performs the abortion that ends her life. But within this disparaging portrait, Yates advances a model of selfhood that contradicts the Romantic individualism on which suburbia was built. April's resignation comes after a meditation on the state of her life, for which she ultimately takes responsibility:

> What a subtle, treacherous thing it was to let yourself go that way! Because once you'd started it was terribly difficult to stop; soon you were saying "I'm sorry, of course you're right," and "Whatever you think is best," and "You're the most wonderful and valuable thing in the world," and the next thing you knew all honesty, all truth, was as far away and glimmering, as hopelessly unattainable as the world of the golden people. Then you discovered you were working at life the way the Laurel Players worked at *The Petrified Forest*, or the way Steve Kovick worked at his drums—earnest and sloppy and full of pretension and all wrong; you found you were saying yes when you meant no, and "We've got to be together in this thing" when you meant the very opposite; then you were breathing gasoline as if it were flowers and abandoning yourself to a delirium of love under the weight of a clumsy, grunting, red-faced man you didn't even like—Shep Campbell!—and then you were face to face, in total darkness, with the knowledge that you didn't know who you were. (304–305)

April closes the note by asking, "how could anyone else be blamed for that?," which might suggest another case of Yates mocking his subjects; after all, the liberal individualism that motivates suburban social contracts would agree that April chose to yoke her life to Frank's and therefore is ultimately culpable for her unhappiness. But the empathy in the narrator's description, coupled with the events of the following chapters, suggests more concern with human nature than with social structures.

More specifically, April's recognition aligns her with the novel's moral position. She realizes that Frank is not some great poet and she not some tortured actress, but rather fallible people sharing space. When she dryly states that "[h]e was—well, he was *Frank*," April realizes that she had been mischaracterizing their relationship for quite some time; "The only real mistake, the only wrong and dishonest thing was ever to have seen him as anything more than that" (303). More than just a simple misidentification, April claims that such thinking leads to a series of compromises that continued until "you were face to face, in total darkness, with the knowledge that you didn't know who you were." The narrative April lays out here, from pretension and expectation to alienation and loss of identity, is not a sign of liberal contractualism. April's malaise stems not from a botched agreement or an individual who has been compromised by others, but rather from a series of self-induced pretensions, a desire for the unreal instead of the actual. The authenticity for which she was working was not that of Rousseau's "true self," but rather that of a person situated in space in relation with other people.

April's soliloquy operates according to a model of authenticity as described by Martin Heidegger.[8] Against Enlightenment visions of selfhood, Heidegger rejects the possibility of the fully sufficient pre-social identity assumed by social contract theorists and claims that all knowledge and consciousness requires relationships with others. Dasein—Heidegger's term for conscious, existing individuals—is never isolated, but is always "Being-in" or "Being-with" something outside of itself.[9] The self, then, cannot be solitary or predetermined; it is always in relation. These relations are necessary because Dasein does not create a world according to his or her wishes, but is "thrown" into a world already populated with subjects, objects, and moods. The experience of being-in-the-world most often involves unreflective interaction with these elements, which finds them "ready-to-hand" (*zuhanden*) or available for use. According to Heidegger, "No matter how sharply we just *look* at the 'outward appearance' of Things…we cannot discover everything ready-to-hand," and therefore must rely on the common understanding of these things (98). According to this logic, then, an individual cannot be in isolation because everything one thinks and knows comes from others.

Being authentic (*eigenlich*), or enacting one's identity, involves interpreting the materials of one's existence in a manner different from his or her neighbors. In a thrown state, Dasein is limited to the opinions of *das man* or the "they": a neuter, faceless reference to indistinct others who are "not this one, not that one, not oneself, not some people, and not the sum of them all" (164). The "they" transmits information about the world, and therefore is a necessary part of becoming, but living only according to the "they" is, for Heidegger, inauthentic; the inauthentic Dasein only superficially interacts with others, uncritically accepting their perceptions. The "they" ensnares Dasein in inauthenticity, which can only be reversed when Dasein brings itself "back to itself from the lostness in the 'they.'" This bringing back to lostness is not a separation from others through mediating agreements, but a recognition of one's factual relation to the "they," taking the form of "an existentiell modification of the 'they'" (312). As Lawrence Vogel puts it, "[t]here is no pure authenticity but at best an authentic appropriation of the authentic. The possibilities one can make one's own do not come from nowhere; they are handed down to one from the factual world to which one belongs" (12). The authentic self, an individual's true identity, therefore requires relation to those in one's proximity, who will provide the "they-self" Dasein modifies "in an existentiell manner so that it becomes *authentic* Being-one's-Self" (313).

April's phrase "face to face, in total darkness, with the knowledge that you didn't know who you were" is particularly telling here as it draws attention to the relationship between existential authenticity and identity. Contemporary identity theorists Charles Taylor and K. Anthony Appiah have expanded on Heidegger's approach by refiguring this process of formation for the modern liberal state. In his re-evaluation of John Stuart Mill's *On Liberty*, Appiah argues that although an individual in a liberal society must be free to pursue his or her own conception of the good, this concept cannot be created in a vacuum because even when we design our plans of life, the material from which we form these plans is wholly unoriginal: "Autonomy, we know, is conventionally described as an ideal of self-authorship. But the metaphor should remind us that we write in a language we did not ourselves make" (156). All stances, including rejections of a particular viewpoint or affinity, require the presence of an other to bring it to our attention. Similarly, Taylor claims that although an individual "can always be original, can step beyond the limits of thought and vision of contemporaries, can even be quite misunderstood by them...the drive to original vision will be hampered, will ultimately be lost in inner confusion, unless it can be placed in some way in relation to the language and vision of others" (*Sources of the Self* 37–38).[10] As this claim indicates, authenticity is always relational and can never transcend the individual's immediate milieu. When we talk about who we are, Taylor notes, we refer to the "background against which our tastes and desires and opinions and aspirations make sense. If some of the things I value most are accessible to me only in relation to the person I love, then she becomes integral to my identity" (*The Ethics of Authenticity* 34). Appiah takes this further by emphasizing the contributions from those we do not choose to have in our lives, arguing that

> the putatively autonomous individual [is] confined to the options that are available to you; and those options themselves represent fixities, a nexus of institutions and practices you did not create yourself. If your values represent what you desire to desire,…what you desire to desire may not be up to you, in the sense that your "will" is the product of forces external to it. (53)

According to this line of thought, it is no surprise that April would "not know who she is" because she asserted an identity that had nothing to do with the facts of her relationship with others.

At first glance, one might assume that because April's recognition of her authenticity leads to despair and death, the novel is cynical about this intersubjectivity, making it seem more destructive than the liberalism he mocks elsewhere. However, a similar recognition occurs in the moments following April's death, in the most clearly ethical moment in the book. For most of the novel, next-door neighbor Shep Campbell has been a pathetic figure who feigns admiration for Frank while lusting after April, a disposition only increased by a drunken sexual encounter between he and April; but her demise incites active and selfless behavior from Shep. Yates accentuates this shift by recounting Shep's behavior leading up to the death, noting that "he hadn't been of much use" to his coworkers and family, behaving instead like an obsessive "lovesick kid" in pursuit of his dream girl (313). But upon learning that she has been hospitalized, Shep abandons his selfish self-loathing and gains "a sense of competence," acting less like a child and more like "a tense, steady paratrooper, ready for action" (314). The paratrooper identity the narrator mentions warrants more attention. Like Frank, Shep had often dreamed wistfully of his younger life, to which his real life with Milly in Revolutionary Hills Estates unfavorably compares, namely his time in the military. But where the paratrooper persona heretofore served as a distraction from his day-to-day life, it works here to heighten his responses to other people. Immediately after learning that April had been rushed to the hospital, Shep refuses to wallow in the self-pity of losing his dream girl or indulge in heroic rescue fantasies; instead he uses "the old combat feeling, the sense of doing exactly the right thing, quickly and well, when all the other elements of the situation were out of control" to propel him into retrieving and caring for his one-time rival Frank (315). Where April's fantasies move her out of the factual world and away from a sense of self, Shep's recognition allows him to construct an identity that has meaning in the world.

According to Heidegger, when individuals witness the transition from Dasein to no-longer-Dasein, they become aware of death as "*the end of Dasein*" and "*Dasein's ownmost possibility*" (303). When one accepts that he or she can never outstrip the possibility of death, Dasein begins to anticipate it. For Heidegger, this anticipation is freeing:

> When, by anticipation, one becomes free *for* one's own death, one is liberated from one's lostness in those possibilities which may accidentally thrust themselves upon one; and one is liberated in such a way that for the first time one can authentically understand and choose among the factual possibilities lying ahead of that possibility which is not to be outstripped. Anticipation discloses to existence that its uttermost possibility lies in giving itself up, and thus it shatters all one's tenaciousness to whatever existence one has reached…Since anticipation of the possibility which is not to be outstripped discloses also all the possibilities which lie ahead of that possibility, this anticipation includes the possibility of taking the *whole* of Dasein in advance in an existentiell manner; that is to say, it includes the possibility of existing as a *whole potentiality for being*. (308–309)

This existing as a *whole potentiality for being* manifests in resoluteness, which is a recognition of both Dasein's immediate existence and the possibilities from that existence, not just the possibilities allowed by the "they." In being resolute, Dasein puts forth an identity, but it is based on relation to what is possible:

> Resoluteness, as *authentic Being-one's-Self*, does not detach Dasein from its world, nor does it isolate it so that it becomes a free-floating "I." And how should it, when resoluteness as authentic disclosedness, is *authentically* nothing else than *Being-in-the-world*? Resoluteness brings the Self right into its current concernful Being-alongside what is ready-to-hand, and pushes it into solicitous Being with Others. (344)

In short, the experience of seeing another person die clarifies the limits of one's life, limits based on real experiences. Death lets individuals find themselves by grounding them spatially and forcing them to base their identities on that grounding.

*Revolutionary Road* repeatedly draws attention to the difference between authentic and fantastic behavior in the portrayal of Shep and Frank's respective responses to April's passing. Frank becomes overwhelmed by it all, and his mad run through Revolutionary Hills Estates culminates in a return to his empty house, where he concocts a ghostly version of April. Unlike the real April—who was, by turns, wistful, bitter, and resigned—Frank's pretend version is kind and comforting, embodying Frank's list of "how to love" that ended their last night together. Similarly, where Frank had thus far abhorred housework—the second chapter prominently features him angrily working in the yard—he now attends to his ghostly wife, allowing his head to "ring with the sound of her voice as he set to work." The fact of his house serves as a further distraction from his existence: "How could she be dead when the house was alive with the sound of her and the sense of her? Even when he had finished the cleaning, when there was nothing to do but walk around and turn on lights and turn them off again, even then her presence was everywhere, as real as the scent of her dresses in the bedroom closet" (324). Conversely, Shep also wrestles with the temptation to reject the reality of her death, largely in the form of an inner voice that told him "This isn't really happening; don't believe any of this," but he refuses to relent. Yates draws attention to this distinction through parallel descriptions, juxtaposing Frank's certainty of his fantasy wife against Shep's attention to the details of the hospital:

> People didn't die this way, at the end of a drowsing corridor like this in the middle of the afternoon. Why, hell, if she was dying that janitor wouldn't be pushing his mop so peacefully across the linoleum, and he certainly wouldn't be humming, nor would they let the radio play so loud in the ward a few doors away. If April Wheeler was dying they certainly wouldn't have this bulletin board here on the wall, with its mimeographed announcement of a staff dance ("Fun! Refreshments!") and they wouldn't have these wicker chairs arranged this way, with this table and this neat display of magazines. (317)

Unlike Frank, Shep uses the reality of his existence to form his identity: "It took him a long time to find his way back, and he would always remember that this was what he was doing—mincing down hallways carrying two containers of coffee, wearing a silly, inquiring smile—this was what he was doing when April Wheeler died" (319). This difference is clear: Frank's refusal to acknowledge April's death results in a form of non-being, while

Shep's willingness to acknowledge both the painful facts of his existence and his neighbor's needs allows him to construct an authentic selfhood.

In both cases, Shep and April both leave behind their pretenses about who they wish they were and who they wish they lived among, and simply respond to those who are actually present. In doing so, they create authentic identities, based on the facts of their existence: April the doting housewife and Shep the man of action. And yet April's identity leads to death, while Shep's compels him to aid his neighbor. The gender dynamics of the Eisenhower era certainly play a large part in these outcomes, but the despair into which April sinks also draws attention to the importance of ethics in such relations: April died, in part, because she received no hospitality.

## CRITICAL HOSPITALITY

At first glance, Shep's behavior might seem unremarkable, the basic obligations one would expect from a friend. However, the context of both the novel and the aforementioned suburban assumptions make Shep's actions more notable. As I have discussed, suburban contractualism prioritizes knowability and rights: members enter into communities with people made similar by adhering to the contracts terms, and they give up certain rights with the understanding that they will gain certain benefits; if the other people do not adhere to the terms and if the benefit is not clear, then there is no reason to form the association. When Shep invites Frank into his house, not only is there no clear gain for him, but it is actually contrary to his interests, as the novel's previous chapter thoroughly outlined the degree to which he pined after April and felt envy toward Frank. Moreover, nearly every character has, up to this point, acted with the same sense of self-interest found in the Laurel Players scene, where the kindness offered was highly contingent and based upon the benefits they would gain from one another. Furthermore, Frank has been made "desperately out of place" by his grief and no longer acknowledges the contract's terms. In this way, Frank has become other to the residents of Revolutionary Hills Estates—a stranger in his own neighborhood—and, therefore, Shep had no contractual obligation to care for him. But where all the other neighbors stay inside their homes and watch TV, Shep takes responsibility and offers hospitality.

The fact that Shep forgoes his rights for the sake of Frank cannot be under-emphasized, as the notion of rights is central to standard definitions of hospitality. Traditionally, as in the Greek concept of *xenia*[11] or in the cosmopolitan vision Immanuel Kant outlines in his essay "Perpetual Peace," hospitality is reserved for strangers who are passing through the land. Normally speaking, Frank is not a stranger to Shep, but that was only true when they both adhered to the contract: they were knowable to one another when they went to cocktail parties, kept up the yard, and held middle-class jobs. But the "desperately out of place" Frank whom Shep invites into his house no longer abides by that contract and is therefore no longer knowable, as highlighted by the narrator's description of him abandoning propriety when he "veered from the pavement, cut across someone's back yard and plunged into the down-sloping woods, intent on a madman's shortcut to Revolutionary Road" (323). Accordingly, Shep's reaction to Frank's strangeness cannot be explained by traditional theories of hospitality as they often operate according to contracts that try to make the stranger familiar by refiguring him in relation to the host. Consider Kant's "Perpetual Peace," which admits the stranger only when he agrees to certain provisions: the stranger "may only claim a *right of resort*"—to "present themselves in the society of others"—but may not "claim the *right of a guest* to be entertained, for this would require a special friendly agreement whereby he might become a member of the native household for a certain time" (106).[12] Kant's theory puts priority not on place but on ownership and imposes a set of requirements: the stranger remains a stranger while in the place that belongs to someone else and must not disturb the assumptions or beliefs of the host, but must accept the presented roles while briefly sharing space.[13]

Shep does not adhere to this distinction and does not extend limited rights to strange Frank. Rather, he invites Frank into his house without reservation, even though his presence worries Milly, and cedes his rights as a homeowner by letting Frank have whatever he needs. Shep's behavior exemplifies critical hospitality because he encounters an other, made into a stranger by the violation of suburban contracts, within his domestic space, even as it unavoidably disrupts his subjectivity and initiates a reconstruction of identity. Shep the homeowner has rights defined by laws, by contracts, and by notions of property, but he abandons them all for the sake of Frank's needs. The invitation disrupts the prior assumptions on which Shep developed his identity, and he must, therefore, reconstruct his selfhood. Rather than define himself by the desires and advantages vouchsafed by his suburban contracts, Shep must authentically respond to the unknowably unpredictable other that Frank, in his grief, has become.

The critical hospitality here is a type of domestic existentialism, where the self is thrown into question by the presence of an other; it is a matter of both ethics and identity.

My concept of critical hospitality follows the model explored in Jacques Derrida's essay "On Hospitality."[14] Derrida's essay troubles the prime distinction assumed in *xenia* and by Kant: that of the host, sovereign in his or her ability to grant welcome, and the guest. This sovereignty posits a certain inviolability of the home, over which the homeowner maintains control; however, the authority on which the homeowner relies is, as Derrida points out, ultimately already violated as the state lends its power to the laws that grant the homeowner the right to welcome or refuse. Moreover, the very knowledge of the right is contingent upon the presence of the guest or foreigner who prompts the question of welcome or expulsion. Accordingly, Derrida argues, the question of hospitality becomes "the very question of being-in-question, the question-being or being-in-question of the question" because the one requesting aid, "putting the first question, puts me in question" (3). So, ultimately, hospitality "is due to the foreigner, certainly, but remains, like the law, conditional, and thus conditioned in its dependence on the unconditionality that is the basis of the law" (73). This presence of the guest necessarily involves a "transgressive step," an impossibility in which "the stranger or foreigner held the keys" to the house, revealing an always implicit reversal:

> It's *as if* (and an *as if* always lays down the law here) the stranger...could save the master and liberate the power of his host; it's *as if* the master, *qua* master, were prisoner of his place and his power, of his ipseity, of his subjectivity (his subjectivity is hostage). So it is indeed the master, the one who invites, the inviting host, who becomes the hostage—and who really always has been. And the guest, the invited hostage, becomes the one who invites the one who invites, the master of the host. The guest becomes the host's host. The guest (*hôte*) becomes the host (*hôte*) of the host (*hôte*). These substitutions make everyone into everyone else's hostage. (123)

"Such are the laws of hospitality," Derrida claims; substitutions that make "everyone into everyone else's hostage" (125). The laws of hospitality by which the guest and host assert and assume certain roles already contain the fragments of their undoing, which can never be exterminated or expelled. Hospitality then is already implied by the mere proximity of others, and this implication undoes any host/guest binary. It exceeds all designations until all that is left are two people, sharing space in a face-to-face relation.

As Derrida's description suggests, the demand for hospitality is ultimately an ethical quandary, which is clear in Shep's act of critical hospitality. The need to care for Frank supersedes Shep's propriety, rights, desires, and even his safety; the look on Frank's face cannot be dismissed on any of those terms: "The way Frank's eyes looked, and the way he huddled and trembled in the seat beside him, had filled him with fear," explains the narrator; "He knew now that all his opportunities for action would soon be over; when he had steered up this final hill to this ugly brown building, he would pass into an area of total helplessness." The face of Frank Wheeler compels Shep to act, a fact that Yates accentuates by contrasting his response to that of Milly, who initially uses Frank's suffering as a cause for gossip or to draw attention to herself—"she had made some sandwiches and set them out in the kitchen, in case anyone got hungry later…She'd been ready to sit up all night with him and—well, read to him from the Bible, or something; ready to hold him and let him weep on her breast; anything"—but she finds herself completely unprepared for "the awful blankness of [Frank's] eyes when Shep brought him up the kitchen steps" (321). In both cases, the vulnerability and surprise of Frank's despair-racked face demands critical hospitality that cannot be ignored by the selfishness of Shep or Milly. They see him and must respond.

The emphasis on the face as the locus of ethical demand recalls the work of Emmanuel Levinas, whose first major work *Totality and Infinity* was described by Derrida as "an immense treatise on hospitality" (*Adieu* 49).[15] Posited as a correction to Heidegger's phenomenology, Levinas insists on the priority of ethics before ontology. Where Heidegger's phenomenology reduces to a division between ready-to-hand (*zuhanden*) objects that one might use unreflectively and present-to-hand (*vorhanden*) objects that one ponders, Levinas claims that such a model becomes totalitarian when applied to real people. Levinas describes this totalizing figure, which collapses all other people and objects into extensions of the self, as "the Same":

> To be I is, over and beyond any individuation that can be derived from a system of references, to have identity as one's content. The I is not a being that always remains the same, but is the being whose existing consists in identifying itself, in recovering its identity throughout all that happens to it. It is the primal identity, the primordial work of identification. (*Totality* 36)

Against the domineering Same, Levinas posits the interruption of the other, who arrives to the Same both as an object and as a surprise that exceeds expectation.[16] In Levinas' phenomenology, the Same's totality becomes disrupted by an encounter with the other's face, which is the sensible manifestation of that person. The face serves as an object for the Same to recognize, while also suggesting an infinite interiority; it is "[t]he way in which the other presents himself, exceeding *the idea of the other in me*" (50). This exceedance disturbs the Same, shattering epistemological assumptions, and the other becomes the one who "is above all the one I am responsible for" (*Entre Nous* 105). As Derrida puts it, "Levinas wants to remind us that responsibility is not at first responsibility of myself for myself, that the sameness of myself is derived from the other, as if it were second to the other, coming to itself as responsible and mortal from the position of my responsibility before the other, for the other's death and in the face of it." (*Gift of Death* 46). And yet it is this very condition that makes the Same "able to respond," a point he states in an uncharacteristically blunt fashion while speaking of Heidegger's relationship of recognition, explaining that "to be human means to have a responsibility for the other":

> The other is properly nothing to me. In French, this is expressed well: *il n'est rien pour moi, il ne me regarde pas* (he is nothing to me, he does not concern me). This 'not-concerning-me' is the non-human. The human enters into being in order to say the ontological absurdity: the other *does* concern me, the death of the other *does* concern me. (Robbins, "Being-Toward-Death" 132)

The demanded response forms the prime ethical moment, in which the Same must decide between to options. The Same can either objectify the other by enfolding the interruption into his or her predeterminations—an act of totalizing objectification that Levinas compares to "murder"—or the Same can welcome even the unknowable and potentially dangerous other, caring for him or her by refusing to impose limitations.

## SINGULARITIES IN SUBURBIA

Because it presents an ethical imperative that cannot be simplified to a contractual agreement or even a moral good—it is no law that commands response but the naked openness of the other's face—Levinas' ethics allows us to reconceptualize suburbia as a setting for stories about individuals interacting with one another. Where the popular view claims that phenomena such as restrictive zoning and what Kenneth Jackson called "America's drive-in culture" have weakened suburbia's "'sense of community' which prevails in most metropolitan areas," resulting in "a reduced feeling of concern and responsibility among families for their neighbors and among suburbanites in general for residents of the inner city," *Postmodern Suburban Spaces* argues that suburban fictions repeatedly imagine a different type of community possible within domestic spaces, one in which critical hospitality refuses individualistic interactions and prompts intersubjective identity construction (272). The stories discussed in this book repudiate and rethink the concepts of Romantic authenticity and contractual community by positing messy and contingent associations within the suburban space, in which neighbors, spouses, and children become other to each other, and thus form new communities in which shared space is the founding element. This approach follows what has been called a "spatial turn" in literary criticism, answering the work done by critics including Edward Soja, Henri Lefevbre, and Fredric Jameson to explore the process of "cognitive mapping" inherent to the reading process.[17] These commentators claim that the spatial relationships represented in literary works undermine what Jameson calls the globalizing impulse of late-capitalist postmodernism, which puts an end to "the bourgeois ego, or monad" and replaces it with free-floating and impersonal "euphoria." The literary critic, Jameson insists, can no longer focus on "the great high modernist thematics of time and temporality," but must attend to the "categories of space" where the self is situated (*Postmodernism* 16–17). But as illustrated in Jameson or Michel de Certeau, this mapping often valorizes the role of the perceiving subject over the perceived object, the work of the all-comprehending Same about which Levinas writes. Tellingly, this spatial egoism lends itself best to the modernist space *par exemplar*, the big city, whether it be the major American cities from which Jameson (via Kevin Lynch) launches his argument or Certeau's "Concept-city," a place of "transformations and appropriations, the object of various kinds of interference but also a subject that is constantly enriched by new attributes" (94). These theorists posit the city as their model, describing the "tactics"—the "calculus which cannot count on a 'proper' (spatial or institutional localization), nor thus on a borderline distinguishing the other as a visible totality"—as a means for making meaning (xix). Suburban fiction, conversely, troubles this "reconquest" (to use Jameson's term) by throwing its central characters into explicitly occupied space; so while Certeau might praise the "walker" as a Bahktinian polyglot whose "enunciative" step variously "affirms, suspects, tries out, transgresses, [and] respects" as it "speaks," suburban fiction often eschews a clear authoritative figure against whom one must resist (99). True, suburbs are administrative spaces, but suburban fiction focuses not on regulations imposed by stoplights or traffic cops, but on neighbors censuring one another. These stories illustrate failures of control that give rise to new, contingent relationships that operate otherwise than an administrator/pedestrian conflict, thereby changing the imaginary nature of suburban rhetoric.

As depicted in the novels studied here, the imagined postwar suburbs better embody Agamben's notion of "taking space," the ethical imperative that operates outside the logic of antagonism by recognizing the coexistence of manifold potentialities in a single place. Within what Agamben calls "easement," the ethical self-posits an identity by making room for the neighbor, and as such, goodness allows for "exteriority and non-latency" to be "the determination and the limit of every thing," while evil is "the reduction of the taking-place of things to a fact like others, the forgetting of the transcendence inherent in the very taking-place of things" (14). Where urban walking rarely becomes more than a "rhetoric," a "process of appropriation of the topographical system on the part of the pedestrian," the being-with and taking-place prominent in suburban fiction allows no rhetorical manipulation or appropriation (Certeau 101, 98). The relationship demands a response that returns the "free *use of the self*" back to the neighbor/guest, treating existence not "as a property" but as "a *habitus*, an *ethos*" (*Coming Community* 27–28).

In repudiating the original designs for suburbia, the distraught Frank running through Revolutionary Hills Estates or residing in Shep's home asserts a different type of spatial arrangement, one that cannot be enunciative or appropriative, but must be inoperative or unavowable. Instead of the Romantic forms of community assumed in suburbia, the types of community posited in *Revolutionary Road* and, in fact, all of those found in this study require a different terminology, something otherwise than the security-minded divisions that spawned the space. I find this terminology in recent continental philosophy, particularly the notion of the singularity, as described variously in works such as Nancy's *The Inoperative Community*, Derrida's *The Politics of Friendship*, Deleuze and Guattari's *Anti-Oedipus* (and its spiritual successor, Hardt and Negri's *Empire* trilogy), as well as

Agamben's *The Coming Community.*[18] Against communities of sameness implied by standard approaches to suburbia, these thinkers emphasize contingency and unknowability, arguing that the pre-social individualism endemic to Western philosophy will inevitably lead to holocaust, as indicated by Agamben's claim that "it is not the city but rather the camp that is the fundamental biopolitical paradigm of the West" (*Homo Sacer* 181). Following Levinas' priority of ethics over ontology, Derrida, Nancy, and Agamben attempt to uncover community founded on difference, resulting in a contingent and non-totalizing society these thinkers call "singularity." The notion of singularity found in Derrida and others is based solely on the face-to-face relation and the radical hospitality it requires. It follows Roberto Esposito's attempts to think community not as "a quality that is added to [member's] nature as subjects," leaving literal ground as the only ground, the shared space of those in proximity (2). Indeed, as Nancy and Blanchot or Hardt and Negri insist, the singular community must be "inoperative" or "unavowable," not designed to achieve a particular goal; a singularity is "a new type of communication that functions not on the basis of resemblances but on the bases of differences" (*Empire* 57). These "whatever communities," as Agamben calls them—in which "whatever" denotes not "indifference" but "non-determination"—best defend the infinite potentiality of their members: "For if it is true that whatever being always has a potential character, it is equally certain that it is not capable of only this or that specific act, nor is it therefore simply incapable, lacking in power, nor even less is it indifferently capable of everything, all-powerful: The being that is properly whatever is able to not-be; it is capable of its own impotence." A "whatever singularity," therefore, "has no identity, it is not determinate with respect to a concept, but neither is it simply indeterminate; rather it is determined only through its relation to an *idea*, that is, to the totality of its possibilities" (*Coming Community* 34, 66). Such a model directly repudiates both the ethos of planned communities found in real suburbs and the for/against binaries assumed by many readers of suburban fictions.

For these philosophers, singularities offer a type of association that eschews the antagonisms inherent in the forms of community described by Western philosophers, particularly social contract thinkers such as Rousseau. Accordingly, singularities avoid the conformity and exclusion so often associated with suburbia as they remove the center to which one must conform or by which one is excluded. Moreover, singularity aptly describes the community formed by Shep and Frank in their moment of critical hospitality. Where the lead-up to April's death gave Shep a clear sense of "doing exactly the right thing," indeterminacy marks his time with Frank. The narration underscores a sense of aimlessness as they move "on the road, going nowhere" in a "sequence of events after that would remain forever uncertain." Shep here does not put his preconceived notions forward, but instead allows his mind to perform "its trick of rolling with the punch," reacting to Frank's concerns in a manner that shows care for Frank (320–321). Although certainly bleak, the image of restlessness and indeterminacy is important. Neither Frank nor Shep knows who one another are, they just know that there is a great need and so respond to one another accordingly. Shep no longer understands himself as April Wheeler's also-ran or as the man who should have stayed in the military, but as the person sitting across from Frank. He becomes the person who does "exactly the right thing" not because it is, in terms of value, empirically right, but because it is the thing that the other person needs. Any history between them, any desires they previously held, any assumptions about who or what they should be are cast aside for the moment of interaction shared between them, and this becomes the founding element of their community. There, within a suburb as cheap and fake as Revolutionary Road Estates, Frank and Shep create a singularity by understanding themselves as fundamentally a people alongside other people.

*Postmodern Suburban Spaces* seeks to find similar examples of fiction writers conjuring suburban singularities, instances where a character's need for hospitality upsets the contractual logic on which another character relied and forces the two to redefine themselves according to the moment of shared space, in a range of texts. This goal sets the book apart from the other studies of suburban fiction, most notably Catherine Jurca's *White Diaspora*, which uncovers instances of "sentimental dispossession"—"the affective dislocation by which white middle-class suburbanites begin to see themselves as spiritually and culturally impoverished by prosperity"—that she identifies as the defining feature of the twentieth-century suburban novel (7). Through these narratives, Jurca argues, suburbanites assume a "homelessness" that obfuscates the myriad advantages they enjoy. While Jurca's incisive readings do effectively highlight the middle-class ennui in novels such as *Revolutionary Road* or David Gates' *Jernigan*, her interpretations too often assume the presence of some "true self" in danger of violation. She reads suburban communities as those "of [the residents'] own making and choosing," in which "racial and class uniformity of the suburb functions...as the condition of community" (9, 8). This interpretive model allows Jurca to address some "questions about the alienation and insecurity of the white middle class," but always in terms of an insider/outsider or authentic/inauthentic dichotomy, overlooking the contingent and multifaceted communities so prevalent in these texts, in which members are not independent agents but strangers sharing space.

Keith Wilhite's recent article "Contested Terrain: The Suburbs as Region" issues a rousing call to understand suburban fiction contrary to Jurca's notions of alienation and dispossession, arguing that such language treats the model as "a reified artifact of Cold War cultural critique" (617). Wilhite positions suburbia as "the endgame and final outpost of US regionalism," which clarifies "the fraught relationship between isolationism and imperialism that has shaped US residential geography and, in turn, helps us rethink the role literary texts play in the postwar project of suburban nation building," through which we see the contradiction between "an isolationist strategy in an era of global expansion, and an imperialist, land-grab campaign within US metropolitan regions" (618–619). For Wilhite, suburban fictions mirror the tensions in this public/private duality, in which characters such as the scattered Lamberts of Jonathan Franzen's *The Corrections* or the multicultural Battle family in Chang-rae Lee's *Aloft* situate their selves on the global stage through suburban living. Likewise, Robert Beuka asserts the prominence of space in his *Suburbia Nation*, understanding the suburbs as Foucauldian heterotopias that stand as "the material counterpart to specific drives and tendencies in American culture apparent from the postwar years onward." Beuka's readings reveal the development of "not only a new kind of physical landscape, but new psychic and emotional landscapes," making suburban fiction "the mirror... through which middle-class American culture casts its uneasy reflective gaze on itself" (2, 4). Insisting upon the contested nature of these terrains, both in their actual implementation and in their cultural acceptance, Beuka claims that attention to place in these stories reveals a middle way between utopian desires and dystopian fears, a complexity often ignored by cultural critics. Re-emphasizing the troubled and plural allows Beuka to analyze suburban fiction as "reflections of our larger cultural sense of suburban place, reflections of the place-specific social dynamics of the landscape that, more than any other, has come to define middle-class American life in the twentieth century" (16).

Despite their notable contributions, both Wilhite and Beuka approach suburban fiction in a similar manner: as a study of individuals in an unreal and ideal space. For these critics, the unease and dissatisfaction commonplace to these narratives are byproducts of the geological machinations of designers and planners, a utopia that ultimately fails. *Postmodern Suburban Spaces* is less concerned with the failure or success of actual suburbs, and more with the way writers of fiction turn a wide range of suburbs into stages for people to dwell among one another, highlighting an aspect of our suburban imagination and opening new ways for thinking about community in the age of American dominance. As such, my project has much more in common with narrowed, genre-specific examinations of suburban fiction, namely Beatrice M. Murphy's *The Suburban Gothic in American Popular Culture* and Katherine Tongson's energetic *Relocations: Queer Suburban Imaginaries*. Both authors read fictions such as Shirley Jackson's stories or Internet artist Lynne Chan's "JJ Chinois" persona as indications of the monstrous, disruptive presence of misfits and outsiders within middle-class neighborhoods, who shatter the divisions assumed by Jurca, Wilhite, and Beuka. Tongson observes the postwar suburb's cultural role as that of the "presumed natural habitat for normativity," reminding readers that inside its "tidy yet nebulous sprawl, even this representational field has been marred by strange and wild things growing where they shouldn't" (5). According to Murphy, these "invasions" lend themselves to horror stories that manifest the "darker, and no less visible, parallel narrative which bore much in common with those which had from the outset shadowed the American dream of progress and optimism: one which perceived suburbia as the physical personification of all that was wrong with American society, a deadening assembly of identikit houses and a breeding ground for discontent and mindless conventionality" (5). Likewise, Tongson's queer theory schema translates these interruptions into a type of revelation and release, highlighting the movements and collisions as different people interact together, a picture best captured by the "pleasure and thrill in the dangerous transaction" of driving through a cloverleaf intersection, "the elaborate dance between drivers destined for different directions, yet forced by design to notice one another as if their lives depended on it, because they do for that instant" (8).

Against these transitional metaphors, *Postmodern Suburban Spaces* looks at the surprisingly static aspects of suburban fiction. I do not mean those who are mired or caught, as understood by the Wheelers at their most melancholy, but the inescapable "here-ness" of people living and dwelling together, the Heideggarian being-with-others (*Mitsein*) that permeates these stories. This study insists on thinking about suburbia as a place where communities are formed, even as they reject the predetermined aspects insisted by most designers. My shift in perspective provides another counternarrative to the forms of community diagnosed by other readers of suburban fiction; where Jurca's "victimization narratives," Tongson's normativity, and Wilhite's globalizing regionalism all emphasize the need for security, they overlook the degree to which this safety is achieved through homogenizing forces. Indeed, mainstays of suburban imagery such as the HOA, gated communities, or even the ever-present nosy neighbor all indicate an incessant push of conformity that has been endemic to American suburbs long before either World War. The increased diversification of suburbia has only intensified this need for homogeneity as relatively arbitrary, economically motivated designations—those blocked from neighborhoods "were undesirable because the subdividers branded them undesirable"—have been exacerbated by the desire for safety, thereby heightening the "deep-seated fears that were embodied in [such restrictions]—the fear of others" (Fogelson 123).[19]

But as two more recent studies of suburban fiction have found, changes in globalization and demographics have fully revealed the unsustainable nature of suburbia. In the introduction to their edited collection *New Suburban Stories*, Timotheus Vermeulen and Martin Dines argue that the very debate over the definition of the word "suburb" indicates the degree to which the model "continually foregrounds contingency and contradiction" (7). Writing about suburban novels after 9/11, Kathy Knapp notes that this contingency allows the fiction to "take its white male protagonist to task for upholding the neoliberal values of individualism, private property ownership, and upward mobility that [...] have both supported and masked white male privilege" (*Unexceptionalism* xv). *Postmodern Suburban Spaces* continues this reappraisal by examining the way dissonance within neighborhoods allows us to rethink the communal imperative behind most American subdivisions. By looking at stories about the tension caused by this insecurity, this book reveals the fact that when Americans think about shared space, they repeatedly call for a radical and critical hospitality.

## CHAPTER SUMMARIES

In the chapters that follow, I will demonstrate that singular communities are far more common to suburban fiction than the predetermined associations most frequently related to the genre. Throughout these stories, contracts are discarded and destroyed in the face of the ineffable and unknowable other, but the result is not simply horror or movement or dispossession;

rather, most suburban fictions feature a being-with and dwelling together that results in an inoperable community, defined only by the presence of the moment. These portrayals call into question the central assumptions about self and society that give rise to real-world planned communities. According to Sue-Im Lee, such relationships are increasingly common to American fiction; where American authors once subscribed to a dichotomy between individual and society, contemporary writers express more of an ambivalence toward the prospects of community. Longing for the benefits offered by an ideal community while avoiding the restrictions and limitations imposed on individuals, these authors seek a community that maintains the "paradoxes, impossibilities, and contradictions" of a "dialectic community without synthesis" (3). Lee finds that many contemporary novels offer a vision of community that neither fully endorses nor fully embraces idealized community, but rather expresses ambivalence toward it: "To be ambivalent is to simultaneously entertain two contradictory attitudes toward one concept. Put another way, ambivalence describes a unique vantage point, of acknowledging the appeal, as well as the undesirability, of any alternative" (21). Rather than be completely "given over" to a particular idea, Lee argues that contemporary novelists offer a deliberative form of community, in which individuals consciously enter into relations with other individuals, willingly accepting the responsibilities this entails while simultaneously holding out the possibility to reject it.

To interpret this ambivalence in suburban fiction and to uncover the critical hospitality that occurs so often, I follow the recent "ethical turn" in literary criticism. A development of the deconstruction and reader-response theories that flourished in the 1970s, narrative ethics combines the two central questions of those disciplines: like deconstruction, it asks "what can we know?" and like reader response, it asks "what can we do?" Accordingly, narrative ethics insists that stories have a reflexive function, that they affect not only the way we understand ourselves and others, but also the way they motivate our actual dealings with flesh-and-blood people in the real world. But unlike standard reader-response criticism, narrative ethics couples its correspondence between the literary and real worlds with Lee's sense of nervousness, an understanding that even fictional characters exceed the reader's interpretive grasp. According to Andrew Gibson, this exceedance is a key element of ethical response, avoiding the totalization common in some forms of narrative, where the narrator—or person ordering the narrative through interpretation—"takes another, others, the world as the object or objects of knowledge and claims possession of them" (26).[20] Adam Zachary Newton's study *Narrative Ethics* makes the connections all the more clear, outlining a process of interpretation that allows a reader to face a text "as one might face a person, having to confront the claims raised by that very immediacy, an immediacy of contact, not of meaning" (11). These approaches recall a number of developments in later reception and narrative theory,[21] which emphasize the problematic aspects of a text in relation to its ability to help the reader interact in the real world and to understand real others. As such, these readings unavoidably involve what Jameson called the "political unconscious," the idea that reoccurring plots and tropes, which he calls "master narratives," have "inscribed themselves in the texts as well as in our thinking about them; such allegorical narrative signified are a persistent dimension of literary and cultural texts precisely because they reflect a fundamental dimension of our collective thinking and our collective fantasies about history and reality" (*Political Unconscious* 34). Jameson's concerns are particularly notable in relation to suburban fiction as both the space and the identities of those within have been heavily influenced and motivated by narratives. But where suburban communal myths often reduced to variations of insider/outsider distinctions, the fictions studied in *Postmodern Suburban Spaces* call for something more contingent and varied, an interpretive process well-suited to narrative ethics.

This emphasis on the symbolic nature of suburban fiction frees me to discuss novels that best relate to the question of community, not those that follow a historical trajectory. This is not to say that the history matters, but rather that the image of suburbia has become untethered from history and, therefore, a discussion of the issues must prioritize the symbolic over the real in order to lead back to the real. For that reason, my choice of novels may seem counterintuitive, as when I talk about race by discussing three works written long after the abolition of racial covenants and the civil rights movements or by reading pieces of satire next to realist and postmodern novels. I have brought these works together not for their historical import, nor as representatives of any particular literary movement. Rather, I have chosen them as particularly useful pieces for talking about aspects of the imaginary communities that still exist.

My first chapter addresses perhaps the most infamous element of suburban association, the racial divisions. "Against Fence Thinking: Welcoming the Racial Enemy" argues that the history of racial violence long associated with the suburbs has been motivated by a liberalism that emphasizes individual action of communal responsibility. Using Carl Schmitt's notion of the friend/enemy distinction, I argue that these texts upset the assurance on which that logic relies to invite a more intersubjective form of community. In Richard Ford's *Independence Day*, the white realtor Frank Bascombe feels compelled to do something for his black neighbors, but his attempt at arm's length engagement is befuddled. In Chang-rae Lee's *A Gesture Life*, Doc Hata uses a series of performances to gain access to his neighborhood, but these gestures separate him from the people who helped shape his identity. Finally, Gloria Naylor's *Linden Hills* forcefully rejects the homogeny driving modern suburbs and posits instead a type of "mirror thinking" where identity is made via relation.

The second chapter, "My Home Is Your Home: Property, Propriety, and Neighbors," expounds upon the correlation between personal property and concepts of the neighbor initiated in the first chapter. I trace suburbia's interest in private property to two dominant discourses: the classical liberal theories of Locke and Kant, which advocate property as a form of protection from invaders, and the concept of dwelling articulated in Heidegger and Arendt, which posits property as a means for developing an isolated identity. Contrasting these approaches to the interactions found in T.C. Boyle's *The Tortilla Curtain*, John Cheever's *Bullet Park*, and John Updike's *Rabbit Redux*, I argue that both philosophies position neighbors as potential enemies, unnecessary and detrimental to one's subjectivity. I contend that the relationships characterized by these novelists can be better described by employing the redefinitions asserted by Kenneth Reinhardt, Eric L. Santer, and Jeremy Waldron. According to these thinkers, the neighbor is not an individual similar to the self, but an other who is in proximity and in need. Following the notions of improper property advanced in Levinas and Esposito, I argue that the houses in Boyle, Cheever, and Updike are not fortresses that exclude, but sites of welcome for the potentially dangerous, but ultimately necessary, neighbor.

It is impossible to envision suburbia's uniform houses without also picturing happy families living inside them; and yet, suburban fictions regularly feature suffocating gender roles, failing marriages, and threatened children. My third chapter, "Domesticated Strangers: Fissures Within the Nuclear Family," examines three portrayals of family: a revolt against traditional contracts in Tom Perrotta's *Little Children*, a family of fear in John Irving's *The World According to Garp*, and a relationship based on impossible promises in Don DeLillo's *White Noise*. These novels struggle to illustrate a type of responsible freedom, a union that differs from both the fear-motivated Eisenhower-era "traditional" family and the egoism inherent to the free love advocated by thinkers like Deleuze and Guattari. These novels demonstrate what Jean-Luc Nancy called "shattered love," a relationship based on obligation to an unknowable other to whom one is joined in familial ties.

Chapter Four "Assimilation and Appropriation: Contest and Collaboration in Global Suburbia" looks at the international implications of the postwar suburb. As vividly illustrated by Richard Nixon's 1959 "Kitchen Debate" with Soviet Premier Nikita Khrushchev, the suburb has become the physical manifestation of the American Dream and a demonstration of exceptionalism for the rest of the world. Accordingly, some immigrants and ethnic groups traditionally excluded from the American community see suburbia as a means to achieving their American Dream, resulting in tensions that have been explored by recent novelists. For example, the Jewish residents in Philip Roth's Weequahic stories might create their own version of the sitcom suburb in hopes of enjoying US culture while protecting their national identities, but novels like *American Pastoral* and *Nemesis* frame the enclave as prohibitive and therefore untenable, just like its White Anglo-Saxon Protestant (WASP) counterpart. Conversely, the Gangulis in Jhumpa Lahri's *The Namesake* find the suburb to be a space of cosmopolitan difference, where they can fashion identities that are neither fully Bengali nor fully American. Finally, Gish Jen's *Mona in the Promised Land* emphasizes the plurality of its neighborhood, in which Mona Chang triangulates her identity in relation to those in proximity: her Chinese parents, her Japanese love interest, her Jewish friends, and her African-American coworkers. By rejecting the notion of a monolithic American character, these stories reaffirm the potential for ethics in suburbia, positioning it as a space not only for cosmopolitan contact, but also for the conflicts and interrupts essential to subjectivity.

*Postmodern Suburban Spaces* reads these stories as acts of imagination, creative responses to real facts of suburbanization that describe and explore more ethical ways of being together in a model that has dominated American popular culture as much as it has its real landscapes. In each of the aforementioned chapters, I identify a key aspect of suburbanization— racism, private property, the traditional family, and American assimilation— and discuss its manifestation in real-world neighborhoods; I then identify the philosophy motivating these practices and examine literary representations that repudiate or rethink that worldview. For this reason, the theories advanced here do not directly apply to real suburbs, and to claim that the communities these authors picture are caused by such a place or likely within it is beyond the scope of my project. I am primarily interested in the fictions various writers create about the space, important because suburbia is very much an imagined community, deeply dependent upon narrative. Those in power initially deployed narratives to imagine the American character of the suburbs, but other writers have been long imagining the difference and strangeness of the suburbs. Once again, fiction can lead the way in describing the suburban character. Whatever else various forces try to ascribe to the suburbs, they are, fundamentally, residential spaces. People live there, they are together there, and as such, their lives—from the mundane play of children and people passing on a commute, to the tragic illustrated by Frank Wheeler's run—become enmeshed with one another. The recognition of this fact motivates the CID or "planned community" as designers attempted to mitigate the risk inherent in shared lives by ensuring that all residents were the same, or at least agreed to the same codes of behavior. They envisioned, and enforced, bourgeois utopias where true Americans could reap the rewards of the nation's prosperity. But fiction has pointed to something else and has understood the proximity inherent in suburbia as endemic to another type of community, one based on shared space. Instead of a utopia, a literal "nowhere," these fiction imagine suburbia as a topos, a place where different people are "now here."

## NOTES

1. The novel was not published until 1961, which puts it after the end of the initial suburban push. However, Yates began working on it during the Eisenhower-era boom; a cold response from publishers delayed the book's release. Accordingly, *Revolutionary Road* deserves attention as one of the first American novels set in the postwar suburb.
2. These and many other similar anecdotes are indexed at the following website:http://realestate.aol.com/blog/2013/09/10/avoiding-hoa-contract-problems/
3. Lucas' website neighborsatwar.com purports to tell readers the very latest in "HOA Amerika," warning readers that "Your freedom really is at risk! Your personal wealth is at risk. Your Constitutional rights are being secretly shredded!"
4. See Costino, "Weapons Against Women: Compulsory Heterosexuality and Capitalism in Linden Hills"; Goddu, "Reconstructing History in Linden Hills"; Montgomery, *The Fiction of Gloria Naylor*; Okonkwo, "Suicide or Self Sacrifice: Exhuming Willa's Body in Gloria Naylor's Linden Hills"; Whitt, *Understanding Gloria Naylor*.

5. See Steinmann and Fox, *The Male Dilemma*; Cammon and Wattenberg, *The Real Majority*; Lemon, *The Troubled American*; Hodgson, *America in Our Time*; Ehenreich, *Fear of Falling*; Warren, *The Radical Center*.

6. Rousseau explains this in "On the Social Contract" by observing, "In every body politic there is a maximum force that it cannot exceed, and which has often fallen short by increasing in size. The more the social bond extends the looser it becomes, and in general a small state is proportionately stronger than a large one" (167).

7. In his reading of *The Reveries of the Solitary Walker*, Roberto Esposito argues that, despite his desire otherwise, Rousseau "cannot live in isolation because that isolation expresses in a reversed form the irreducible need for sharing." Because Rousseau's existence "isn't anything except the irrepressible radiating and spilling out in what doesn't belong to his existence, but of which it nevertheless is a part," Esposito explains, he cannot "bring himself to hate even those whom he believes are persecuting him…How can one hate someone, even one's worst enemy, when each participates in what is constitutively shared?" (60).

8. In a way, April's behavior throughout the novel could be characterized as what Jean-Paul Sartre called "bad faith." The connection, however, is still clear as Heidegger was a direct influence on Sartre, though the former attempted to distance himself from existentialism. See Heidegger's "Letter on Humanism" as a response to Sartre's claims of affinity.

9. Taylor Carman makes a distinction to the familiar translation of Dasein that I use, which is worth noting here. Rather than think of Dasein as a simple existing, Carman argues that the Heidegger intends the word to be "more eventlike than objectlike, its 'being' more like a gerund than a substantive" (41). This distinction emphasizes the specificity of Dasein, so that when Heidegger makes claims like "Dasein is its disclosedness," Carman claims that the phrase does not indicate the way an individual sets out an identity that he or she wishes to perform. Rather, the phrase indicates the specificity of place around the subject: "particular Daseins are particular livings of particular lives" (42).

10. While Taylor does allow for "absent partners," people whose ideas and actions inspire us without our ever having actually met or interacted with them, an identity still requires the interaction from a real, face-to-face other to respond to an identity being enacted by an individual.

11. The notion of hospitality, of course, has a long literary and philosophical history, perhaps demonstrated earliest in the ancient Greek concept of *xenia* or guest-relation. *Xenia* requires hosts to treat guests with respect and care, as illustrated in Homer's *Odyssey* when Odysseus receives hospitality from the Egyptian king he has invaded because the king "feared the wrath of Zeus, the god of guests" (14.318). But while *xenia* may, on the

surface, appear open and welcoming, it cannot be neglected that its "duties are conceived of in astonishingly uniform term: it is as if everyone recognized how a *xenos* should behave in each specific situation"; hospitality, according to this law, is only to be given by the host and received only by the stranger, thereby reifying their roles (Herman 118).

12. While unquestionably the most influential thinker of hospitality in the Enlightenment, Kant is far from the only one working on the topic. See Peter Melvilles' *Romantic Hospitality and the Resistance to Accommodation*.

13. More recently, cosmopolitan thinkers, including Seyla Benhabib, Jürgen Habermas, and K. Anthony Appiah, have been adopting Kantian principles to the current moment of late capitalism. See Benhabib, *The Rights of Others*, Habermas, *The Inclusion of the Other*, Appiah, *Cosmopolitanism*.

14. Some readers, most notably Martin Hägglund, have attempted to separate Derrida's later work from Levinas' influence, offering a more "atheistic" version of hospitality in which even the welcome involves an element of violence. See Hägglund, *Radical Atheism*.

15. In its original French, Levinas distinguishes between autre and autre, the wholly other and the tangentially other. Most translators mark the distinction by capitalizing the word "other" when describing the tangentially other and "Other" when denoting the wholly other. For the purposes of my study, I am referring solely to the wholly Other, but for the purposes of readability will not be following the capitalization model.

16. My use of the word "object" may be a poor one and reflects the often contradictory nature of Levinas' philosophy. Hilary Putman's introductory discussion to Levinas' debt to Judaism may help explain the manifestation of the face by reminding the reader that Levinas tends to speak of the Other in terms usually ascribed to God. With that in mind, the face for Levinas is more a "trace," not an actual physical object: "Just as we never see God, but at best traces of God's presence in the world, so we never see the 'face' of the other, but only its 'trace." (45).

17. See *Spatiality* by James Talley for an impressively thorough and concise primer on the topic.

18. Maurice Blanchot's *The Unavowable Community*, a direct response to Nancy's *The Inoperative Community* and a further discussion of George Battielle's work, is another important work in this conversation. However, because it concerns itself more with the role of literature and myth in community formation and less with the act of singularities, I have focused my attention on the other three works.

19. Nicolaides and Weise's *The Suburb Reader* collects a number of documents to construct a powerfully succinct history of CIDs, HOAs, and the legal challenges raised against them. The chapter entitled "Our Town: Inclusion and Exclusion in Recent Suburbia" is of particular interest. See also

Lassiter, "Suburban Strategies: The Volatile Center in Postwar American Politics," and McGirr, *Suburban Warriors: The Origins of the New American Right.*

20. Against this form of narrative, Gibson reminds us of the spatial relationship between storyteller and receiver (other/Same) in Levinas: the ethical relation emerges "not as my knowledge dominates the other, but as the moral height of the other dominates me" (49, 57).

21. See Iser, *Literary Anthropology,* Robbins, *Altered Reading: Levinas and Literature*; Miller, *The Ethics of Reading* and *Others*; Phelan, *Living to Tell About It*; Schwab, *The Mirror and the Killer-Queen: Otherness in Literary Language*; Schweickart, "Understanding an Other: Reading as Receptive Form of Communicative Action."

## CHAPTER 1

# Against Fence Thinking: Welcoming the Racial Enemy

Early in Neil LeBute's 2008 thriller *Lakeview Terrace*, Los Angeles police officer Abel Turner takes new neighbor Chris Matson on a tour of their cul-de-sac. Abel pretends to do so as a form of friendly welcome, but he actually plans to show Chris that "not everybody up here is someone you want to live next to," a point he underscores by suggesting that some of his fellow homeowners are wife-beaters or drug dealers. Realizing that he, by virtue of his mixed-race marriage, is included among the undesirables, Chris confronts Abel by saying, "We're here, okay? And we're counting on being here in a few years." In response, Abel admits a degree of tolerance in the larger world while still insisting upon some privacy and sovereignty at home. "I've got nothing against you, or her. LAPD, I work with all kinds...I lay my life down for those guys," Abel explains, before clarifying: "But that's where I work; this is where I live." The remainder of the film consists of Abel using both his acceptance as a respected member of the community and his power as a police officer to terrorize Chris, employing tactics drawn from real-world examples of what Jeannine Bell calls "anti-integrationist violence," legal and extra-legal actions designed to be "strong statements about what residential communities should look like and who the perpetrator wants to see as part of his private, neighborhood life" (6). The twist, however, comes from the racial designations: Abel, played by Samuel L. Jackson, is black and Chris, played by Patrick Wilson, is white. The role reversal, intended to heighten the terror for white members of the audience and to lambaste weak, "everybody just

© The Author(s) 2016
J. George, *Postmodern Suburban Spaces*,
DOI 10.1007/978-3-319-41006-7_2

get along"–style American liberal politics, also underscores the ridiculousness of the movie's overall over-the-top tenor.[1] But despite its absurdity, *Lakeview Terrace* effectively illustrates the tension between the rhetoric and the history of suburban racial integration. Racial inequality has long been a defining characteristic of the imagined postwar suburb, drawing from real-world phenomena such as covenants that restricted the sale of property to certain ethnicities, the proliferation of "white flight" in the 1960s and 1970s, and the high-profile shootings in this second decade of the 2000s. These incidents continue despite legal and social shifts that seem to mitigate such practices, such as the 1948 Shelley v. Kraemer decision that outlawed racial covenants and a growing suburban immigrant population. This imaginary plays out, argue observers, in the way homeowners have sublimated the criteria for exclusion into a more communal discourse, one that restricts those deemed detrimental to the community's way of life, who most often happen to be persons of color.

Given its central place in the popular perception, racial violence has unsurprisingly figured heavily in suburban fiction, but few have done so as powerfully as Gloria Naylor in her 1985 novel, *Linden Hills*. Early in the story, the two young African American men who serve as poet guides through Naylor's hellish neighborhood, "White" Willie Mason and Lester "Baby Shit" Tilson, stop outside a school, where the latter launches a lament regarding the fences he finds surrounding him. These types of barriers, he claims,

> get you used to the idea that what they have in there is different, special. Something to be separated from the rest of the world. They get you thinking fences, man, don't you see it? Then when they've fenced you in from six years old till you're twenty-six, they can let you out because you're ready to believe that what they've given you up here, their version of life, is special. And you fence your own self in after that, protecting it from everybody else out there. (45)

Although the scene takes place outside a schoolyard, Lester's speech serves as a useful tool for engaging with fictional portrayals of racial exclusion. In this chapter, I will argue that the "fence thinking" Lester so eloquently deplores represents another variation of the contractual thought that dominates suburbia; in the same way that contracts assert standard of similarity, racist exclusions assert that non-whites are intrinsically and unchangeably dissimilar. Using the concept of the political as articulated by Nazi jurist Carl Schmitt, which understands community to be formed on the basis of a friend/enemy distinction, I will demonstrate that the emphasis on conformity and exclusion on which suburbia is based invites the racial violence that has marked its history. The three novels I examine here will refute this ideology by picturing moments of critical hospitality that undermine the subject positions that sustain fence thinking. Richard Ford's *Independence Day* deals with gentrification from the Caucasian perspective, with a narrator who tries to extend welcome to non-whites while unsuccessfully maintaining his normative position. Similarly, the Asian narrator of Chang-rae Lee's *A Gesture Life* ingratiates himself to his white neighbors by refusing responsibilities to his family and loved ones, who eventually force him to rethink his behavior. Finally, *Linden Hills* features characters who replace fences with intersubjective mirrors, imagining a community that understands other people, even undesirable people, are necessary to create an identity.

## DEFENDING SUBURBAN WAYS OF LIFE

As discussed in the preceding chapter, proponents of explicit neighborhood contracts consider them practical applications of classical social contract theory. The members of the community—in this case the homeowners—determine its character and devise a legal framework to protect it. They justify this arrangement by appealing to notions of freedom and equality, of individual agency to choose one's associations; however, a cursory glance at the application of this ideal in suburban America reveals a history of exclusion and often outright violence directed at non-WASPs, primarily African Americans. The third act of Lorraine Hansberry's 1959 play *A Raisin in the Sun* powerfully illustrates the effects of this phenomenon, in which a racist HOA prevents the African American Younger family from purchasing a house in an all-white Chicago suburb. The HOA representative makes his appeal on the grounds of familiarity and identity, stating that "a man, right or wrong, has the right to want to have the neighborhood he lives in a certain kind of way. And at the moment the overwhelming majority of our people out there feel that people get along better, take more of a common interest in the life of the community, when they share a common background" (III). Tellingly, Lindner only mentions race in passing, directing most of his appeal to notions of individuality and homeowner's rights. According to this logic, the expulsion of the Youngers is only an accident of space, a moment of localized self-rule divorced from larger social and racial issues.

Several observers have traced the history of suburban racial exclusion
to these liberal ideologies. David M.P. Freund argues that the racial covenants of the pre-war period and the violence and white flight of the
postwar decades are rooted in nineteenth-century racial science, which
"figured prominently in the early planning movement because urban
congestion and unregulated development were often associated with
migrant blacks, immigrant Asians, and immigrant Europeans, the populations whose cheap labor (and often squalid living conditions) made the
era's rapid industrial and commercial growth possible" (55). As these
theories fell out of favor, a new myth based on white achievement and
government aid to African Americans during the Civil Rights movement
took its place, which understood white success as the inevitable result of
its people's predilection to homeownership, and the need for government intercession as evidence of non-whites' inherent inability to care
for property. With these myths in place, whites "justified racial exclusion
by invoking what they viewed as nonracial variables: protecting the housing market, their rights as property owners and, linked to both, their
rights as citizens"; so when they refused hospitality to potential neighbors of color, they did so on the grounds of something other than race
(8–9). "White suburbanites (and urbanites) still discriminated against
blacks after World War II because they were black," Freund writes,
"However, whites increasingly believed that they were discriminating not
because black people were inherently different but rather because black
people—for whatever cultural or market-driven reason—posed a threat to
communities of white property owners" (12–13). This history results in
what Brooks and Rose have called "ghost doctrines," in which the connotations of exclusion still inform property law, remapped into language
of communal cohesion. Ironically, racial covenants were more common in
"white neighborhoods where the neighbors were reasonably well off but
did not necessarily have particularly strong internal norms among themselves," and less necessary in those with a cohesive identity (8–9). They
stem from an ideology that allows "owners to tailor their control over
neighboring uses, and because these restrictions are ostensibly private
and consensual, they can do so in considerably greater detail than would
be possible through publicly imposed constraints like zoning. Even more
than public regulations, residential restrictive covenants allow home buyers to pick and choose among packages of limitations, knowing that the
limitations will stick with the properties even when some of the neighbors
sell" (48). As this emphasis on tailoring demonstrates, the language of

individualism that "haunts" these ghost doctrines invites exclusion for those who do not belong. As Freund succinctly puts it, "Suburban officials and homeowners learned to see political autonomy and land-use control as practically synonymous" (219).

The connections between "political autonomy" and "land-use control" that allow communities to choose their own character have remained a stumbling block for those who have tried to forcibly integrate suburbia. The most prominent example is George Romney, the former Michigan governor and director of the Department of Housing and Urban Development (HUD) during Richard Nixon's first term. Despite resistance from both suburbanites and an administration preparing to orchestrate a re-election campaign built on support from conservative homeowning whites, Romney—who had witnessed firsthand the disarray caused by exclusion in Detroit suburbs—made de-segregation a primary departmental goal. Declaring that "[w]e've got to put an end to the idea of moving to suburban areas and living only among people of the same economic and social class," Romney executed "Operation Breakthrough" in 1968, a HUD mandate to help African Americans purchase houses in middle-class neighborhoods (qtd. in Lamb 63). Operation Breakthrough took a punishment/reward approach to integration, allowing "localities [that] waive restrictive requirements in their building codes and zoning ordinances" to receive "low-income housing" and to be given "highest priority when applying for other forms of HUD assistance"; however, if the city refused this carrot, "Romney threatened to rely on the stick as well, cutting or even revoking HUD assistance to communities refusing to cooperate" (Lamb 64). The policy angered homeowners and their representatives, as indicated by Georgia congressman Fletcher Thompson's warning that HUD "must end" initiatives like Operation Breakthrough or "suburbanites would make every effort to over-turn the administration, which they believed was denying them their quality of life and devastating their property values" (Lamb 67). And as Fletcher predicted, suburbanites from Macon, Georgia to Warren, Michigan launched sometimes violent protests to express their dissatisfaction. The latter, within Romney's own home state, provided a concise example of the backlash he received as Warren residents resented HUD's 1970 decision to suspend the funds on which the working-class town relied. Although Romney did his best to frame the HUD's actions as a defense of citizens already in Warren—"Look, we're not going to bring any people here…We're not going to ask you to provide housing for anyone other than those who want to live in

Warren"—mayor Ted Bates responded with language that characterized the Department as a bunch of meddlers who want to use Warren "as a guinea pig for integration experiments" (qtd. Bonastia in 106–107). The mayor's rhetoric underscores the assumption driving the racial exclusion: he is not barring African Americans, but rather protecting the rights of his community. If the community deems African Americans as too other to join, so be it.

Despite this incident and the many others like it, recent data seems to endorse Romney's vision. The economic prosperity of the mid-90s has created what Brookings analyst Audrey Singer calls "twenty-first-century gateways," in which the suburbs of Charlotte, North Carolina and Phoenix, Arizona replace the ethnic ghettos of New York and Detroit. On a more disparaging note, Brookings researchers also find that the economic downturn impacting suburbia has "cut across the blue and red political divide," making suburbs into the "quintessential political battlegrounds" (Berube "Shifting"). And yet, high-profile acts of violence remind us of the persistence of "ghost doctrines" and the ideologies on which they are based. In February of 2012, neighborhood watch volunteer George Zimmerman trailed, wrestled with, and eventually fatally shot unarmed African American teenager Trayvon Martin, who was walking back to his home in a Florida gated community. In November of the following year, African American motorist Renisha McBride was shot and killed by Theodore Wafer after she knocked on the door of his suburban Detroit home in the middle of the night, looking for help for her disabled vehicle. Both of these cases differ from traditional stories about suburban violence in important ways—Zimmerman identifies himself as Latino, and Wafer's possible senility may have contributed to his actions—but the assumptions are familiar. The African American victims are labeled threats simply because of their race and their presence; in both cases, the shooter feared for his life because an other had entered a space in which they were not allowed. In that way, these incidents correlate with traditional anti-integrationist violence, which share a primary assumption that "offenders do not want minorities in their neighborhoods because they feel that the very presence of minorities will lead to the ruin of the offender's white neighborhood in a variety of ways" (Bell 107).

To better address this connection, particularly in light of the violent need for security and the emphasis on "ways of life" discussed here, I turn to the political theology of Nazi Jurist Carl Schmitt. It may seem irrelevant, if not outright inflammatory, to equate the behavior of American suburbanites to Nazi ideology, but Schmitt's vision of community based on exclusion, to say nothing of his emphasis on the possibility of war, provides terminology to analyze the "color-blind" racial violence enacted by some suburbanites, particularly as imagined by authors of suburban fiction.[2] According to Schmitt, the legal structure founded in the state "presupposes the concept of the political"—that is, the communal interactions that are codified in law—and all of these "political actions and motives can be reduced" to the division "between the friend and enemy" (19, 26). Simply put, the friend and enemy are understood according to their relationship to a community's perceived way of life. Although individual members enforce the nomenclature by identifying friends and enemies they encounter—"Each participant is in a position to judge whether the adversary intends to negate his opponent's way of life and therefore must be repulsed or fought in order to preserve one's own form of existence"— Schmitt stresses that these designations are not founded on personal biases; "the morally evil, aesthetically ugly or economically damaging need not necessarily be the enemy; the morally good, aesthetically beautiful, and economically profitable need not necessarily become the friend in the specifically political sense of the word"; so while it may be "advantageous to engage with him in business transactions...he is, nevertheless, the other, the stranger; and it is sufficient for his nature that he is, in a specially intense way, existentially something different and alien, so that in the extreme case conflicts with him are possible" (27). This emphasis on the metaphysical aspects of the enemy, as a figure who—despite the decisions or aspects of any one individual (save the sovereign) represents all that is antithetical to a group—gives his thought a universality that helps us think about communities in the USA.

For example, the language of the first Federal Housing Administration (FHA) zoning handbook echoes Schmitt's emphasis on the communal enemy. These guidelines, writes Kenneth T. Jackson, specially highlight the similarity according to communal aspects by advocating "suitable restrictive covenants" used to avoid "inharmonious racial or nationality groups" in neighborhoods (208–209). According to David Fruend, the FHA's guidelines allow the community to decide for itself who or what is considered inharmonious: "In other words, if a city council or zoning board declared a particular land use to be a threat to the community's safety and welfare, and if it created restrictions that outlawed or controlled that use, the courts were instructed to accept the community's judgment. Once local elites identified a particular land use to be inharmonious, the law said that it was so" (87). It is this idea that Abraham Levitt, founder of the postwar suburb Levittown, invokes when he defends racial contracts; he identifies himself as "a Jew" with "no room in my mind or heart for racial prejudice," but also insists that "if we sell one house to a Negro family, then 90 or 95 percent of our white customers will not buy into the community...This is their attitude, not ours" (Kushner 106). Levitt's rationale here embodies both the non-racial discrimination identified by Fruend and the disavowals attempted by Mr. Lindner in *A Raisin in the Sun*, who expressed personal admiration for the Youngers while insisting that a community could decide who it admits or rejects. This line of thought recalls Schmitt's insistence that "the enemy is solely the public enemy, because everything that has a relationship to such a collectivity of men, particularly to a whole nation, becomes public by virtue of such a relationship," and as such, the enemy "in the political sense need not be hated personally" (28–29). According to this logic, the feelings Linder or Levitt or any other suburbanite might have about would-be African American neighbors is irrelevant, because they are fundamentally enemies and would be better off among their own friends.

Schmitt's theories also help explain the acts of violence that accompany suburban exclusion. Schmitt repeatedly insists upon the practical reality of his political concept, arguing that the friend/enemy designations have meaning "precisely because they refer to the real possibility of physical killing" and "remain a real possibility for as long as the concept of the enemy remains valid" (33). It is important to recall here that the first Levittown subdivision, which sparked the suburban boom of the last 70 years, was a product of war: it was facilitated by industrial techniques perfected in World War II, first inhabited by vets returning from the front, and promoted by the US government as an alternative to Soviet-style communism. Furthermore, the anti-integrationist violence described by Bell is justified by concerns about security, as indicated by the defenses launched in the Martin and McBride shootings: they were real enemies who were viewed as actual threats, and action must be taken. Rhetoric surrounding suburbia focuses on the reality of the enemy, of the barbarian in the city, and the "inevitability" of killing—in the proliferation of private firearm ownership to defend one's family, in the erection of gates and employment of private security firms, in the covenants that determine who may live within a neighborhood—and continues to operate according to the friend/enemy distinction.

Finally, Schmitt's intellectual history as a social contract theorist is particularly helpful when examining the disruption of contractualism illustrated in suburban fictions about racial plurality. Once again, these suburban contracts—explicit or implicit "ghost doctrines"—serve to make individuals legible as friends or enemies to their neighbors. The person who shares a group's way of life will demonstrate him or herself to be a friend, not only in performing the role of a "good neighbor"—for example, mowing the lawn, owning the proper mod cons, adhering to social standards—but also in being understood as capable of being a good neighbor. If they fail to uphold these terms or if, as Fruend has found, they are predetermined to be incapable of doing so, then they are expelled. But suburban fiction rarely portrays relationships in such clear and static terms, and rejects the friend/enemy distinctions that allow for suburban racial exclusion by telling about people who find their assumptions called into question and are forced to redefine themselves in relation to the other they did not want.

This is particularly true of the three novels examined in this chapter. Although they are all written well after the Civil Rights period and they each take place in very different types of neighborhoods, they share a desire to re-examine the potential for intersubjective community in American suburbs in a way that disrupts standard racial thinking. Unlike postwar suburban works written more closely with the Civil Rights era—such as the aforementioned *Raisin in the Sun* (1961), Updike's 1970 novel *Rabbit Redux* (which I will address in the following chapter), or Bruce Jay Friedman's *Stern* (1962)—these works explicitly engage with the concepts of welcome and assimilation, thereby foregrounding tension between hospitality and friend/enemy distinctions. Frank Bascombe of Richard Ford's *Independence Day* uses his "friend" position to extend welcome to African American neighbors, but his interactions with them disrupt his clean dichotomies. Similarly, in Chang-rae Lee's *A Gesture Life*, Asian immigrant Doc Hata uses his house as a demonstration of his "friend" qualities, a designation that cannot mitigate the obligations he owes to others. Finally, Willie and Lester of Gloria Naylor's *Linden Hills* document the violent downfall of an African American suburb founded on its own exceptionalism while advocating an intersubjectivity that requires a plurality. Each of these stories feature incidents of critical hospitality that refuse the clarity of the friend/enemy distinction as characters are forced to acknowledge and often take responsibility for others whose very presence repudiates their autonomy. By repeatedly imagining the abandonment of the friend/enemy distinction, these authors preference communities that eschew the security and homogeny so desired by Schmitt and by historical suburbanites in favor of singularities where shared presence—not racial signifiers—is the binding element.

## "AMERICA LIKE IT USED TO BE, ONLY BLACKER": RICHARD FORD'S RACIAL IN-DEPENDENCE

Frank Bascombe, the sportswriter-turned-realtor protagonist of Richard Ford's *Independence Day* (1995), seems like an odd place to begin talking about race in suburbia. A white middle-class hero in the tradition of Updike's Harry Angstrom or Walker Percy's moviegoer Binx Bolling, Bascombe enjoys all the privileges of the modern American lifestyle: multiple careers that afford him a great deal of financial autonomy, largely pleasant relationships with his ex-wife and children (to say nothing of those with a number of girlfriends), and ownership of several properties. Despite this luxury, Bascombe finds himself constantly beset by the same ennui that plagued his forerunners Bolling and Angstrom. In *Independence Day*, Bascombe gives a name to his condition: the "Existence Period," during which he "ignore[s] much of what [he does not] like or that seems worrisome and embroiling, and then usually see[s] it go away." It is a stance of extreme disassociation, in which he finds himself increasingly "willing to let matters go as they go and see what happens. Perhaps they'll even get better. It's as possible as not" (10–11). Critics have been quick to note that Bascombe's Existence Period certainly has its roots in philosophical thought, specifically American transcendentalism and pragmatism, but that he twists these traditions "to his own solipsistic view of the world" (Chernecky 170). In particular, Bascombe's desire to face reality and live a self-sufficient life requires him to reject "as emotionally perilous the possibility of living a life connected to others and to his past and instead embraces an existence devoid of such complexities. He banishes from his mind any kind of attachment that might make him vulnerable to other people." (Walker 135). The novel's central plot, concerning a trip Bascombe and son Paul take to the Baseball Hall of Fame in Cooperstown, New York, illustrates the ethical problems of this ideology, culminating when Paul sustains an injury that calls upon the talents of a wide range of people, including those Bascombe would rather forget. The need for others intensifies his own culpability in Paul's injury, leading him to take responsibility in a manner that he had never done before; "It is my fault.

Sure it is," he admits, "When your kid gets his eye busted, that's your fault. I was supposed to help manage his risks" (396). This realization of his own involvement in other people's lives leads into a recognition of his place within the larger community and the necessity of relating to people as they are, not as he wishes they would be.[3]

Ford's readers have long since noted the importance of space in the writer's work, a curiosity stemming from reoccurring characters who live between places and from the author's own wanderlust.[4] It is appropriate, then, that his most well-known works take place within suburbs that experience transition: the largely black suburb Wallace Hill—which is experiencing its own "bright flight," in which young, upwardly mobile African Americans abandon the neighborhood for better surroundings—and his own neighborhood of Haddam. The critical hospitality required by these characters differs from that of other figures in Bascombe's life, as he remains constantly aware of their racial difference. As such, these interactions address the contractual aspects of Bascombe's highly limited interactions with African Americans and recall both the history of suburban racial violence outlined above and Schmitt's friend/enemy distinction. Bascombe's position as a "friend" motivates each of these interactions, and while he unquestionably wishes to help black characters overcome their "enemy" status, his Existence Period self-interest prohibits him from authentically responding to them as properly unknowable others. In each case, Bascombe assumes that his tenants, his former lover, and his potential client are simply black variations of himself, signatories to the same social contract, albeit in darker ink—part of his wish to keep "America like it used to be, only blacker" (24). When Bascombe relates to these characters, he unwittingly reinforces the friend/enemy distinction by trying to make them like him. As Kathy Knapp puts it, *Independence Day* imagines "sentimental *re* possession: Frank makes the case for commitment to rather than disavowal of the suburbs, with himself in the center" (*Unexceptionalism* 13). While this tactic works with some of his neighbors, the black characters he encounters often refuse to be defined as variations of him, behaving in a manner that confounds contractual fence thinking.

The most pronounced of the three plots concerns an act of sentimental repossession as Bascombe attempts to join a primarily African American space by purchasing a pair of rental houses in the black neighborhood Wallace Hills. One of the houses, formerly rented by an elderly African American couple with whom Bascombe enjoyed a congenial relationship, remains empty until the end of the novel, where it serves as the

resolution to a long plot about Bascombe's frustration with two cantan-
kerous white clients. The other house is occupied by the family of Larry
McLeod, an inhospitable and potentially violent former Viet Nam vet who
rejects Bascombe's friendly overtures. As related in his first-person narration, Bascombe frames Larry's contempt as grave ingratitude, but his
language also reveals the egoism motivating his involvement in Wallace
Hills. This condescension is evident as he relates his first experience with
Wallace Hills, which he presents as a type of "discovery" on his part:
"I'd passed down this street and the four or five others like it in the dark-
town section of Haddam at least five hundred times in the decade and
a half I'd lived here, and didn't know a single soul." Bascombe tries to
rhetorically compensate for this ignorance by understanding the oppression the African American citizens have experienced via the discomfort
he felt upon first moving to Haddam, when he and his wife feared that
their neighbors had "some secret insider knowledge we didn't have simply
because we'd shown up when we did—too late—yet unfortunately it was
knowledge we could also never acquire, for more or less the same reasons." Worse, he smugly couples this condescension with a "deep appreciation for the sense of belonging and permanence the citizens of these
streets might totally lack in Haddam (through no fault of their own), yet
might long for the way the rest of us long for paradise" (26–27). Each
of these examples feature Bascombe operating according to friend logic,
presenting himself as a cultural insider who understands the terms of the
contract and wishes to extend that same set of behaviors to others, as if
they were a people simply waiting for him to reach out. He joins them in
proximity, not to establish a face-to-face relation, but to extend to them a
limited welcome based on his understanding. This line of thought negates
the subject's sense of autonomy and treats them as would-be friends for
which he is the catalyst that brings them to fruition.

To achieve this similarity, Bascombe invokes the language of limited
hospitality. He explains his ignorance about the black citizens of Wallace
Hill as a lack of welcome, admitting, "I had been invited into no one's
home, had paid no social calls, never sold a house here, had probably
never even walked down a single sidewalk (though I had no fear about
doing it day or night)" (26). Similarly, he thinks of his behavior as a type
of equal exchange, stating that the least he could do was "help make two
families feel at home…though they and their relatives might've been here
a hundred years and had never done anything but make us white late-
arrivers feel welcome at their own expense" (28). This language allows

him to shape Larry's inhospitality as the problem in the relationship, and thereby minimize his own culpability. He sarcastically feints humility when realizing, "I deserve to be paid money for letting him live in my house," and later complains that his rent payment "is being held hostage to the McLeods' ingrown convictions regarding privacy and soleness" (150, 423). He intends the phrase "Larry McLeod and I have not much enriched or broadened each other's world-views" as a bit of understatement that hangs blame for the failure squarely on Larry's unwilling shoulders, but his imagined solution to the problem highlights his own limited hospitality: "I should've hauled them over for a cookout the minute I closed on their house, gotten them into some lawn chairs on the deck, slammed a double margarita in both of them, served up a rack of ranch-style ribs, corn on the cob, tomato and onion salad and a key lime pie, and all after would've been jake" (28, 128). In each of these cases, Bascombe understands hospitality as a matter of friendliness in which he gives property and benefits and the recipients show due gratitude for the kindness he offers. But the empty rental property on one street and Larry McLeod's violent refusal on the other symbolize the shortcomings of such assumptions, indicating that Bascombe's worldview cannot fully explain the residents of Wallace Hill.

A scene recounting Bascombe's frustrated attempted to collect rent from Larry depicts this ignorance. Bascombe dwells within the neighborhood certain of his rights as a homeowner and of the community's appreciation for the economic assistance he provides. But when they do not react in a suitably grateful manner, Bascombe imagines himself bereft of rights or welcome, as "a criminal" who "peer[s] through the front window into the living room" (119). This feeling intensifies when Myrlene Beavers, an elderly woman who enjoyed a pleasant relationship with Bascombe before succumbing to dementia, mistakes him for a prowler and calls the police. Bascombe hopes to resolve this misunderstanding via both legal rights, telling the officers that he is the homeowner and reminding himself that he has "a right to see [inside of the rental house] under extraordinary circumstances," and his presumption of belonging, but both strategies fail. Neither the police nor the citizens of Wallace Hill recognize Bascombe for who he claims to be. The episode ends when police calm the situation and Myrlene suddenly returns to addressing him as Bascombe the landlord, but this does little to assure him of his status. He still describes Myrlene as "traitorous" and gives Larry's wife a "betrayed" look (125). More than an inconvenience, Frank senses the degree to which his limited hospitality is recognized or accepted by others. In his mind, he has made them friends by giving them part of his entitlement to the American suburban dream, which should erase, if not all hard feelings toward white Americans, at least hard feelings toward him. But the characters fail to stay in such roles and, in doing so, exceed friend/enemy binaries.

The murdered realtor plot further emphasizes the phenomenological undoing of Bascombe's friend position as it highlights his inability to properly describe her, or himself in relation. Clair DeVane, "a perfect little dreamboat" with whom he was linked, "briefly but intensely," exists as a spectral figure who haunts Bascombe's narrative, appearing obliquely at key points, including the opening passage in which he introduces the reader to Haddam. He mentions Clair's murder in a curt, matter-of-fact aside—"roped and tied, raped and stabbed"—counting the death as just one of the unfortunate events from which Haddam was feeling a "new sense of a wild world being just beyond our perimeter," including it among anecdotes about plummeting property values and untrimmed trees (211, 4). This tendency repeats almost every time he mentions her, as when he tries to reduce her experiences—left with two kids after husband runs off with another woman, Clair moved to Haddam (where "she didn't see many people who looked like her") and worked her way from receptionist to agent—into a "good story: human enterprise and good character triumphing over adversity and bad character" (142). And yet, despite these constant apparent slights, Bascombe muses upon her again and again, never able to fully describe or fully forget her. He can neither make sense of her murder—"there's no proof nor any reason to imagine anyone would need to kill as sweet a soul as Clair was for their purposes to win out"—nor does he understand his affair with her, which she considered "exactly wrong and doomed" (144, 211). At times, he tries to dismiss her as a one-off oddity, suggesting that she "had not fully existed in anyone's life but her own" and that their time together was a fleeting dream "entirely founded on Clair's being a total impossibility," and elsewhere casts her as a stock character in his personal development, "a featured player in some Existence Period melodrama of my own devising" (145, 215). This indecision, combined with her frequent reappearances in his narrative, reveals that she haunts Bascombe, thereby calling his independence into question. In this way, Clair remains, in Levinas' terms, an unthemtizable other, an individual who cannot be reduced to knowability by an observing subject. Without the ability to make sense of Clair,

Bascombe cannot properly think of himself as a friend or an enemy, nor can he articulate the influence she has had on him.

The stakes of this lack of clarity are particularly evident in a short scene midway through the novel, in which Bascombe makes a sales pitch to an African American trucker called Tanks. Once again, we see at work the transitory factor central to Ford's fiction, as Bascombe and Tanks have nothing in common, and yet find themselves sharing space together when watching detectives investigate a murder that occurred at the motel where they are staying. Though a seemingly inconsequential chance encounter, the pair's brief time in proximity encapsulates the shortcomings in Bascombe's Existence Period. When Tanks expresses interest in buying a house, Bascombe launches a sales pitch based on a myriad of assumptions he makes about his would-be client. But despite an alleged concern for "misrepresentation," Bascombe is mostly interested in being understood, not in understanding. He takes offense at Tanks' admission that he assumed that realtors "was all crooks," but does not answer in kind because of his adherence to a contractual version of the "golden rule," reminding himself that "I wouldn't want to do anything to you that I wouldn't want done to me—at least as far as realty goes" (209). Unconcerned with misrepresenting Tanks, Bascombe feels confident enough in his knowledge of the other man to imagine him "snugged up in his high-tech sleep cocoon, decked out (for some reason) in red silk pj's, earphones plugged into an Al Hibbler CD, perusing a Playboy or a Smithsonian and munching a gourmet sandwich purchased somewhere back down the line and heated up in his mini-micro"; when Tanks asks a vague question about property values in his current hometown of Alhambra, California, Bascombe offers an enthusiastic "you're in great shape," despite the fact that he has "never been in Alhambra, [does not] know the tax base, the racial makeup, the comp situation or the market status" (202–203). Bascombe's confidence goes so far that he dismisses Tanks' very legitimate worry that he would be "the only pea in the pod" if he moved to Haddam; when Tanks asks, "You got any niggers down there in your part of New Jersey?" Bascombe offers an unfounded answer, "Plenty of 'em." Although Bascombe is "awfully sorry to have said that," his Existence Period removal demands that he does not shift his language and continue with the pitch, which ultimately fails (209). Like Larry McLeod and Clair DeVane, Tanks is unmoved by Bascombe's tactics, refusing to accept his vision of fences, even when he professes to open them.

Ford emphasizes the insufficiency of the contract by repeatedly drawing attention to the circumstances of Bascombe and Tanks' interaction, particularly the murder investigation happening in the motel. Bascombe claims that he and Tanks "aren't socializing here" but only "bearing brief dual witness to the perilous character of life and our uncertain presences in it," and that without the death, "there's no reason for us to stand here together" (202). He intends the phrase to have an air of solemnity appropriate to the situation, framing him and Tanks as uninvolved bystanders, but Ford does not allow the men to enjoy non-participant status. Bascombe's social solitude is disrupted when the victim's wife exits an adjoining hotel room and inserts herself into the space shared by Bascombe and Tanks; in this moment, the pair become "her companions of a sort," who watch her "with distant compassion." The description that follows recalls Levinas' emphasis on the disruption of the face: "Her face comes up, light catches it so that I see the look of startlement on her fresh young features. It is her first scent, the first light-glimmer, that she's no longer connected in the old manner of two hours ago but into some new network now, where caution is both substance and connector" (208). Although he recognizes the demand made by the woman's face—"I, of course, could connect with her—give a word or a look"—Bascombe refuses her on the grounds that "it would only be momentary, whereas caution is what she needs now, and what's dawning," and he even tries to placate his guilt by limply telling himself that the "lesson of caution" that the wife has learned "at a young age" is "not the worst thing" (208). As this woefully pathetic summation suggests, Bascombe's irresponsibility is insufficient to the facts of his present situation, which Ford positions as a repudiation of the Existence Period contracts.

The failure of contractualism that he experiences in that most impermanent space forces Bascombe to understand the limitations of places such as suburbia. The happy life in Haddam or the Caucasian-focused experience in Wallace Hill that Bascombe had fashioned for himself falls apart because he realizes that place "may only seem to provide a refuge; it is finally, as Ford himself believes, totally barren of meaning, totally arbitrary in essence, until a person breathes significance into it by occupation, thought, memory, and a history shared with someone else" (Walker 170). By the end of the novel, Bascombe comes to this realization and recognizes his place within the larger society; the final scene finds him standing "in the crowd...feel[ing] the push, pull, the weave and sway of others" (451). The man who had embraced suburbia and real estate as a means for avoiding the complications of other lives accepts his entanglement in them, and while Paul's injury is the clearest impetus of this change of heart, the resolution to the Markham subplot connects the engaged, responsible Bascombe to his experiences with African American suburbanites. For commentators such as Ian McGuire, the Markham plot mirrors Bascombe's failed attempts to maintain a pragmatic distance from the people around him. Like Bascombe, the Markhams "are psychologically paralyzed by an awareness of their own previous errors of judgement" and must learn to live in present reality (24). Although he fails to see the similarity to his own situation, Bascobme labels the Markhams' trepidation a case of the "realty dreads," the longing for a perfect house and neighborhood that sets impossible standards impossible. Accordingly, the Markhams tend to find some reason to reject each property Bascombe shows them, despite his attempts to "draw them back toward a chummier feeling, make them less anxious both about the unknown *and* the obvious: the ways they're like their neighbors (all insignificant) and the happy but crucial ways they're not" (57–58). By the end of the story, the Markhams' dreads have lost them all other options, leaving them with one tenable property: the Wallace Hill rental house across from Larry McLeod. In the midst of his arguments with the Markhams, Bascombe asks himself, "[I]s there any cause to think a place—any place—within its plaster and joists, its trees and plantings, in its putative essence *ever* shelters some spirit of as proof of its significance and ours?" His answer is direct:

> No! Not one bit! *Only other humans do that,* and then only under special circumstances, which is a lesson of the Existence Period worth holding onto. We just have to be smart enough to quit asking places for what they can't provide, and begin to invent other options...as gestures of our God-required but not God-assured independence. (442, emphasis mine)

To put it another way, Bascombe comes to understand that significance or meaning comes not from sheltering one's self through constructs, whether they be houses or contracts; rather, it comes through relating with other people in proximity, specifically other people as they are. To try to hold out and wait for other options results in the meaningless life he found himself leading when trying to just "let things go" in his Existence Period.

The fact that Bascombe makes these observations while moving the Markhams into Wallace Hill, the all-black neighborhood he planned to defend by acting as a benevolent landlord, indicates the importance of the African American characters in bringing Bascombe to this state of independence. Finally recognizing his own tenuous claims to insider status, Bascome's position on unfamiliar ground forces him to forego the separation between the insiders and the outsiders, or to hold them to specific knowable states, and rather take the space and the people as they are—they are black residents next to an empty house—and respond accordingly, without pretensions about how they will (or should) act in response to him. In fact, Bascombe's silence about his plans for Wallace Hill—save for an off-hand comment about all houses having history, a statement made to evade Joe Markham's "two-bit subterfuge for broaching the race issue" via a few off-hand remarks—indicates a notable change of heart regarding others (419). Instead of endlessly narrating about the lives of people he has not taken the time or space to know or offering them highly limited faux-hospitality, Bascombe simply stays silent and exists. He enters the push and pull of others without trying to define them, or himself, first.

By prioritizing relation over definition, by coming to face those in proximity in all of their difference, Bascombe forgoes the contractualism that has motivated suburbia's racial history. Racial covenants, white flight, and even some integration mandates—not unlike those Ford portrays in Bascombe's Wallace Hill plan—require clear recognition of insider and outsider, neighbor and stranger. By silently merging the black and white spaces, looking for in-dependence instead of asserting a contract, Ford imagines a different type of relation, one that accepts both unknowability of being with others and the interrelation between people sharing space that gives those spaces significance.

## A QUANTITY KNOWN: STASIS AND DWELLING IN *A GESTURE LIFE*

Where Tanks refuses Frank Bascombe's qualified welcome, Franklin "Doc" Hata—the Korean-born, Japanese-raised narrator of Chang-rae Lee's 1999 novel *A Gesture Life*—discovers that, despite being the only Asian in an all-white middle-class suburb of Bedley Run, "it seemed people took an odd interest in telling me that I wasn't *un*welcome" (2–3). In fact, for Doc Hata's neighbors, his ethnicity has become "both odd and delightful to people, as well as somehow town-affirming" (2). Of course, this acceptance was not simply bestowed upon him by the virtue of his existence; rather, it was something Doc Hata had to labor to earn.

Aware from the beginning that he was "a foreigner and a Japanese" living on a white, middle-class American street, Hata strove to meet and even exceed his neighbor's expectations so that his presence did not frighten the homeowners, but gave them "the reassuring thought of how safe they actually were, how shielded, that an interloper might immediately recognize and so heed the rules of their houses" (44). As this reference to "heeding the rules" suggests, Bedley Run operates according to an unspoken but no less strict neighborhood contract, one that Doc Hata internalizes by establishing his own house, a "two-story Tudor revival at number 57," which he renovated from a dilapidated relic into "one of the special properties in the area" (16). But as with Bascombe's Existence Period, these gestures raise troubling ethical problems as his behavior becomes an excuse to ignore the needs of those he encounters, including his own daughter. This issue stems from another instance of contractualism based on a friend/enemy distinction, as indicated by the many divisions that occur throughout the novel: from Hata's position as the sole Asian in Bedley Run, to the relation between Bedley Run and its adjoining (but considerably more economically troubled) suburb Ebbington, to the conflict between the Japanese Imperial Army and Korean comfort women that appears in flashbacks. A multi-racial immigrant, Hata is well aware of the mental dissonance caused by Schmittian politics, but he assuages this discomfort by internalizing its logic, using propriety to gain acceptance. But as he tries to construct this identity, other people—even those he considers enemies—repeatedly call him into responsibility, disrupting his solipsistic existence. For the citizens of his town, which underwent its own economic reformation in the 1960s and changed its name from Bedleyville to the "more affluent-sounding" Bedley Run, Hata's project of self-improvement and self-possession embodies the suburban ethos of autonomy—literal self-naming—and of individualism.[5] When a realtor declares, "Doc Hata *is* Bedley Run," she indicates the extent to which he has fully established himself as the community's friend (136).

The central aspect to Doc Hata's friendship performance is his house and the studious housekeeping he performs to ingratiate himself with his neighbors. Hata's emphasis on his home as a means of acceptance into the larger social milieu recalls the "domestic fiction" genre, which was particularly popular among nineteenth-century middle-class women. In her study *Neodomestic Fiction*, Kristin J. Jacobson argues that though elements of the genre still continue, novels after 1980 have shifted from stories that imagine stability and safety in the home—that tend to "categorize the home as either a haven or a trap"—to those that "promote, rather than attempt to resolve, instability and heterogeneity" (31, 29). For Jacobson, *A Gesture Life* is one such "queered" novel.[6] Jacobson claims that Hata's "views on homeownership…suggest that where he tweaks suburban alienation to his advantage, he reproduces suburban control…When Doc Hata paints his estranged, adopted daughter's bedroom, his penchant for control, perfection, and, by implication, domestic security emerges" (174–175).

I would like to slightly adjust Jacobson's claim to argue that Hata's need for control and the process of identity construction in which he engages are all byproducts of his desire to establish "friend" status, to make himself knowable to his neighbors and therefore accepted. As the title suggests, Hata undertakes a number of gestures to "prove" his adherence to the standards of friendship, most importantly his devotion to housekeeping. As he tells readers, "in regarding one's own house or car or boat one can discover the discretionary pleasures of ownership…and thus have another way of seeing the shape of one's life, how it has transformed and, with any luck, multiplied and grown" (136–137). It is not surprising, then, that when Hata errs and puts his house in danger by falling asleep in front of the fireplace and starting a small fire in his den, he experiences "the peculiar sensation" that he is "already dead and a memory…walking the hallways of another man's estate" (139). To be sure, part of this domestic attention stems from Hata's desire to enact the neighborhood contract, but even that behavior is part of the "good neighbor" identity he cultivates, as these demarcations serve as the primary terms of interaction between his fellow residents.[7] In Bedley Run, he explains, "being neighbors means sharing the most limited kinds of intimacies, such as sewer lines and property boundaries and annual property tax valuations…on the whole an unwritten covenant of conduct governs us, a signet of cordiality and decorum, in whose ethic, if it can be called such a thing, the worst is to be drawn forth and disturbed" (44). Doc Hata's housekeeping, then, is based on the Schmittian logic: by keeping his home in good condition and participating in the rules and expectations of the other citizens, Hata can enjoy peace and solitude.

Like Bascombe, Hata wishes to extend his friend status to outsiders, namely a Korean orphan named Sunny, who he adopts into a privileged lifestyle in the USA. He brings her into his home, thereby providing shelter for her and a space to enact his identity as a benevolent father. Doc Hata reflects on this achievement early in the novel, acknowledging that he has always wished to be in a situation like the one I have steadily fashioned for myself in this town, where, if I don't have many intimates or close friends, I'm at least a quantity known, somebody long ago counted. Most everyone in Bedley Run knows me, though at the same time I've actually come to develop an unexpected condition of transparency here, a walking case of others' certitude, that to spy on me on my way down Church Street is merely noting the expression of a natural law. *Doc Hata*, they can say with surety, he *comes around*. (21)

But where his property and propriety have allowed him to become this "quantity known," a symbol of his neighborhood's diversity and individuality, Doc Hata admits that his life has become somehow unsatisfactory. The long-strived-for rapport he has crafted has become "discomfiting" and he finds that the "happy blend of familiarity and hominess and what must be belonging is strangely beginning to disturb me" (21–22). Hata's admission undermines the promises of friendship, as the very things that are supposed to give him a rich life—including an enclosed private space from which he can form a public persona—have become dissatisfying and confining.

Lee foregrounds the source of Hata's unhappiness with a striking intertextual passage. After his usual swimming routine is interrupted by a moment of existential nausea—"I suddenly have the thought that I'm not swimming in my own pool at all, but am someplace else, in a neighboring pool or even a pond"—Hata seeks solace by retreating into his house, where he recalls a short story "about a man who decides one day to swim in other people's pools, one after a another in his neighborhood and town, which, as described, seems very much like Bedley Run" (23). The story is, of course, "The Swimmer" by John Cheever, and Doc Hata's identification with the protagonist Neddy Merrill is revealing. Hata and Merrill do share some surface qualities, as both are intensely private and wish to avoid society's unnecessary excesses; but where Hata finds even the possibility of swimming in someone else's pool sickening, Cheever's Merrill eschews property rights and embraces impropriety, climbing over walls, going through gates, and pushing aside hedges. Merrill's improper behavior would be unthinkable for Hata, and while it does ultimately cost him his home—he returns to find the lights off, the doors locked, and the place abandoned—it also opens him to a new relation with his neighbors, one that goes beyond the usual alcoholic daze of cocktail parties.

By invoking Neddy Merrill, Lee draws a stark distinction between Cheever's protagonist and his own, reminding readers that the former undergoes a type of transfiguration while Hata remains unhappily familiar: Merrill experiences literal ecstasy (*ex*-stasis) while Doc Hata stays cloistered within "in the *peerless* quiet of the pool" (23 emphasis mine). For philosophers like Levinas and Jean-Luc Nancy, consciousness requires ecstasis, as the event moves the subject from solitary ipseity to a recognition of a reality beyond one's individual subjectivity. According to Levinas, the all-objectifying Same who reduces everything to his or her understanding does so because he or she has no true relation: "this relation does not become an implantation in the other and a confusion in him, does not affect the identity of the same, its ipseity, does not silence the apology, does not become apostasy and ecstasy" (*Totality* 41–42). For Nancy, who insists that community is "neither a work to be produced, nor a lost communion, but rather as space itself, and the spacing of the experience of the outside, of the outside-of-self," ecstasy is the basis of community and of selfhood. Via ecstatic interruption with an other, the individual realizes the limits of his or her subjectivity. For this reason, "consciousness is never mine...I only have it in and through the community," and this community is "the ecstatic consciousness of the night of immanence, insofar as such a consciousness is the interruption of consciousness" (*Inoperative Community* 19). Nancy's philosophy directly contradicts the foundation of Schmitt's friend/enemy distinction, which understands imminence as similarity within a group and the expulsion of others. For Levinas and Nancy, however, others are required for identity; it is exposure, not exclusion, that makes the self.

It is a concept that Hata should understand well, given his experiences with racism in World War II Japan. Before becoming Doc Hata of Bedley Run, he was Lieutenant Jiro Kurohata of the Japanese Imperial Army, a medical officer charged with preparing "volunteer" Korean comfort women to perform sexually for his fellow soldiers. Within the framework of actual war, Schmitt's friend/enemy logic becomes particularly pronounced: beyond the larger East/West dichotomies at work in World War II, Kurohata's Korean ancestry and Japanese adoption make him a type of enemy masquerading as a friend, a point often made by his cruel commanding officer, Captain Ono. Ono underscores this outsider status when he starts flying a black flag outside the camp infirmary to summon Kurohata. As the narrating Hata explains, the flag is both a pun and an insult; "Hata is, literally, 'flag,' and a 'black flag,' or *kurohata*, is the banner a village would raise by its gate in olden times to warn of a contagion within" (224). As a Korean in the Japanese army, Kurohata is himself the contagion, the disease that must be purified. However, this very mark against him becomes the means of connection when one of the comfort women, a Korean named Kkutaeh or "K" forges a relationship with Kurohata on the grounds of their shared heritage; specifically, she begs him "as a countryman" to "take your gun from your holster and put me down right now" (238). Even as the two of them become close to one another, divulging their pasts and making plans about their lives after the war, Kurohata not only refuses to take responsibility for K and honor her request, but even takes sexual advantage of her and interprets her lack of resistance as willing participation. In a telling exchange, K—having killed Captain Ono—again begs Kurohata to kill her; when he refuses, she tells him, "You are a decent man, Lieutenant, but really you are not any different from the rest" (300). In one regard, her statement confirms Kurohata's desires, to no longer be the diseased outsider or black flag, but to finally be recognized as Japanese; on the other, her claim demonstrates the degree to which he has harmed others—even those he claims to love—in this pursuit. This history reveals Hata's Bedley Run friendship project to be nothing more than an attempt to avoid responsibility for prior actions, to distance himself from the loveless father or inhumane soldier that he has been. The house serves as a facade to distract from that past and to maintain facile, gesture-based relationships with his neighbors, in which he will never have to worry about exposure. So while Hata might find his current identity too confining and unsatisfying, it does have the advantage of evading a terrible past. However, the evasion does not last as suburbia becomes the ground for moments of critical hospitality. People with whom Hata shares space refuse not only the distinctions he attempts to enforce, but also the coherence of the identity he has constructed. In fact, it is the very presence of enemies that helps him construct his sense of self.

The first interruption comes from a person who, on the surface, seems to be another friend: fellow Bedley Run homeowner Mary Burns, with whom Hata has a brief romantic relationship. By the time he and Mary meet, Hata had well developed his distancing gestures, but instead of simply accepting his externals, "Mary Burns, somehow, decided to breach that peace with [Hata]," employing a Neddy Merrill-like impropriety: Mary breaks the "buffer of fine landscaping and natural vegetation, of whitewashed horse fence and antiqued stone walls" and steps on the lawn to speak with Hata, "doing nothing to camouflage or otherwise hide" (44, 48). In undoing the sanctity of the landscape that Hata has created and interrupting the spacial divisions he has constructed, Mary forces Hata to recognize the insufficiency of his polite exterior. Her attempts to engage with him emotionally draw attention to the ethical stakes of his behavior. As a widower with significant familial problems, Mary needs more from Hata than a swimming companion and a weekend date, but whether the topic of conversation is the inevitability of death or Mary's difficulties with Sunny, Hata refuses to give anything more than pat answers. And while Mary eventually wearies of trying to pry an honest reaction from Hata, their relationship has a lingering effect on him, eventually providing the means for his reunion with Sunny. This unavoidable disruption makes Mary a bad neighbor, if not an enemy by Schmitt's standards, because she does not allow Hata the peace he wants; her memory haunts him and calls him into question, even after she has left his corporeal presence. He cannot exercise his autonomy or choose his identity for himself, because he must contend with the irrepressible thought of her disappointment. In the same way the specter of Clair DeVane brought Frank Bascombe into authentic responsibility, Mary proves too puzzling, too infinite, for Hata to merely dismiss. Her memory exposes his poor behavior.

Most importantly, Mary draws attention to Hata's irresponsible treatment of Sunny, describing her as "a woman to whom you're beholden...as if she's someone you hurt once, or betrayed and now you're obliged to do whatever she wishes" (60). In some ways, he is "beholden" to Sunny, as he hopes that he can transfer "the ambivalent ethical relation between Doc Hata and K to the adoptive relation between Hata and Sunny"; however, it would be more accurate to say that Sunny is beholden to K, or Hata's memory of K, as she must always live up to the person he betrayed (Jerng 53). Sunny, of course, fails to do so, and although he never verbalizes his disappointment, Hata does admit that he wishes she were "somewhat appreciative of the providence of institutions that brought her from the squalor of the orphanage—the best of which can be only so happy—to an orderly, welcoming suburban home in America, with a hopeful father of like-enough race and sufficient means" (73). This phrase "like-enough race" signals a prejudice that Hata does not explicitly articulate, but is implied in his opinions of others, particularly Sunny. Hata's narration obliquely positions Sunny as racially other, with passing references to her dark hair and skin: "I had often asked her if she would take better care with her skin...but in those days it was desirable to be tanned and dark as one could get, and Sunny was one who never had trouble in that regard" (31). Even when Hata recounts their first meeting, he recalls seeing not the Korean he imagined, but a "skinny, jointy young girl, with thick, wavy black hair and dark hued-skin...the product of a much less dignified circumstance, a night's wanton encounter between a GI and a local bar girl" and how her "hair, her skin, were there to see, self-evident, and it was obvious how some other color (or colors) ran deep within her" (204). Doc Hata's disappointment with Sunny's racial makeup becomes even clearer when combined with the fact that, when looking for Sunny at a party, he was struck "immediately" that "a number of the partygoers were black and Puerto Rican; colored people were a rare sight in Bedley Run, especially at social events, and never did one see such 'mixed' gatherings" and his "next thought was that Sunny wasn't simply involving herself intimately with all these men white and brown and black, but was living with them as well, with no other company but theirs" (102). This racial concern only becomes exasperated when Sunny's attendance at parties in the economically depressed suburb Ebbington brings her into contact with African American boys, leading to a striking scene in which Hata, driving to one such party to retrieve his teenage daughter, finds her first dancing for and then kissing a black boy named Linc. Although any family member may feel some discomfort at witnessing such an intimate act, there is a touch of racial prejudice in Hata's wish that "she were just another girl or woman to me, no longer my kin or my daughter or even my charge" (116). Sunny, who was intended to be a further aspect of his friendship project, of repeating this identity of Asian acceptance in the USA, instead aligns herself with an unwelcome blackness.

Accordingly, Sunny's various acts of rebellion cannot be understood as simple teenage behavior problems, but rather demands for critical hospitality directed at the man who extended a highly limited invitation when he brought her into his house. "Sunny, I'm afraid, always hated the house," Hata tries to tell readers, but Sunny reframes the opinion to emphasize Hata's expectations, as in an argument concerning a piano she no longer practices:

> "I'm saying, you like having it around for what it says. About me. How I've failed."
> "That's not in the least true."

"Sure it is," she answered, almost affably. But there was real defeat in her voice also, a child's broad welling of it.
I told her, "If anything, Sunny, I should see it as a symbol of my own failure, in inspiring the best in you."
"That's right. I've failed doubly. First myself, and then my good poppa, who's loved and respected by all." (26, 31)

Instead of aiding Hata's identity project, Sunny, like Mary, refuses to be a figure in Hata's solitary self-development, and in fact levels the most direct attack on her father's performance: "You make a whole life out of gestures and politeness," she charges, claiming that his neighbors regard him as nothing more than a "'good Charlie' to organize the garbage and sidewalk-cleaning schedule" (95). So where Hata intended Sunny to further secure him as a friend, his treatment only solidified her as an enemy, chasing her out of his house and into Ebbington for a 14-year estrangement. Even after they begin to reconcile, the adult Sunny insists on limiting Hata's interactions with her mixed-race son Thomas. To protect her son from her father's racism, Sunny instructs Hata, "I don't want you to tell him there was a connection," and makes him refer to himself as "Franklin," for whom Sunny once worked (212). Prompted by a desire to leave his unsatisfying home and create a bond with Sunny and Thomas, Hata—who has labored so much to construct his identity—accepts Sunny's description of him, refusing the terms of distinction he once used.

According to Hamilton Carroll, "Hata's attempt to write himself into the nation fails because it is displaced by the return—as traumatic subjects—of the people he abjects in the constitution of his narrative," and while Carroll refers largely to K and Sunny, I would include Mary in the category, as she also displaces Hata's acceptance (595–596). More specifically, the radical hospitality insisted by "enemies" Mary and Sunny confound the distinctions by which Hata had operated his life. Admitting that he behaved like a monster and a terrible father, Hata ends his story by admitting that he has been misrecognized by the neighborhood that claimed to know him. He is not a distinguished retiree and respected member of his community, but a horrible villain, whose likeness should be a sign of evil:

But it is not. And I do not live in broad infamy, nor hide from righteous pursuers or seekers of the truth. I do not mask my face or screen my doings each day. I have not yet been banished from this earth. And though nearly every soul I've closely known has come to some dread or grave misfortune, I instead persist, with warmth and privilege accruing to me unabated, ever securing my good station here, the last place I will belong. (345–346)

By recognizing himself as both an enemy and a friend, Hata acknowledges the impossibilities of the distinctions on which he relied. Without these clear signifiers, Hata chooses to abandon fence thinking by abandoning his house, and the novel ends with him "outside looking in" at his house, which is now "alive and full" with other people (356). By engaging with others and not hiding behind the gestures of good-neighborliness, Doc Hata takes responsibility for who he is, for what he has done, and thereby responds to the factuality of the world around him. No longer stuck in his pool, Hata rejects his stagnant existence and experiences the ecstatic.

## THINKING FENCES, THINKING MIRRORS

Although, as *A Gesture Life* shows, Hata certainly experiences racism, his ability to adopt and dismiss fence thinking is, in part, a consequence of his race and class. As a member of the Asian "model minority," the assumptions foisted upon Hata differ from those placed upon other non-whites entering the suburbs. As shown earlier in the chapter, African Americans have long been subjected to concentrated exclusion via anti-integrationist violence and government mandates. The frustration that *Linden Hill's* Lester expresses about the fences that surround him captures the feeling of alienation created by these friend/enemy distinctions, a central theme of Naylor's novel. The titular neighborhood is a postwar suburb reserved for successful African Americans, one that embodies Bascombe's vision of "America, only blacker" in the most disturbing manner. It is the project of Luther Nedeed and his nearly identical son, men who purchased a tract of "hard sod only good enough to support linden trees," built shacks upon it, and rented them to "murders, root doctors, and bootleg preachers who were thrown out of the South" (2, 5). Under the control of Nedeed and four generations of his sons and grandsons—each named Luther Nedeed and each alike in appearance and temperament—Linden Hills became a "showcase," an "ebony jewel that reflected the soul of [surrounding white dominated] Wayne County but reflected it black" (9). But as much as the present-day Linden Hills, overseen by Luther Nedeed V, has become the premier space for the black middle class, it is also a Dantean hellscape filled with people who ransom their identities for the sake of material gain: a black executive worries that his attraction to woman of color will damage his reputation, a homosexual man abandons his partner to marry the daughter of a business associate, a preacher denies his faith to make crowd-pleasing sermons, a historian chronicles the development of Linden Hills in a manner that flatters the Nedeeds. Starting with Luther Nedeed, each of these characters draw strict divisions between insiders and outsiders, those who embody the spirit of Linden Hills and those whose presence threatens their ethos. In this way, *Linden Hills* is very much communal grotesque, an image of a group who internalizes the same logic that deems them unwelcome and directs it against a new set of enemies. An unquestionably bleak novel, *Linden Hills* vividly illustrates the self-destructive aspects of fence thinking by suggesting that the need to eradicate the other ultimately leads to suicide. But by presenting the neighborhood through the perspectives of poet guides Lester and Willie—the former a third-generation Linden Hills insider and the latter raised in the adjacent urban slums—and that of Luther V's enslaved wife Willa, Naylor imagines another type of suburban community, in which the unwanted and antagonistic are essential to one's identity.

Issues of community have always been at the center of Naylor's work, beginning with her 1982 debut, *The Women of Brewster Place*. For critics such as Susan Meisenhelder and Barbara Christian, Naylor's focus on African Americans, particularly lower-class women, indicates support for a monolithic group identity.[8] While the genesis of Linden Hills, a blacks-only space made on otherwise rejected land, might seem to endorse these readings, the novel is more interested in illustrating failures of connection, which often occur exactly because they preference sameness and affinity over difference and plurality. The novel borrows the structure of Dante's Inferno, with the streets of the suburb corresponding to the rings of Hell. Naylor places the residents on their respective streets/rings because, as she explains in a conversation with Toni Morrison, they have "given up" key aspects of their identities: "The first are ties with family, then ties with community, ties with their religious and spiritual values, then ties with their ethnocentric sense of self" (Naylor and Morrison 46). While this language may suggest a fear of race-betrayal, the actual "sins" committed by residents are acts of irresponsibility, the refusal to care for other people.

These irresponsible acts often involve fence thinking, as shown in the scenes of Luther II transforming his neighborhood from a refuge for the unwanted to an exceptional space. Breaking from the cool, observational tone employed through much of the chapter, the narrator adopts fiery language to characterize the omnipresence of white oppression: "white money backing wars for white power because the very earth was white—look at it—white gold, white silver, white coal running white railroads and steamships, white oil fueling white automotives" (8). The narrator continues in that register when explaining Luther II's own desires, thereby framing him not just as a victim, but as an equal participant. When Luther II pictures himself as a "beautiful, black wad of spit right in the white eye of America," he imagines not simply separation from the larger culture, but also an antagonistic force in which he can be a "fly in that ointment, a spot on that bleached sheet" (8–9). But Luther also couches his complaints in paternalist language—ridiculing African Americans stuck "digging another man's coal, cleaning another man's home, rocking another man's baby...the maids, mammies, and mules who were bringing the price of that sweat back to his land and his hands"—which reveals the egoism of his communal vision (8). When Luther II speaks of "his people," one assumes he refers to simply African Americans, and his complaints about those who "were always out of step, a step behind or a step ahead, still griping and crying about slavery, hanging up portraits of Abraham Lincoln in those lousy shacks" seem to indicate frustration with those who refuse to be their own wads of black spit. However, the larger context reveals that Luther intends to adopt his own fence thinking and to follow these forms of oppression in constructing his neighborhood, changing the designation "his people" to mean people who belong to him. In turning Linden Hills into "a showcase," Luther insists on having the right type of people within the neighborhood, taking "extreme care to weed out anyone who threatened to produce seeds that would block the light from his community" by separating those who "would be the most eager to work with him on the future of Linden Hills" from the "madmen like Nat Turner or Marcus Garvey" who had "rooted themselves in the beliefs that Africa could be more than a word; slavery hadn't run its course; there was salvation in Jesus and salve in the blues" (11–12). As this passage indicates, Luther has no interest in "taking this wedge of earth and try to turn it into a real weapon against the white god"; rather, he wants to plan a community that would foster a particular identity, reserved for particular people. When Luther's indirect discourse describes Linden Hills as "a place where people had worked hard, fought hard, and saved hard for the privilege to rest in the soft shadows of those heart-shaped trees," his worldview recalls that of Hansberry's Mr. Lindner (16). He establishes an ethos of success and achievement, and excludes all who fail to embody it.

Despite the extremes to which the Nedeeds go to maintain their calcified jewel of a neighborhood, the novel repeatedly highlights difference within the suburban space. Luther V imagines that the homogeneity of his neighborhood "reflect[s] the Nedeeds in a hundred facets" so they could "take those splintered mirrors and form a mirage of power to tor-ment a world that dared think them stupid—or worse, totally impotent" (16). But the first chapter features several instances of people misreading zoning laws or misplacing fences, so that the "boundaries contracted and expanded over the years to include no one, and then practically everyone in Wayne County" (1). The contours of the identity that Luther con-structs as a foundation for his neighborhood becomes similarly blurred when rumors about him spring up, bringing into question everything from the source of the Nedeeds' fortune to the color of Luther I's eyes, which were "assigned every color except red" (3). These imprecise color designations, critics have noted, are particularly important, as the neigh-borhood's forms of exclusion and inclusion are, at their base, formed on ocular, racial evidence. When Luther Nedeed tries to establish "what a black space should be," argues Luke Bouvier, he remains "within the same problematic as the white racists they are supposedly defying, for they con-tinue to naturalize and essentialize the rhetorical figure of race" (140, 142). Likewise, Keith Sandiford notes that the "signifiers of [Luther's] monomania—concern for name, lineage, and political continuity—point to the qualitative conditions of critics and anxiety that constitute the psy-chological substructure of gothic," which are undone by Naylor's inter-textual and polyvocal method (197).

More than an example of dramatic irony, the play of signifiers under-mines the very assumptions on which the community is built. The Nedeeds design Linden Hills for "their blacks," but the content of this blackness is disrupted throughout the opening chapter, beginning with the introduc-tion of protagonists "White" Willie Mason and Lester "Baby Shit" Tilson. Both names refer to the character's skin color and both were adopted as a form of resistance: Willie is teased for his dark black skin—"Didn't ice get so cold it turned hot? And when you burned coal, it turned to ash; so if Willie got any darker, he'd just have to turn white"—while Lester is called "Baby Shit" because of "the milky-yellow tone in his skin" (24). The boys not only claim their names to diffuse aggression, but also use them as a form of transgression: Willie's whiteness recalls Derridian *dif-férance*, while Lester's name blurs the line between decent and obscene language—"A real cuss word and nobody could get into trouble from the principal or anything for saying it: if it's his name, it's his name, so what could the teachers do about it?" (25). Contrast this fluidity to the racial implications of Luther Nedeed V's treatment of his wife Willa, whom he locks in the basement because she bears him a white son. Luther assumes infidelity, but the fault is actually his, because he did not follow "the pattern of his fathers and married a pale-skinned woman," and instead chose a woman who was "better than pale—a dull, brown shadow." Their white son is an enemy sprung from the seed of friends, a "ghostly presence that mocked everything his fathers had built" and, to Luther, foretells "the destruction of five generations" (18). The dramatic irony at play, then, reveals that the founding racial ethos is tentative and contingent.

This emphasis on contingency within a hegemonic space prepares the way for Willa's ascent from the basement, which becomes an act of critical hospitality when she demands that Luther respond to her as the housewife she wishes to be. Throughout most of the novel, her husband subsumes her identity into his—she is not even named until the last 25 pages of the novel—but she regains a sense of self by examining mementos left behind by the wives of previous generations' Luther Nedeeds: a cookbook, a Bible, and a photo album. As she reads, she recognizes her own struggle in that of the wives, which allows her to assert her own version of the housewife identity. She solidifies this self-actualization by climbing the stairs and cleaning the house. This development surprised even Naylor, who had initially conceived of the character as "this very conservative upper-middle class black woman" who would "just get up, walk out of there and say, 'No, this is shallow. This is not for me.'" But as the character developed, she took on an identity unexpected by her creator.[9] "What her self-affirmation became was acknowledging her conventional position," Naylor explains, "[I]f you realize these are the alternatives and that is what I choose to do, then that's fine" (Naylor and Morrison 16). The narration foregrounds Willa's agency in the recovery of her identity, declaring that "she had made herself" alive, and insisting that her "marriage to Luther Nedeed was her choice, and she took his name by choice" (278). The fact that she chooses this role even though "[m]any women wouldn't have chosen it" uncovers a communal aspect to this triumph of autonomy: she may have formed a selfhood that was "rightfully hers, that she had worked hard to achieve," but she came to it through relations with other people (280). Without exposure to friends like the other Nedeed wives and her enemy Luther, Willa would not have the material to make herself into a housewife.

The narrator underscores this intersubjectivity via the mirror imagery that reoccurs throughout *Linden Hills*. In addition to Nedeed's desire to make Linden Hills into a jewel that reflects his image, the novel's opening epigraph provides a tonally contrary example with a poem in which Lester's grandmother warns him not to sell "that silver mirror God/propped up in your soul." Conventional wisdom would suggest that mirrors serve an intrinsically narcissistic function by only displaying the self to the self, and such an aspect certainly occurs in Willa's scene; Naylor herself explains that she had "actually invented a mirror" for Willa, because if the character realized that she "had a face, then maybe she had other things going for her as well, and she could take her destiny in her own hands" (Naylor and Morrison 31). But at the same time, Naylor's comments gesture toward the dialogic nature of this mirror, as the wives' accounts, specifically the photo album with the face of Luther IV's wife Priscilla McGuire scratched out, compel her to discover her own face and, eventually, assume her housewife persona. Even Willa's acceptance of the housewife identity, a plot point that has earned her charges of essentialism, is not a creation of her own, but a decision to adhere to a script made by others.[10]

This intersubjectivity alters the important image of Grandma Tilson's silver mirror. In the poem, Grandma Tilson warns Lester, "You ain't gotta die to go to the real hell...Uh uh, you just gotta sell that silver mirror God/propped up in your soul...to the highest bidder." A fitting beginning to a story about social climbers in middle-class hell, the poem seems to operate according to a Rousseauist concept of a fully formed, pre-social self, in which conformity is the root of all evil. Under this interpretation, acting like other people is tantamount to selling your soul, and therefore deserves punishment in Linden Hills. But Willa's conformist authenticity and actualization through relation problematize this assumption, and draw attention to the communal nature of these sins committed; after all, the heritage the characters abandon includes "ties with family, then ties with community, ties with their religious and spiritual values, then ties with their ethnocentric sense of self." In other words, the sinners all abandoned the people who helped make them who they were for the sake of short-term material gain. With that in mind, the "Silver Mirror" is not simply a recognition of yourself, but the recognition of yourself in context, of another person holding the mirror up for you. This relational valence underscores the degree to which the residents of Linden Hills do, in fact, reflect Nedeed: they adopt a fence thinking that welcomes friends who support their goals and shun those who present complications.

This notion of intersubjectivity illuminates the novel's bizarre final chapter, in which Willie and Lester—hired by Luther to help him decorate the family Christmas tree—bear witness to Willa's emergence from the basement and the destruction of the Nedeed house. Willa's appropriation of the housewife identity repudiates Luther's xenophobia, as she chooses to take the identity not as part of his grand scheme of sameness, but as a response to her knowledge of the other Nedeed wives and her own desires. The narration of the scene emphasizes the role of both the mirror and the face in Willa's reclamation of selfhood. Willa's ascent corresponds with the moment when Luther, having spent the evening extolling the virtues of his lifestyle, orders Willie and Lester to look at the decorated house as proof of its glory; but when Willie turns to observe, he "saw what Willa saw," the narrator states: "There in the mirror next to the open kitchen door was a woman, her hair tangled and matted, her sunken cheeks streaked with dirt" (298). Willie recognizes her as wild and strange, but "Luther Nedeed made two mistakes that cost him his life: he thought Willa was leaving the house, and he read the determination in her eyes as madness" (299–300). Luther's life has been spent cultivating relationships only with those who reflect his face and avoiding those who are different, and so he fails to recognize Willa as anything other than a "fly" in his ointment. Accordingly, the fire that destroys them both illustrates the ultimate result of fence thinking. In his attempt to create a neighborhood that accepted a strictly interpreted set of friends and abolished unwanted enemies, Luther in fact destroyed himself, burning down the foundation he fashioned. What could have been a space of freedom from oppression, itself a rebuke to the ideologies that deemed him as unwanted, it instead assimilated the suicidal logic that resulted in the end of his life, and of Willa's. The only eulogy read for the brave experiment of Linden Hills, the black showcase that only demonstrated the equality of evil, comes from Willie, who babbles in horror that none of the residents—those who otherwise promised allegiance to Luther—attempted to save him. The novel ends with Willie and Lester walking away from the remains of the Nedeed house and telling one another "They let it burn" as they move past fences:

> Each with his own thoughts, they approached the chain fence, illuminated by a full moon just slipping toward the point over the horizon that signaled midnight. Hand anchored to hand, one helped the other to scale the open links. Then, they walked out of Tupelo Drive into the last days of the year. (304)

These closing lines highlight a contrast to two possible worldviews. The fact that neighbors who once aligned themselves with Nedeed did nothing to stop the house from burning shows just how much they have learned to reflect Luther: like him, they care more for their sense of propriety than for other people. In creating a perfect friend replica, then, Luther creates his own destruction. Conversely, Willie and Lester support each other by joining hands and work together to move through the ever-present fences. The communal aspect of Willie and Lester's duo illustrates a mirror thinking that operates differently from the fence thinking cultivated by suburbia.

That said, there is no question that Naylor intends the suicidal image of the Nedeeds burned alive in their own house to be not only "the end of Linden Hills," but also the end of suburbia. As a writer, she invokes the language of exclusion and antagonism often associated with the space. Accordingly, when she writes a speech for Lester that imagines a way of being that contradicts fence thinking, it moves him away from the suburb where he has lived his entire life:

> "Maybe," Lester said softly, "maybe there's a middle ground somewhere. For me as well as you. I know I can't keep living off my mother forever. And it costs money to keep up a house even if there's no mortgage. There's repairs and property taxes. But..." He sighed. "But I don't know why it must be one or the other—ya know, ditchdigger or duke. But people always think that way: it's Linden Hills or nothing. But it doesn't have to be Linden Hills and it doesn't have to be nothing—ya know, Willie? I mean, in spite of all the propaganda and those ads and crap that Nedeed floods the world with, there are other places to live. But it's sorta easy to forget that. I mean, what's so special about this place? Just look at it. This is the end of Linden Hills and look at it." (283)

The other place to live here is clearly not a modern suburb, but the fact that they came to this recognition—and indeed, all of their recognitions about themselves—within the suburbs suggests that burning buildings and bodies need not be the *only* end of Linden Hills. For suburbia to become a place hospitable to other people, it would require designers and residents to abandon their adherence to contractualism and to friend/enemy distinctions, something that seems unlikely in the wake of the Trayvon Martin and Renisha McBride shootings. It would require residents to admit the unknowable difference in everyone with whom they dwell. However, the fact that Naylor—along with Ford and Lee, and other writers—imagines this abandonment and imagines singularities within suburbia, where people gather together and relate to one another as neighbors sharing space, is worth noting. If someone like Bascombe can allow the unknowable others in his presence to frustrate his ideas about selfhood, if Doc Hata can abandon his identity based on gestures and instead care for the aspects of others that he finds repulsive, if Willa can find her heritage in a collection of mementos—in short, if the refusal of fence thinking imagined by these authors can occur in a real suburb, then there may be no need for the Willies and Lesters of the world to go elsewhere. They can be welcomed into the community, necessarily changing the notions of friends and enemies.

## NOTES

1. Lakeview Terrace is the road on which Los Angeles Police officers detained and assaulted African American truck driver Rodney King in 1991. King's famous question—"Can't we all just get along?"—is explicitly referenced and casually dismissed during one of Chris and Abel's many confrontations.
2. It may seem inflammatory, but it is not unprecedented. In *The Feminine Mystique*, Betty Friedan famously called the house of a suburban wife "a comfortable concentration camp" (XX). More practically, though, Brooks and Rose note that "larger public opinion grew wary of racial restrictions in light of the Nazi and fascist actions in Europe, again especially during and after the Second World War, in which many minority citizens fought, and some died, in service to the United States" (5).
3. In an interview with Wendell Smith, Richard Ford explains that writing the Bascombe trilogy—which also includes *The Sportswriter* (1986) and *The Lay of the Land* (2006)—forced him to acknowledge the importance of suburbia. Though he believes that there are "lots of things to dislike about the suburbs," he finally had to admit that "people don't dislike them," and rather than attack the region with a Keats-like screed, Ford decided that "it might be more interesting surgery on the suburbs to talk about them in unironic terms" (Smith 53–54).
4. Elinor Ann Walker puts it best in the first line of her study on Ford: "Richard Ford likes places, so much that he has moved many times and has owned residences in Louisiana, Montana, and Mississippi." (1).
5. See Moraru, "The Other, the Namesake: Cosmopolitan Onomastics in Change-rae Lee's *A Gesture Life*."
6. Not coincidentally, each of Lee's first three novels—*Native Speaker* (1995), *A Gesture Life* (2001), and *Aloft* (2004)—explore this instability within a suburban setting, as suburbia's obsession with external performance and interior individuality provides Lee with a useful metaphor for infinity and exteriority. Lee contrasts a largely urban story about ethnic espionage in *Native Speaker* against a sitcom suburb, in which protagonist Henry Park finds his attempts to assimilate frustrated by his white wife's demands, his immigrant father's foreignness, and the accidental death of his son Mitt.

Turning his successful landscaping business over to his son, Jerry Battle of *Aloft* considers the neighborhood a place of endless entanglement and expectation, which he irresponsibly evades by taking to the skies in his commuter plane. Even Lee's most recent novel *The Surrendered* (2010), which splits its time between a Korean village and various urban locales, opens with an image of refugees first seeking shelter in and then looting and destroying a farmer's house.

7. In her study *Double Agency: Acts of Impersonation in Asian American Literature and Culture*, Tina Chen identifies Hata's behavior as an act of "impersonation," a practice unique to post–World War I Asian Americans. Chen distinguishes between acts of imposture and acts of impersonation, observing that stereotypes that regard Asian Americans as either members of a "model minority" (a non-white group who embraces mainstream ideals of upward mobility, politeness, and civic duty) or as potential spies and a "yellow menace" position them as "imposters": "frauds who pretend to American identity by performing, with an intent to deceive, the rights and responsibilities of citizenship" (18). Building off of attempts to "make imposture something other than a mark of foreignness, secrecy, of falsehood," while still recognizing the performative and fractured nature of Asian American identity, Chen rejects "the logic of imposture—a logic biased on binary notions of 'real' and 'fake,'" to suggest that we think of Asian American performance as "a politics of impersonation." Impersonation, Chen argues, offers "more than a way of thinking about the performance of identity as that which is either essentialized or constructed: it affords us a paradigm for considering the mutually constitutive dimensions of identity and performance—the im-personation that is not about performing someone's else's identity but about performing into being a sense of one's personhood" (7–8). Where imposture indicates a stable self under an inauthentic mask, impersonation indicates a dialogic of performance and perception, where both viewing and viewed parties participate in the construction of self.

8. See Meisenhelder, "'The Whole Picture' in Gloria Naylor's *Mama Day*," and Christian, "Gloria Naylor's Geography: Community, Class, and Patriarchy in *The Women of Brewster Place and Linden Hills*."

9. Naylor often talks of her characters as if they were autonomous agents, even to her. In another interview on the same topic, Naylor states that she had envisioned Willa as part of "some great feminist dream," but was "absolutely floored" when Willa "climb[ed] up those stairs and start[ed] cleaning house." She claims that she "stopped writing for about two weeks because [she] was so angry," but later states, "Thank God I had enough sense to go back to the book and let her do what she wanted to do" (Conversations 156).

10. "The problem lies, I think, in Naylor's essentialism. Her essentialistic model of womanhood, centered in a biological self-determination…errs in the same way Luther's mythic model does. By describing Willa as a powerful queen ant, Naylor recreates an historically contingent subject as a mythic matriarch. Like Luther's myth, Naylor's essentialism threatens to invert but not to dismantle patriarchy. By merely flipping the binary oppositions of a partriarchical/matriarchal system, Naylor fails to free Willa from a system which defines her as an absence: Willa might escape the basement but she never leaves the house. In the end, Naylor's seemingly radical revisioning of history proves to be limited. Willa's autobiographical history recuperates her past and her self-identity, but it posits no alternative system, no movement beyond. Willa might deconstruct the system, but it is Willie who offers a vision of a new order. As the efficacious historian, Naylor can finally only imagine a black male poet." (Goddu 226).

CHAPTER 2

# My Home Is Your Home: Property, Propriety, and Neighbors

At the climax of the 1961 *The Twilight Zone* episode "The Shelter," Dr. Bill Stockton and his family huddle inside the bomb shelter they built in their basement, hoping that it will protect them from both the oncoming Soviet bomber planes and their neighbors' attempts to break down the door. The escalation is a classic *Twilight Zone* twist, as the episode opened with quite a different scene: Dr. Stockton and the same neighbors who now threaten him gathered in his kitchen to celebrate his birthday, proclaiming him a good friend, a skilled physician, and an integral part of the community. I open with "The Shelter" because the story highlights important aspects to narratives about the relation between neighbors and property. First, "The Shelter" illustrates two dominant concepts about property in the USA: those that imagine the house as a fortress against invaders—"a man's home is his castle," as the saying goes—and those that use property to welcome specially chosen intimates. These concepts simply reduce the contractualism discussed thus far to a smaller set of associations, operating according to a logic that maps the distinction between knowable signatories and dangerous non-signatories into a separation between internal friends—those invited into the home—and external enemies, from whom the house provides protection. Second and more distressingly, "The Shelter" conflates the neighbor with the enemy, more real than even the invading Soviets, as neighbors are always already outside the door and ready to do harm. In "The Shelter" and many other suburban fictions, the encounter with the dangerous neighbor leaves one homeless, forced to forego security.

J. George, *Postmodern Suburban Spaces*,
DOI 10.1007/978-3-319-41006-7_3

More than just a horrific element to titillate audiences, however, this homelessness trope functions much like the repudiation of fence thinking discussed in the previous chapter, a theme that questions the ability to accurately recognize the neighbor. In these stories, characters use their propriety and their property to establish a subject position above and against others, but when that sense of propriety is disrupted, the characters experience a more contingent—and, I contend, more ethical—type of community, in which the neighbor is welcomed and cared for despite the danger inherent in the hospitable act.

This chapter traces this logic of the neighbor specifically to dominant Western approaches to property as articulated by two related philosophical traditions: the emphasis on the exterior as defense stems from the classical liberal tradition, in which property is an extension of social contract theory; the second notion, which imagines property as a space for intimacy and nurture, correlates to the concept of dwelling advanced by Heidegger and Arendt. While the latter approach might seem less antagonistic, both theoretical models posit identities formed in solitude, separated from all but a qualified few, an assumption critiqued and transformed by moments of hospitality in suburban fiction. This chapter focuses on three novels that feature this transformation, through various types of homelessness. I begin with T.C. Boyle's *The Tortilla Curtain* and John Cheever's *Bullet Park*; although the two books seem to have very different plots and conflicting views of private property—Boyle's novel describes the increasing violence caused by the construction of a gate around an affluent neighborhood on the Mexico/California border, while Cheever's story features a gleefully stereotypical company man enjoying the company of his neighbors in suburban New England—they both highlight the antagonism inherent in these philosophies. But as I will demonstrate, both novels also refigure the role of property and propriety in suburban relationships, imagining homes as places of welcome, not as a means of defense. This redefinition has implications for the figure of the neighbor, which—drawing from the ethical philosophy of Levinas and Esposito and from studies of the neighbor by Kenneth Reinhard, Eric L. Santer, and Jeremy Waldron—I explore with a reading of *Rabbit Redux* by John Updike. I will argue that although others are impossible to predetermine and therefore frightening, they must be welcomed as their presence provides a necessary element for consciousness. Private property can be used to provide this welcome, thereby transforming the suburban home from a defense against enemies into a shelter that allows singularities to occur.

## War in the Living Room: *The Tortilla Curtain*'s Porous Border

Several factors influenced suburbia's expansion from a privileged location for the wealthy few to the dominant residential model in the USA, including the development of the highway system and increased industrial efficiency in World War II, but the primary motivator was the concept of private property. While Americans have debated the role of property since the colonial period, the topic became particularly prevalent during the twentieth century. President Herbert Hoover made the issue a central goal of his administration and began to institute programs to increase owner occupancy even while serving as Secretary of Commerce under Presidents Harding and Coolridge. From his "Better Homes" movement to his 1928 campaign slogan, "A car in every garage and a chicken in every pot," Hoover insisted that private property was integral to the American ethos and devoted himself to improving the country's housing. However, Hoover was not interested in mere shelter, nor did he intend to increase public housing; rather, when the President touted "better homes," his assumption was "that a better home was an owner-occupied home" (Ronald 140).[1] Despite the institution of programs like the Federal Home Loan Bank, Hoover's attention to a specific type of house and neighborhood—giving preference to "all-white, all-Protestant neighborhoods" and "segregated subdivisions, enforced by deed restrictions, and sometimes separated by walls from neighborhoods where people of color resided"—resulted in fewer successes, and any meager gains made were soon undone by the Great Depression (Hayden 125). Hoover's efforts did whet the public's appetite for home ownership, which only increased in response to Depression-era foreclosures. The question of home ownership became integral to Roosevelt's New Deal reforms, prompting him to include a housing credit in the 1944 GI Bill. But as GIs began returning from the front, often with young families in tow, this credit only exacerbated the demand and led to a full-fledged housing crisis.

In response, legislators proposed public and private solutions. The most prominent public solution was the Greenbelt project, a government-sponsored development in Maryland, designed to be "surrounded by a belt of open land to prevent sprawl" and to be "characterized by decent housing and a high level of social and educational services" (Jackson 195). As opposed to the individualism associated with modern suburbia, "[c]ooperation encompassed every aspect of town life" in Greenbelt;

"residents organized transportation, created citizens' associations, founded a journalism club that put out the local newspaper, and established baseball teams, a dramatic club and a credit union. Meetings took up so much of people's time that in 1938 residents passed a town motion declaring a meeting moratorium from Christmas to New Years Day" (Baxendall and Ewen 73). Worried that public housing would diminish rental rates and home sales, a number of interested parties opposed the project and advocated private housing, including developers Abraham Levitt & Sons. The Levitts had their own solution to the housing crisis, namely their Levittown subdivision in Long Island, and they joined other developers to engage in a smear campaign designed to discredit the notion of public housing.

The Levitts found a powerful ally in Senator Joseph McCarthy, who presided over the hearings of the US Senate Joint Committee Study and Investigation of Housing. Already exhibiting the staunch anti-communist stance for which he is now known, McCarthy made the housing crisis into an ideological battle. Where the private housing industry had been criticized for "its outmoded methods and inability to provide mass housing," the government was "experienced in building low-income housing, and the public (and most members of Congress) assumed the government would continue to provide public housing for working- and middle-class renters" (Baxendall and Ewan 91). Against these assumptions, McCarthy and the Levitts invoked Hoover's ethos of private homeownership as a type of achievement and indication of self-sufficiency. Public housing would inevitably lead to an erosion of personal responsibility and self-sufficiency, they argued, but private property would help strengthen the individual, wither government dependence, and even combat the oncoming threat of communism; as William Levitt proclaimed, "No man who owns his own home and lot can be a communist" (qtd. in Kushner xiv). McCarthy's arguments—and political gamesmanship—proved more effective than those in support of public housing: "The housing hearings served as a public forum to attack government-sponsored public housing, alleged lazy and inefficient union laborers, local building codes, and gray marketeers," resulting in a "new coalition forged between political conservatives and the master builders [which] would define the parameters of suburban postwar housing" (Baxendall and Ewan 104). The Greenbelt project was soon shut down, while Levitt and Sons established two more Levittowns in New Jersey and Pennsylvania, instituting a model that would come to dominate American residential landscape.

Given the history of private property in the USA, it is no surprise that McCarthy's rhetoric better resonated with Americans. Although the country's founders certainly debated the methods of establishing and regulating private property, the concept itself was never in question.[2] Among the many sources from which Jefferson, Madison, and Hamilton drew to construct the country's property policies, the clearest single influence was John Locke, the theorist who best "furnished a clear-cut rationale for independence from England" (Siegan 47). Unlike his fellow social contract theorists Hobbes and Rousseau, Locke insisted that property existed in a state of nature, prior to the establishment of society or government. As explained in *The Second Treatise on Civil Government*, Locke believed that the common becomes private when mixed with the *"labour* of his body, and the *work* of his hands, which are both properly his" (19, emphasis original). Locke frames this appropriation as a moral good, as it fulfills God's command to cultivate and make use of creation: "[t]he common is of no use...he who appropriates land to himself by his labour, does not lessen, but increase the common stock of mankind" (19, 23). Locke's property theories "planted the seeds for a perspective about the sanctity of human rights that in time bore fruit in the formation of a limited constitutional government," which remained potent long after the Revolution and guided the debates about the ratification of the Constitution (Seigan 49).

The Enlightenment philosophy of Immanuel Kant, whose thought influenced the American transcendentalists and mirrored the founders' liberal individualism, expounds on Locke. Kant does not define property as a right because, he claims, *"[f]reedom* (independence from being constrained by another's choice), insofar as it can coexist with the freedom of every other in accordance with a universal law, is the only original right belonging to every man by virtue of his humanity" (30).[3] One can exercise this freedom by asserting that an external thing belongs to him or her, to the extent that "I could be wronged by another's use of a thing *even though I am not in possession of it*" (37). If one person could be wronged when another uses an external thing, Kant notes, then private property necessarily places all others "under obligation to refrain from using that object of my choice, an obligation no one would have were it not for this act of mine to establish a right" (44). In the state of nature, no such agreement is possible and property is limited to what one physically possesses; but in civil society, these agreements are enforced by a greater will, that of the government: "So it is only a will putting everyone under obligation, hence only a collective general (*common*) and a powerful will, that can provide everyone this assurance" (45). This tension between individual freedoms and the rights of others is a key point of convergence between Kant and the founders, as both he and "Revolutionary-era Americans, demanded reciprocal dependence so that no free citizen had 'rights of coercion over others which are not symmetrical with their rights over him'" (Shain 188).

This relation between freedom, restriction, and property advocated by Locke and Kant informs not only American political rhetoric, but American literature as well, which often portrays property as the cause of all manner of conflict.[4] Battles over property open and drive much of James Fenimore Cooper's *The Pioneers*, as Natty Bumpo's house serves as the site of conflict where he defends his property from the meddling of a local legislator. Not much later, Frank J. Webb's *The Garies and Their Friends* describes a race riot in Philadelphia in which the protagonists defend themselves by turning the house into a literal fortress, storing guns in the kitchen, hiding civilians in the closet, and firing on attackers from the upstairs bedroom window. Similar contests of ownership book-end Charles W. Chesnutt's *The Marrow of Tradition*, as white suprema-cist Major Delamere makes his stand against racial integration by refusing entry to African American Dr. Miller. Stories as diverse as James' *The Turn of the Screw*, Richard Mattheson's *I Am Legend*, and William Styron's *The Confessions of Nat Turner* invoke horror by describing menacing assail-ants invading the house and terrorizing homeowners. The trend is even more apparent in the recent genre of suburban fiction. As Cathrine Jurca says of Sinclair Lewis's *Babbitt*, another house-centric novel, in suburban fiction, "The boundaries between outside and inside, public and private, are already under assault" and continue "to shape what is meant by *home*" (66). Consider the intra-suburban violence marking Robert Coover's "The Babysitter" and Joyce Carol Oates's *Expensive People*, or the disorder outside Junior's house in Charles Burns' *Big Baby*, not to mention slasher films like John Carpenter's *Halloween* or Wes Craven's *The Last House on the Left* and *A Nightmare on Elm Street*.

The violence prevalent in these property-centric narratives is not a mere genre convention. Rather, I suggest that these stories reveal the antagonis-tic nature of liberal theories of private property, the exclusion inherent in the American individualism extolled by McCarthy. As with the contracts discussed in the previous chapter, these theories begin with the assump-tion of an enemy, of an attacker who wants to steal or destroy the property of others, an assumption that invites insular and defensive communities. This defensive stance informs many American stories about property, and becomes particularly evident in fictions set in the suburbs—a well-populated domestic space in which neighbors interact on a daily basis. One of the more powerful examinations about the liberal approach to property is T.C. Boyle's 1995 novel *The Tortilla Curtain*, which depicts the escalating struggle between Delaney Mossbacher, a self-proclaimed liberal humanist living in the upscale Arroyo Blanco Estates, and Cándido Rincón, an illegal immigrant struggling to scrape together enough money to rent an apartment. Despite their attempts to avoid one another, the two men find themselves frequently thrown together, and each considers the other a threat to his property.[5] Most of Boyle's novels explore the shortcomings of idealists, and certainly, critics have read *The Tortilla Curtain* as a satire of upper-class Democrats. However, I contend that Boyle's sharpest critique is reserved for the desires and actions associated with land tenure, as Cándido and Delaney (and in fact every character in the novel) are thrust into conflict, despite their initial indifference toward one another, because they pursue private property.

Although certainly exaggerated for dramatic effect, I do not consider the conflicts featured in *The Tortilla Curtain* anomalous; in fact, I assert that they are a logical extension of liberal property rights. Consider Kant's explanation of the relational nature of property claims: because a physical object "has no reason and no means to object to its relation to the possessor," Kant states that private property laws "do not legislate the relation between an individual and an object but an individual *against others* who make claims to an object" (59 emphasis mine). When one gains property, Kant states, the possessor gains not the right to the actual object, but rather a right

> *against a person*, namely right against a *specific* physical person, and indeed a right to act upon this causality (his choice) to *perform* something for me; it is not a *right to a thing*, a right against that *moral person* which is nothing other than the idea of the *choice of all united a priori*, by which I alone can acquire *a right against every possessor of the thing*, which is what constitutes any right to a thing. (59, emphasis in original).

In other words, the right to property necessarily requires a restriction against others and binds their freedoms. This antagonism is equally clear in Locke's thought; although he distinguishes between the pre-social state of nature and a Hobbesian "state of war"—an inevitable condition of "*enmity* and *destruction*" between those who come into contact with one another—his description still emphasizes the potential for conflict. Locke characterizes the pre-social savage's independence in terms of the processes by which "*one man comes by a power over another*" when the latter violates the law of nature, a right extended to every man who "*hath a right to punish the offender and be executioner of the law of nature.*" But when entering into society, these "governors of *independent communities*" agree "together mutually to enter into one community, and make one body politic" (10, 13–14 emphasis original). In contrast to both the state of nature and the state of war, society is positioned as an antidote to fighting: "To avoid this *state of war*...is one great reason of men's putting themselves into society, and quitting the state of nature" (16). Prescribing society as a deterrent to aggression, Locke frames others nearby—neighbors—as nothing more than aggressors *en potentia*, restrained only by the conventions of society. One comes to the other, then, not as a necessary part of making a life—property and labor all exist prior to socialization—nor as a necessary element of one's consciousness.[6]

This assumption of unessential others provides a central theme in Boyle's satirical rendering, as he puts the language of exclusion and contract in the mouths of blissfully unaware suburbanites who conceive themselves as agents similarly executing their rights as citizens. The central conflict stems from a proposal to build a gate around the neighborhood for vague reasons of "safety" and "property values," and Boyle repeatedly undermines his characters' platitudes with a plot that throws the characters together, refusing any type of exclusion and, therefore, redefining the terms by which property gains its meaning. Consider the following scene, late in the novel, in which Delaney encounters a Mexican named José Navidad, who has (unbeknownst to Delaney) been hired to distribute fliers advertising an upcoming neighborhood association meeting.[7] On the surface, Delaney's comments to him seem ordinary to any property owner expelling a trespasser: "I want to know what you think you're doing here...This is private property. You don't belong here"; but, upon closer inspection, it becomes clear that Boyle is invoking and deconstructing liberal contractualism. The odd, overly qualified nature of the first part of Delaney's injunction foregrounds the epistemological stakes of his command, asking not what José is actually doing, but rather what he "thinks" he is doing. The distinction assumes that José is intrinsically in error—his presence is empirically wrong, a mistake on José's part—and, more importantly, puts Delaney in a position of judgment; regardless of the answer José gives, Delaney has already decided, as the free indirect discourse leading up to the quotation reveals, that he imagined that José had stolen "the Cherrystones' silverware in there, their VCR, Selda's jewelry" (228). The formulation highlights the division of power inherent in the relationship between the two, as Delany—who first takes notice of José—operates as a perceiving Same (to use Levinasian terms) who accuses the other he notices ("I want to know"), not allowing him to explain himself or present himself on his own terms, but only to confirm or deny Delany's hunch.

Delany strengthens his demand by invoking his "right" to accuse in the second half of his comments, beginning with the declaration, "This is private property." By reminding José that they stand on private property, Delany not only invokes the law—thereby threatening a presumably illegal immigrant—but also of his own rights of privacy, to limit one off and to remove one's self. Delany therefore considers himself a type of sovereign in relation to José, and Boyle's narration underscores the domineering arrogance Delaney practices in response to the "invader"; by simply sharing proximity, Delaney assumes, José is "mocking him, bearding Delany right there in *his own* community, right there on *his own* street" (228, emphasis added). The last line in Delany's rebuke—"You don't belong here"—re-emphasizes Delany's assumed sovereignty and puts it in spatial terms; by assuming the right to tell José that he does not belong in that space within Arroyo Blanco Estates, Delany also asserts his own position as one who does belong and one who enjoys all attendant benefits, including the right to remove. And so, within this small passage, Boyle recalls liberal notions of property by understanding property as a right against someone else: it is Delany's, and therefore cannot be José's.

But even as he calls upon this language, Boyle immediately works to undermine and satirize the logic, starting with the very space on which Delany stands. José trespasses not on Delany and Kyra's territory, but on that of his neighbors, the Cherrystones.[8] All of the evidence that Delany marshals, then, and the ontological position he assumes are undone by José's presence, particularly when the accosted man reveals the contents of his satchel—not the Cherrystones' possessions, but fliers that he had been hired to distribute. More than a simple gag or a moment of cosmic justice against Delany's temerity, the reversal reveals a fundamental flaw in liberal contractualism—the assumption that all involved are clearly identifiable agents who have "signed" the contract. These moments of confusion become a reoccurring theme throughout the novel: realtor Kyra takes possession of a house she is selling for out-of-town clients, invoking homeowners' rights to chase away trespassers; "illegals" like José,

Cándido, and América are regularly hired and brought into the neighbor-hood to perform manual labor; Boyle even devotes an entire subplot to a wealthy embezzler under house arrest in the suburb. These confusions of insider/outsider—or, to use Schmitt's terms, "friend/enemy"—status complicate the entire notion of a wall, highlighted by Delaney's lament that the wall "might keep *them* out, but look what it keeps in" (224). His indistinct use of pronouns is telling; the liberal pursuit of private property, as exemplified by Locke and Kant, has resulted in a widespread mistrust of one's neighbor, forcing residents to consider everyone a potential enemy.

Boyle uses this confusion to increase the tension of the novel's climax, in which Delaney confronts Cándido at his camp in the valley:

> Because at that moment something fell against the side of the shack, some-thing considerable, something animate, and then the flap was wrenched form the doorway and flung away into the night and there was a face there, peering in. A gabacho face, as startling and unexpected and horrible as any face leaping out of a dark corner on the Day of the Dead. And the shock of that was nothing, because there was a hand attached to that face and the hand held a gun. (351)

Boyle's inversion here is obvious, making the one who once proudly asserted his rights as a property owner into the type of invader he cursed. Moreover, where his paranoia heretofore compelled him to conceive of others as enemies in waiting, mistaking landscapers for thieves and mur-derers or framing Cándido, whom Delaney hits with his car in the opening pages, as a "jack-in-the-box who'd popped up in front of his bumper and ruined his afternoon," Delaney and his gun now pose a real, empirical hazard to Cándido and his home (7). But Boyle shows little interest in simply exchanging the oppressor for the oppressed, and instead highlights the antagonistic nature of the combatants' property claims. By locating the narration in Cándido's perspective, Boyle positions him as the prop-erty owner who assumes an antagonistic right; moreover, the narration highlights the ocular evidence of the observing Cándido, whom the invad-ing Delaney objectifies, repeatedly calling him "something" and describ-ing his "gabacho face" as "startling and unexpected and horrible." Boyle underscores the confusion by switching back and forth between the two men's perspectives as the shack and its occupants are swept away by a mudslide. The dueling focalizations make the confrontation not just a struggle against nature, but also a battle of antagonists as the ground they wish to claim washes out from underneath them.

The shifting perspectives amidst a wildfire and mudslide that destroy the property underscore the impossibility of liberal contracts, which—in one form or another—posit government as a means for defending property. The presence of unknowable others, inside or outside the confines of the suburb, throws the entire notion of agency and contract into question: legally, Cándido has no right to put his shack in Topanga Canyon; morally, Delaney has no right to destroy the Rincóns' shelter and expose an infant to the elements. But contracts do not apply here, as they are not the self-interested, rational participants assumed by Locke or Kant. Rather, they are constantly in relation to each other. As has happened throughout the novel, the two should have nothing to do with each other, and yet there they were, sharing proximity and entangled in each other's lives. Boyle reinforces this point in the novel's final lines; as Cándido realizes that his child has died, he notices a "white face spurge up out of the black swirl of the current and the white hand grasping at the tiles." Although Delaney is an enemy who has raided his home and who was indirectly responsible for the death of his daughter, although he embodies the very threat suburbanites envision and used to persecute immigrants like the Rincóns, Cándido "reached down and took hold of it," thereby saving Delaney's life (355). Cándido's actions operate according to a form of relation otherwise to the antagonism that has dominated the novel, an interdependence distinct from "the novel's formulaic representation of cultures as self-contained and sharply delineated, asymmetrical worlds" (Schäfer-Wünsche 405). Although certainly less antagonistic, this alternative logic is not some sunny, "Pollyanna" optimism—Cándido's decision to take Delaney's hand excuses or solves nothing: Delaney's house has still been destroyed and his neighbors have still turned against him; Cándido is still not welcome in the USA and his daughter is still dead.

But with the loss of literal ground comes also the removal of property. If it was property by which they once defined themselves, then the novel imagines the loss of that ground as the means for reforming identities. The narrator uses apocalyptic language to describe this undoing—"The mountain roared, the boulders clamored"—and highlights the destruction of the home: "Cándido heard the rush of water ahead and saw the lights of the development below them, riding high on the wave of mud that hammered the walls flat and twisted the roofs from the houses and sent him and America and little Socorro thundering into the void" (355). With all else removed, the characters only have their relation with each other. Boyle cleverly leaves the ending ambiguous, with no indication of how Delaney will go back to the remains of his charred home or what Cándido will do, having lost his child along with his few possessions. But it does end by reinforcing a different form of relation once the property has gone. Delaney can only define himself here as a person facing Cándido, and Cándido can only define himself as a person facing Delany. In that moment, they both require hospitality from each other, despite the antipathy they earlier experienced. They end as the sole constituents of one another's identities, right there in that place. The novel in no way glosses over the painful aspects of this new relation, but neither does it present it as avoidable. The two have been sharing space throughout the novel, and it was largely possessions—the house and car that Delaney owned, the shelter and appliances that Cándido wanted—that drove them into conflict. The lack of these items does not mean that conflict is now forever avoided, but it does indicate that the new prime element of their identities is the relation with one another, a relation that has been present, but obscured by fences and walls. Delany and Cándido have formed a singularity, and as such, there's no telling what will happen next. But Delaney's need compelled Cándido into responsibility, and as the only one present, Cándido could not avoid that responsibility. Throughout *The Tortilla Curtain*, the defense of private property pushed neighbors into conflict with one another; and yet at the end of the novel, after the property has been destroyed, they behave not as antagonists asserting rights, but as people in proximity—neighbors.

## *BULLET PARK*: THE CONTEMPTIBLE CLOSING OF DOORS

Although it was written more than 20 years before *The Tortilla Curtain* and takes place in a more middle-class New England suburb, John Cheever's 1969 novel *Bullet Park* also focuses on property and neighborliness, so much so that the very first chapter features a realtor—the evocatively named Mr. Hazzard—introducing a "stranger" to the neighborhood. As he goes about his sales pitch, preparing the stranger to purchase some property, Hazzard also lays out the rules of Bullet Park, giving him a sense of the expectations that come with ownership. Hazzard includes in his list an interesting and odd scene, in which he switches his perspective to an unnamed teenager, who stands at a precipice above Bullet Park and unleashes the following diatribe:

> Oh damn them all…Damn the bright lights by which no one reads, damn the continuous music which no one hears, damn the grand pianos that no one can play, damn the white houses mortgaged up to their rain gutters,

damn them for plundering the ocean for fish to feed the mink whose skins they wear and damn their shelves on which there rests a single book-a copy of the telephone directory, bound in pink brocade. Damn their hypocrisy, damn their cant, damn their credit cards, damn their discounting the wilderness of the human spirit, damn their immaculateness, damn their lechery and damn them above all for having leached from life that strength, malodorousness, color and zeal that give it meaning. Howl, howl, howl. (5–6)

Anyone familiar with suburban fiction will recognize the teenager's jeremiad. Countless stories—from early postwar books like David Reisman's *The Lonely Crowd* or Bruce Jay Friedman's *Stern* to modern television dramas like *Weeds* or *Breaking Bad*—feature shallow suburbanites mindlessly "discounting the wilderness of the human spirit." But where other writers would make this teenager the wry, disaffected hero of their novel, Cheever's narrator dismisses him and instead lingers on the middle-aged Wickwires, who labor to get out of bed after a weekend of debauched cocktail parties. "There was nothing hypocritical about the Wickwires' Monday mornings," declares the narrator, "and so much for the adolescent" (9). In affirming the authenticity of the Wickwires, who seem to project false personas against their true alcoholic selves, over that of the blunt, truth-telling teenager, Hazzard presents a warning for the stranger: if you own property here, you will interact with odd people.

Cheever's fiction highlights the absurd in the banal, portraying dynamic characters who form their identities through relations with others in proximity. Although Cheever had pursued this project since the publication of his 1958 collection *The Housebreaker of Shady Hill and Other Stories*, 1969s *Bullet Park*, his final suburban work, best demonstrates his complex method. The titular neighborhood brings Eliot and Nellie Nailles, a married couple who insistently defend bourgeois American values, together with Paul Hammer, a wanderer who wants to shock suburbanites out of what he considers an unreflective stupor by publicly immolating the Nailles' teenage son Tony. As Hammer enacts his plan, the Nailles fret about Tony's depression, a deep malaise brought on by an uncharacteristic moment of rage from Eliot. Both crises are resolved through the intervention of Swami Rutuola, a Baltimore-born mystic who embodies all of the extra-suburban otherness that the Nailles find so repulsive. In learning to recognize the seemingly benign Hammer as a threat, the would-be suburbanite Tony as different, and the markedly odd Rutuola as necessary, Eliot gains a new understanding of who he is as a suburbanite. As these and other redefinitions indicate, Hazzard's caution sets up a major theme for the book, as the lesson he tries to teach the stranger, later revealed to be Paul Hammer, must be learned by the protagonist Eliot Nailles as well. Eliot understands ownership of a suburban home to be part of a larger project of identity construction, one in which the property signals a type of propriety to the neighbors, to which he expects them to adhere. This does not make Eliot an anti-social man; in fact, he is quite generous with his neighbors, weeping when they die and gladly giving money when they fall on hard times. But, like Bascombe and his sense of conditional hospitality, the care Eliot reserves for only his neighbors reveals an ethical shortcoming in his sense of neighborliness. Over the course of the novel, Eliot and his wife Nellie discover that their selfhoods, founded on a contemptible exclusion and limited welcome offered to neighbors who meet predetermined agreements, confounded by numerous calls for critical hospitality, demanded by those they would consider outsiders, those they consider neighbors, and even their own son. In this process of development, the Nailles refigure the use of their house as a place to welcome bizarre neighbors and to create a selfhood with them.

Christened the "Chekov of the suburbs," Cheever explores the frustrated longings of the middle class in the USA, employing the mundane settings and character types common to satires but mixing them with a pathos-leaden surrealism and a profound sympathy for his subjects, setting the mold for contemporaries John Updike and Raymond Carver, as well as modern authors such as Rick Moody, A.M. Homes, Chang-rae Lee, Tom Perrotta, and Jonathan Franzen.[9] Although Cheever manages to avoid being lumped in with middle-brow icons like Oprah Winfrey or Drs. Spock and Phil, the critical response to his work has been checkered. A number of readers, including Clinton S. Burhans, Jr., Robert G. Collins, and Lars Andersson, find his fiction glib and simplistic, too beholden to "an affirmative view of suburbia that lacks the subversive analysis of society common to many forms of realism" (Andersson 441).[10] *Bullet Park*, with its seemingly uncomplicated good-versus-evil plot and cheery ending—after Eliot rescues Tony and Hammer is arrested, the narrator simply declares "everything was as wonderful, wonderful, wonderful, wonderful as it had been"—has been particularly maligned (245). Collins dismissively calls the novel a "mad comedy, and more horrible for it" (7), while Michael D. Byrne claims that *Bullet Park* reveals Cheever's attitude toward suburbia to be one of "complete ambivalence," in which the trite ending "lingers in the imagination like an unsolved riddle or a confusing joke—or a paradox whose complexity is irreducible" (86).

Despite this chilly reception, the publication of daughter Susan Cheever's memoirs *Home Before Dark* in 1984, followed by the release of the author's letters in 1988 and his journals in 1991—collections that revealed his struggles with alcohol and depression, as well as his repressed bisexuality—sparked a re-evaluation of his work, in which readers found a more nuanced view of his most prominent setting. As Timothy Aubry observes, because "the very essence of suburban experience is to be included/excluded, Cheever is in a difficult position as a satirist. To critique or mock suburbia, to feel or pretend to be outside suburbia, is the essence of what it means to be a suburbanite, so the more he jabs, the more he implicates himself as a part of the company he is critiquing" (69). But Cheever does not mock or jab at his characters as much as he illustrates their constant shortcomings, dramatizing the chasm between their actions and their intentions. He lends "a sympathetic eye" to these flaws because, Keith Wilhite explains, "the private spaces of suburbia create an equivocal geography peculiar to the human trespasses and the tenuous nature of middle class life" (216–217). As members of an artificially "planned community," such characters necessarily embody some degree of superficiality; but Cheever is less interested in exposing the façade, and instead accentuates the idiosyncratic and pathetic nature of its inhabitants, focusing on the way the neighbors interact with one another.

*Bullet Park* protagonists Eliot and Nellie Nailles trouble the standard assumptions about suburbia because they gladly embody middle-class conventions, appearing to the casual observer to have, as the narrator puts it, "less dimension than a comic strip" (25). Eliot is proud of his job as a middleman at a mouthwash company, he espouses the virtues of the nuclear family, and he expresses concern for his neighbors, while Nellie is a homemaker who embraces conservative morality and traditional gender roles. Antagonist Paul Hammer gives the impression of an equally broad character, a self-styled cosmopolitan and cultural avenger, inspired by his mother's faux-radicalism to combat mundane suburban lifestyles. But Cheever extends these stereotypical elements far beyond comic simplicity, giving the characters an absurdity that belies any potential flatness: Eliot recites his company's slogans with a near-religious devotion, adores his wife to a degree that others find "morbid, aberrant and devious," and will employ violence to protect and raise his son Tony in the manner he sees fit (24). Hammer's disgust with the "squalor, spiritual poverty and monotony of selfishness" he associates with middle-class USA exceeds mere condescension; he plans to find a paragon of that lifestyle—"some young man, preferably an advertising executive, married with two or three children, a good example of a life lived without any genuine emotion or value"—and then "crucify him on the door of Christ's Church" (168–169). These are neither the shallow, sunny moralists of television sitcoms nor the materialist straw men peddled by satirists; they are as multifaceted as those who dwell in any other living space. As the narrator insists, these characters "had erotic depths, origins, memories, dreams and seizures of melancholy and enthusiasm" (25).

While Cheever's housebreakers and swimmers are unquestionably sad and frustrated, they are a far cry from the self-centered fools implied by other popular portrayals of suburbanites. Accordingly, Cheever satirizes neither the place nor the people, but rather their egoistic behavior, which is often founded on the middle-class home. When Hammer, trying to gain his neighbors' confidence, adopts local customs like attending church, volunteering in the fire brigade, and throwing a cocktail party for everyone on his street, Cheever does not depict his affiliations as one-dimensional because suburban communities are inherently deficient. Nor does a critique of Eisenhower-era gender roles manifest in Eliot's hyperbolic fear of the train he takes from Bullet Park to the city, a fear he bravely battles in order to "fend for Nellie and his son" and not leave them defenseless, "besieged by enemies—cold, hunger and fear—refugees from a burned city" (123). Rather, Cheever's portrayal belittles Hammer's utilitarian parties and Eliot's "urbanphobia" because these actions distract the characters from the reality of people in proximity. This distinction is most clear in a scene in which Nellie attends an avant-garde play at a downtown theater and is offended when a male actor undresses onstage. Nauseated by the actor's impropriety and by the audience's apparent apathy, Nellie feels acute dislocation: "Had she gone mad?...Boarding the bus, she looked around for the reassuring faces of her own kind, looked around desperately for honest mothers, wives, women who took pride in their houses, their gardens, their flower arrangements, their cooking" (31). She describes her trip home as not only a narrow escape from danger, but as the recovery of her identity:

> Boarding the train was a step in the right direction. She was going home and she would, in the space of an hour, be able to close her door on that disconcerting and rainy afternoon. She would be herself again, Nellie Nailles, Mrs. Eliot Nailles, honest, conscientious, intelligent, chaste, etc. But if her composure depended upon shutting doors, wasn't her composure contemptible?

Contemptible or not, she felt, as the train moved, the symptoms of restoration. When she left the train at her stop and walked through the parking lot to her car she arrived back at herself. (32)

To be sure, Cheever renders the scene with comic disapproval, but it is not Nellie's gardening or cooking that the narrator finds contemptible; rather, he condemns her exclusion, her shutting of doors and showing affinity for only the "faces of her own kind." Nellie, like Eliot and Hammer, refuses to engage with those who dwell with her; she wants to form her identity only with those similar to her, and Cheever's narrator parodies her ridiculous solipsism. More than simple self-indulgence, the behavior in these scenes operates according to a syllogistic formula: if Nellie runs from the city to the suburb, she will be safe; if Hammer acts the role of a "normal" suburbanite, he will not be suspected. By closing the door in her home and returning to the garden and house in which she takes so much pride, Nellie can recover her identity and be safe again. The faces of her own kind are those who perform the domestic duties she recognizes, and those are the people who will be welcomed. In other words, she feels safe and welcome in private, but threatened in public.

This division between the public and the private, the *oikos* and the *polis*, has long been a mainstay of political philosophy. As Hannah Arendt explains in her genealogy of the *vita activa*, ancient Greeks and Romans affirmed the essential separation between the public and private spheres; the public sphere, manifested in the *polis*, was the space of plurality and engagement with difference, while the private sphere, manifested in the *oikos*, was the space of the hidden and confidential. Where engagement with the *polis* was required for a full life—"a life spent in the privacy of 'one's own' (*idion*), outside the world of the common, is 'idiotic' by definition," Arendt reminds readers—the city was filled with difference and was therefore dangerous; in the household, conversely, one could be "primarily concerned with one's own life and survival" (38, 36). However, the enlightenment's valorizing of equality and the authentic subject muddles the separation between public and private—in response to this exposure, Arendt argues that the concept of the intimate has risen to oppose the social. The intimate, Arendt explains, performs the crucial requirements that once belonged to the private, in which the essential but immaterial activity of labor can be achieved. In Arendt's estimation, labor—the biological and intelligent human activity most closely associated with consciousness and identity construction—must be performed in isolation, without the demands of the public sphere and of society.[11]

For Arendt, the modern sense of private property is implicated in the rise of the social. In fact, Arendt argues that society was founded by "an organization of property-owners who, instead of claiming access to the public realm because of their wealth, demanded protection from it for the accumulation of more wealth" (68). Despite this detrimental element of property, Arendt believes that it has become necessary precisely because it has abolished the private. After the establishment of society,

> the four walls of one's private property offer the only reliable hiding place from the common public world, not only from everything that goes on in it but also from its very publicity, from being seen and being heard. A life spent entirely in public, in the presence of others, becomes, as we would say, shallow. While it retains its visibility, it loses the quality of rising into sight from some darker ground which must remain hidden if it is not to lose its depth in a very real, non-subjective sense. The only efficient way to guarantee the darkness of what needs to be hidden against the light of publicity is private property, a privately owned place to hide in. (71)

Because the intimate requires a space to act without demands, to test one's potentiality, private property is the most reliable protection from neighbors.

Arendt derives this notion from her teacher Heidegger, who asserts that dwelling is an essential part of being human. In his "Letter on Humanism," Heidegger identifies homelessness as the primary affliction of modern humanity, the result of both technology and the priority of action over thought associated with Sartrean existentialism. For Heidegger, homelessness "consists in the abandonment of Being by beings. Homelessness is the symptom of oblivion of Being. Because of it the truth of Being remains unthought" (*Basic Writings* 252). In response, Heidegger calls for a "homecoming," in which individuals rediscover their grounding through authentic dwelling, the process by which humanity gives meaning to the spaces and objects with which one factually interacts: "The proper dwelling plight lies in this, that mortals ever search anew for the essence of dwelling, that they must ever learn to dwell" (363). Heidegger further expounds on this philosophy in "Building Thinking Dwelling," describing dwelling and building—of occupying and developing a piece of land—as a way of securing what he calls "the fourfold": the earth, sky, divinities, and mortals. In other words, dwelling and building give a land meaning by associating a people with the land they possess and by making objects like buildings and houses. Because dwelling "is always a staying with things," it is the private object, away from the demands of the social, in which the private identity is formed and prepared to interact with the exterior world (353).[12]

As indicated by their interactions with one another and with neighbors at house parties, the Nailles happily create their identities within the intimate space of their home: not only does Nellie wish to escape the dangerous world by retreating to her home, but Eliot also possesses "a domesticated organ with a love of home cooking, open fires and the thighs of Nellie" (24). At the same time, they feel threatened by the presence of those they do not want in their private space. Consider the following scene, in which Tony invites an older widow from the city, with whom he has begun a romantic relationship, to lunch in the Nailles' house. Her presence in his home offends Eliot, even more than her "seduction" of their teenage son, because he interprets her visit as an affront to his homeowner identity:

> The sexual authority that Nailles imagined as springing from his marriage bed and flowing through all the rooms and halls of the house was challenged. There did not seem to be room for two men in this erotic kingdom. His feeling was not of a contest but of an inevitability. He wanted to take Nellie upstairs and prove to himself, like some old rooster, that the scepter was still his and that the young prince was busy with golden apples and other impuissant matters. (96)

In this way, Tony acts as a Levinasian other, whose presence interrupts the Nailles' assumptions and whose "odd" desires expose them to alternative possibilities. Although Hammer chooses Tony as his sacrificial representative of middle-class banality, the teen is, in fact, largely uninterested in his parents' lifestyle, preferring the potentialities he associates with urban spaces. Cheever illustrates Tony's growing alterity in a scene in which he and Eliot go golfing. When Tony dismisses the idea of going to school, Eliot urges him to conform, insisting that "you had to observe some of the rules of the game" (116). Tony responds by dismissing the "rules of the game" and, by extension, the constituent elements of Eliot's identity:

> So then he said, "Maybe I don't want to get married. I wouldn't be the first man in the world who didn't want to get married, would I? Maybe I'm queer. Maybe I want to live with some nice, clean faggot. Maybe I want to

be promiscuous and screw hundreds and hundreds of women. There are other ways of doing it besides being joined in holy matrimony and filling up the castle. If having babies is so great why did you only have one? Why just one?"...So then he said that I had got to understand that he might not want to come home at dusk to a pretty woman and play softball with a bunch of straight-limbed sons. He said he might want to be a thief or a saint or a drunkard or a garbage man or a gas pumper or a traffic cop or a hermit. (117–118)

When Tony goes one step further and belittles the mouthwash business, Eliot swings his club at his son. As someone who defines himself as a loving and responsible father, the action disturbs Eliot: "I was very angry. I couldn't understand how my only son, whom I love more than anything in the world, could make me want to kill him" (118). Although he does not realize it, Eliot wanted to kill his son because he defines his life so completely by his personal concept of suburbia, based not on the factual reality of his home—after all, outside of Eliot and Nellie, who but Tony has more claim on the household?—but in his own ideals. So when Tony aligns himself with the city and disrupts Eliot's assumptions, he becomes unrecognizable to his father; in the course of one conversation, Tony shifts from beloved son to some unknowable other.

Eliot's reaction sends Tony into a great depression, forcing him to be bedded in his room, and troubles Eliot to the point of alienation. Both of these affects recall the ecstatic experience of Doc Hata in his pool, revealing a key problem within the notion of dwelling: the solitary life is unfulfilling. While Arendt retains the Ancients' disgust for a completely isolated life, her division between intimate and social spheres simply refigures the liberal's emphasis on the pre-social self, imagining the self formed in isolation from others. Arendt frames the influence of others into the private as a type of homogenizing "mass hysteria," under which "we see all people suddenly behave as though they were members of one family, each multiplying and prolonging the perspective of his neighbor." Though they are all "imprisoned in the subjectivity of their own singular experience," it is an oppressed subjectivity, under which only one perspective is permitted (58). When Arendt claims that property is vital to exclude the public or when Heidegger valorizes a piece of ground, they assume the presence of voyeurs looking upon the subject and they believe that this gaze harms the self. These thinkers characterize the exposure to others as a laying bare, a nakedness before a firing squad of observers, and never consider that exposure might be integral to the identity formation process. Even Heidegger, who, as demonstrated in the previous chapter, insisted that all consciousness is in relation to the factual world, invokes an egocentric approach to property.[13] As Donald J. Gauthier explains, Heidegger's emphasis on the home space informs his ethics, in which he traces the term ethics to ethos or abode, thereby defining ethics as an allegiance to one's country. In building structures in which Dasein dwells and constitutes a self, Gauthier notes, "the builder's relationship with the earth takes precedence over his relationship to the other" (109). To dwell, to form the self, then, one must exclude and hide from others.

Despite the horrific nature of Eliot's attack, then, the hospitality he eventually gives Tony becomes the first step out of his house and into interactions with those from whom he once hid. Tony's potential death prompts the Nailles to forego their antipathy toward outsiders and to welcome a mystic healer called Swami Rutuola. Juxtaposed against the two local doctors who first attempt to heal Tony, Rutuola is markedly other to the Nailles, and this alterity poses a significant problem for them. Cheever's narration foregrounds the difference between Bullet Park and Rutuola's Greenwich Village, and highlights the profound discomfort Nellie feels when seeking the Swami's help. Mirroring Nellie's previous experience in the village, when she witnessed the offending play, Cheever stages her trip to the Swami's apartment as another struggle for identity, this time with different results. As before, Nellie feels lost and decentered; she tries to compare the area to "the rooms of her own house," but is overtaken by the "alien reek of the hallway—the immemorial reek of such places," which seemed "to strip her of any moral reliability." In the same way Nellie ran from the theater before, her instinct here "was to turn and go"; but in her condition of being-toward-death that follows Tony's sickness, she accepts that "her duty was to climb the stairs" (128). Cognizant that her prior "shut-door composure" was contemptible, Nellie abandons the sheltered housewife persona she so carefully crafted: "She seemed to be saying goodbye to herself at a railroad station; standing among the mourners at the edge of a grave. Goodbye Nellie" (128–129). Initially, Nellie tries to recreate the social contract and take on the role of a person who belongs in the downtown building, like a census taker or a relief worker; but her need exceeds the terms of any contract and her simultaneous ignorance of and reliance on the others she encounters make predeterminations impossible. Where Nellie's previous concept of the authentic identity occurred in isolation, an ideal based only in her own ipsetic desires, the reality of

Tony's impending death pushes her resolution to the facts of the space in which she dwells. She no longer thinks of herself as a woman victimized by undesirables, but as a person coming for help: "She was a woman with a sick son, looking (at the advice of a thief) for a magician" (129). In short, she relates to the people and objects with whom she shares space and understands her authenticity as that of the person within that milieu.

Where Nellie recreates her identity in a place she hates, Eliot has his persona disrupted in the place he loves, his home in Bullet Park. Desperate to help Tony, Eliot welcomes Rutuola—who Cheever gives both an indeterminate race ("a light-skinned Negro") and an indistinct accent (his was "a rootless speech")—into the neighborhood to perform his mystic rituals (130). Upon entering the Nailles' house, he asserts his control over it, locking Eliot and Nellie out of their son's room and insisting he not be disturbed, and he begins his work by cleaning Tony's room. Eliot does not shun the Swami, but responds to his presence—even if this response is frustration or doubt—and thereby allows his assumptions to be shattered. Where he once tried to beat the otherness out of his son, Eliot here relates to a person he does not understand but ultimately needs. Cheever illustrates the change with a scene in which Eliot, after Tony has been healed, prepares for a party. Earlier, he demanded that his family adhere to the social contract and "obey the rules of the game," specifically insisting that no one should walk around "bare ass"; but Eliot now feels "a powerful reluctance to dress" and fantasizes about a life spent wearing only "a fig leaf, a tiger skin, [or] nothing at all" (240). The presence of others has opened him to possibilities he had not previously considered, and even if he ultimately rejects these possibilities, this rejection, as Appiah and Taylor argue, is given significance through his relation to those differences.

The heightened action of the final chapter brings all these disparate characters together within Bullet Park, but the novel's closing line undercuts any sense of climax or enduring resolution. Against the blackly comic descriptions of Hammer drugging and abducting Tony and of Eliot breaking into the church with an ax, Cheever ends his story on a falsely cheery note: "Tony went back to school on Monday and Nailles—drugged—went off to work and everything was as wonderful, wonderful, wonderful, wonderful as it had been" (245). At first glance, this ending seems trite, a dismissively chipper hand-wave to the disturbing events that preceded it. But this reading overlooks the incongruity in Cheever's description of Eliot and Tony—the father has become a drug addict and the son, his body wasted by entropy, still has no zeal for the school to which he returns—and it ignores the important qualifying phrase "as it had been." This closing phrase declares that the pluralistic neighborhood that closes the novel is the same that opened it. This revelation does not mean that the subdivision remains as flatly intact as it was before, but rather that Bullet Park was always multifarious and incoherent; the alien reek was not imported with Hammer and the Swami, but was already present with the Wickwires and the Nailles. The house, then, becomes not a place to exclude the strange other, but a space to welcome the strange neighbor. The "wonderful, wonderful" ending suggests that house parties will continue in Bullet Park, but now the Nailles participate in them by using the space to meet the oddities who are already there.

## RUNNING IN PLACE: PROPERTY AND IMPROPRIETY IN *RABBIT REDUX*

Raymond Carver's oft-anthologized story "Cathedral" posits a use for private property that differs from those advocated by Locke and Kant or Arendt and Heidegger. Throughout the story, the unnamed narrator complains that his wife's longtime friend, a blind man called Robert, will be coming to stay in his house. The narrator considers the invitation an affront to his rights as a homeowner and resents having to change his lifestyle to accommodate a disabled person. However, during their first night together, the narrator extends a modicum of hospitality toward Robert when, while watching a television program about cathedrals, he attempts to explain the images on screen. When the narrator's descriptions fall short—"The truth is," he explains, "cathedrals don't mean anything special to me. Nothing."—Robert suggests that they learn by drawing one together: Robert puts his hands over those of the narrator, who performs the sketch with his eyes closed (372). Where the narrator spent of most of the story disgusted with the notion of even touching Robert, he now acquiesces, and the event shocks the narrator and alters his perceptions, leaving the previously pugnacious homeowner speechless and grateful. As befitting an attempt to understand a religious structure, the encounter brings the narrator into the presence of something ineffable, something unknowable and infinite. Crucially, the narrator foregrounds the importance of the house in his retelling of the incident: "My eyes were still closed. I was in my house. I knew that. But I didn't feel like I was inside anything" (375). The narrator's movement from house to cathedral reveals a change in his concept of the home space: by allowing Robert to disrupt his assumptions—to displace his sovereignty as homeowner, to touch and relate to him—the narrator realizes the ecstasy of the infinite.

Although the narrator only achieves a metaphorical homelessness, Carver's story belongs with other suburban fictions about the loss of property. These stories feature the destruction or abdication of home and yard, but I do not believe that they necessarily reject the notion of property. Rather, I argue that they assert moments of critical hospitality, which reveal a longing for the improper ecstasy undergone by Carver's narrator. To achieve this ecstasy, suburbanites must redefine their concept of the neighbor from a potential enemy kept away by fences and yard lines to an other on whom the subject relies.

Jeremy Waldron, himself no stranger to the question of private property, offers just such a redefinition in his reading of the Biblical parable of the Good Samaritan.[14] Against usual categories of neighbor-ness that put greater emphasis on fealty and similarity, Waldron argues that neighbor-ness is determined by proximity:

> The idea is that these three travelers are each bound morally to the man who fell among thieves by virtue of being in his immediate vicinity—in his "neighborhood" (in the crudest geographical sense of that term) when he is in desperate need. Never mind ethnicity, community, or traditional categories of neighbor-ness. They are there and that makes them his neighbors. (348)

Proximity also alters the ethical duties of those involved, as the Priest and the Levite who passed by the injured man committed no evil until they "went out of their way" to avoid helping him (343). Noting that "there was no antecedent special relationship between the man who fell among thieves and the Samaritan that might ground a traditional duty to rescue"—and in fact, the races of the two men made them enemies—Waldron insists that this lack "doesn't mean that their relation was wholly abstract"; rather, Waldron explains that the relationship between the Samaritan and the injured man "at that time and in that place was morally significant in its particularity, and special by virtue of the immediate concrete circumstances of their encounter at that particular moment in that particular place" (346). According to Waldron's position, the neighbor is an ethical, spatial designation, not a legal status, and therefore anyone with whom one shares space becomes one's neighbor and cannot be evaded because of Kantian *prioris* or Heideggarian antipathy.

Waldron's redefinition corresponds with recent work by Kenneth Reinhard and Eric L. Santer, who advance a political theology of the neighbor. Both Reinhard and Santer borrow the philosophy of Carl Schmitt, which asserts that "the exception in jurisprudence is analogous to the miracle in theology" (*Political Theology* 36). In his search for the secular miracle, Santer argues that the commandment to love the neighbor is as important as the commandment to love God, and therefore the neighbor has the same right to suspend the law as the sovereign. Like the sovereign, the encounter with the neighbor is a secular miracle, which disrupts normality and undoes any sense of communal unity. Because "there is really no such thing as self-analysis; one cannot give to oneself the possibility of new possibilities," the neighbor's role is paramount: "Something must *happen*, something beyond one's own control, calculations, and labor, something that comes from the locus of the Other" (123). Similarly, Reinhard imagines the neighbor as "a mode of political relation that would not be based on the friend-enemy couple, but on the neighbor as a third term, one that is obscured by Schmitt's binary opposition, but that is no less central to religious discourse, sociality, and political theology" (13). The neighbor "materializes the uncertain division between the friend/family/self and the enemy/stranger/other," located on the intersection between the Schmittian injunction to expel the enemy and the Biblical command to love the enemy (18). Where Schmitt's theory is based on a boundary—albeit one that can be transgressed by the sovereign decision—Reinhard describes the neighborhood as a place that is "infinite in its openness, its lack of boundaries, and its *lack of* obsession with the otherness of the other" (70). But even then, the neighbor is a particular, a limit based on the proximity of space, of the face to face. As a mix between the ethical and the political, the neighbor is the infinite other made particular by the presence of the ineffable.

The redefinition given by Waldron, Reinhard, and Santer recalls the ethics of Levinas, who states that the "responsibility for the Other...commands me and ordains me to the other, to the first one on the scene, and make me approach him, makes me his neighbor," thereby provoking "this responsibility against my will, that is, by substituting me for the other as a hostage" (*Otherwise* 11).[15] This command by the other means that the neighbor cannot be excluded, even by the conventions of law or morality, but must be welcomed into the home of the subject and must be given shelter. Levinas' insistence on welcoming the homeless separates him from Heidegger, his forerunner and greatest influence. Like Heidegger and Arendt, Levinas asserts the primacy of the home space, claiming that dwelling "is not the simple fact of the anonymous reality of being cast into existence as a stone one casts behind oneself; it is a recollection, a coming to oneself, a retreat home with oneself as in a land of refuge, which answers to a hospitality, an expectancy, a human welcome" (*Totality* 156). But Levinas insists that the "privileged role of the home does not consist in being the end of human activity but in being its condition, and in this sense its commencement," because the "inwardness" of subjectivity "opens up in a home which is situated in that outside—for the home, as a building, belongs to a world of objects. But this belongingness does not nullify the bearing of the fact that every consideration of objects, and of buildings too, is produced out of a dwelling" (152–153). By emphasizing the "worldliness" of the home, the fact that it is not a solitary possession but, as Kant reminds us, a claim made in relation to others, Levinas underscores subjectivity's reliance on, not opposition to, neighbors:

> The Other—the absolutely other—paralyzes possession, which he contests by his epiphany in the face. He can contest my possession only because he approaches me not from the outside but from above. The same can not lay hold of this other without suppressing him. But the untraversable infinity of the negation of murder is announced by this dimension of height, where the Other comes to me concretely in the ethical impossibility of committing this murder. I welcome the Other who presents himself in my home by opening my home to him. (171)[16]

Where alternative property theories frame the neighbor as an invader or a voyeur, Levinas posits the neighbor as a necessary element of the home and, by extension, the self. Where Heidegger frames the self as a type of rootedness and connection to the land, Levinas counters that the home "is the very opposite of a root. It indicates a disengagement, a wandering [*errance*] which has made it possible, which is not a *less* with respect to installation, but the surplus of the relationship with the Other, metaphysics" (172). Therefore, while the self is certainly constituted within the shelter of the home, the home is not a shelter *from* the neighbor but a shelter *for* the neighbor:

> The possibility for the home to open to the Other is as essential to the essence of the home, as closed doors and windows. Separation would not be radical if the possibility of shutting oneself up at home with oneself could not be produced without internal contradiction as an event in itself, as atheism itself is produced—if it should only be an empirical, psychological fact, an illusion. (173)

Once again, the neighbor is not a legal designation, but a present other who carries the indications of infinity. It is this concept of the neighbor portrayed in Carver's "Cathedral," the unwanted other whose presence in the house both undoes the rights of the property owner and provides the miraculous exposure to infinite.

Despite Carver's intriguing depiction, the absolute welcome advocated by Levinas and others raises a number of questions that the short story simply does not address. In hopes of providing a larger discussion, I would like to close this chapter with a reading of John Updike's *Rabbit Redux*. At first glance, *Rabbit Redux* might seem like an odd text to find such an argument, as the novel, and in fact all of Updike's Rabbit Tales, have a reputation for being sexist, racist, and jingoist.[17] Though that characterization might be true, I contend that these undesirables represent the wildly untethered ego of Updike's protagonist Harry "Rabbit" Angstrom, who, as a middle-class male, occupies not only a national normative position, but also a suburban normative position. But where the common reading of the Rabbit novels understands Harry's egoism as a consequence of his running, his escape from the crowding presence of others, I argue that, in *Rabbit Redux*, his egoism stems from his house and neighborhood. This centrism motivates Rabbit's decision to allow Jill, an under-aged prostitute who ran away from her upper-class family, and Skeeter, a troubled black Viet Nam veteran, into his house. But while Harry intends to use his house to exert his moral and social superiority over others, his exposure to Jill and Skeeter alters his perceptions. As present and infinite neighbors, the two exceed Harry's expectations, disrupt his moral high ground, and break his identity as accepted neighbor. Harry loses his house in the process, but he gains a new and more ethical subjectivity, one that responsibly engages with others.

Without question, property plays an important role in each of Updike's Rabbit novels: *Rabbit, Run; Rabbit Redux; Rabbit Is Rich; Rabbit at Rest;* and *Rabbit Remembered*.[18] Most readers tend to focus on Harry's restlessness, emphasizing his penchant for running from familial, moral, and spiritual responsibilities, and while some critics have championed Rabbit as a continuation of American individualism, aligning him with Huck Finn, George Willard, and other great American escapees, other commentators have seen him as a grotesque critique of middle-class American values.[19] Indeed, in an oft-quoted passage, Updike himself claimed that his mission was to "transcribe middleness with all its grits, bumps, and anonymities" (*Assorted Prose* 186). He puts the matter more directly in an interview with *Time*, declaring,

> My subject...is the American Protestant small-town middle class. I like mid-
> dles. It is in middles that extremes clash, where ambiguity restlessly rules.
> Something quite intricate and fierce occurs in homes, and it seems to me
> without doubt to examine what it is. (*Conversations* 11)

But more than a middleness, I argue that *Rabbit Redux* displays a centrism, a position of power that Harry occupies because of his property
status, situated between the upper-class Penn Parks and the lower-class
Brewer and Mt. Judge.

Harry clearly demonstrates this centrist attitude when, at the outset of
his relationship with Skeeter and Jill, he treats them as nothing more than
representative enemies; positioning them as something on the dangerous
fringe, he sees himself as a bastion of, if not the good, then at least the
norm. Updike vividly illustrates this judgment with the fantasies Harry
entertains as he rides the bus from downtown Brewer back to the suburbs:

> It's as if, all these Afro hair bushes and golden earrings and hoopy noises
> on buses, were the seeds of some tropical plant sneaked in by the birds who
> were taking over the garden. His garden. Rabbit knows it's his garden and
> that's why he's put a flag decal on the back window of [his car] even though
> Janice says it's corny and fascist. In the papers you read about these houses
> in Connecticut where the parents are away in the Bahamas and the kids
> come in and smash it up for a party. More and more this country is getting
> like that. As if it just grew here instead of people laying down their lives to
> build it. (13)

For Sally Robinson, Harry derives this hostility from the "increased visibil-
ity of women and people of color in Rabbit's world," which have in turn
heightened awareness of his own privileges as a white male, attention that
"brings with it a loss of power, as the norm is revealed to be contingent
and its position fragile" (345). Faced with the growing social enfranchise-
ment of minorities and women, and with the impression that "the new
heroes of American culture are not 'ordinary' white men like Harry, but
the various groups who organize collectively around rights and against
injustices," he tries to tap into "the well of Middle American alienation
and 'disenfranchisement,' and imagines himself as a victim because he is
white and male" (350). Furthermore, Harry's garden narrative—in which
African Americans are foreign scavengers and rich liberals are derelict
groundskeepers—frames him as not just a victim but also a defender of
the good, a role bestowed upon him by his status as a homeowner.

By basing his selfhood in his suburban home, the mod cons at Harry's disposal transform him into a King in his castle: offending garbage is swept away (sometimes leaving a sweet stink "because the Penn Villas sewers flow sluggishly"), food is at the ready and quickly prepared (even by a husband whose wife is working late), and a myriad of images leap from the screen into Rabbit's fantasies (25). Moreover, as if to advance Updike's mission to "transcribe middleness," Harry's neighborhood Penn Villas is located between the urban Mt. Judge/Brewer area where he once lived and Penn Park, the affluent inner-ring suburb he longs to join. Harry considers his inclusion in the thoroughly middle-class subdivision a personal achievement, allowing him to abandon the Brewer of his youth to uncivilized minorities, to his dying mother, and to his impotent father, who he dismisses as "one of the hundreds of skinny whining codgers in and around this city, men who have sucked this same brick tit for sixty years and have dried up with it" (4–5). Conversely, Harry maintains a complicated, Babbitt-esque relationship with Penn Park, sometimes desiring the company of its residents—he expresses relief when a couple from the upper-class neighborhood joins him in an unfamiliar restaurant—and later proclaiming, "I hate those Penn Park motherfuckers...If I could push the red button to blow them all to Kingdom Come...I would" (285). Harry's centrism, then, the position that calls him to battle the encroaching others, is based not just in his race, gender, or class, but also in his role as a suburban homeowner.

Although he does not necessarily articulate an overt plan—and in fact questions himself immediately after allowing them to stay—his homeowner status informs all of his initial interactions with Jill and Skeeter. His visit to Jimbo's Friendly Lounge, the bar where he first meets the duo, is predicated on this distinction, as his co-worker invited him there and introduced him to Jill because he "lives in this fancy big house over in the fanciest part of West Brewer, all by himself, and never gets any tail" (132). The language of homeownership permeates his first thoughts of Jill: "*She'll ooze in the letter slot,*" he thinks upon seeing her, and explains her defensive attitude as "pulling rank" because "[h]e is Penn Villas, she is Penn Park" (129). When they return to his house, Harry counters Jill's aggressive sexuality by directing her through the rooms of his house:

"Where's the bathroom?"
"Take off your clothes here."

The command startles her; her chin dents and her eyes go wide with fright. No reason he should be the only scared person here. Rich bitch calling his living room tacky. Standing on the rug where he and Janice last made love, Jill skins out of her clothes...She treads lightly on his carpet, as if watchful for tacks. She stands an arm's-length from him, her mouth pouting prim, a fleck of dry skin on the lower lip. "And you?""Upstairs." He undresses in his bedroom, where he always does; in the bathroom on the other side of the partition, water begins to cry, to sing, to splash. (142–143)

Similarly, Skeeter appears in Harry's house as a "set of shadows in the old armchair [that] has been with them ever since their marriage" (205). Property metaphors shade everything from Skeeter's taunts—"I screwed your bitch"—to Harry's justification for hostility toward Skeeter, comparing their altercation to lifting "the metal waffle-patterned lid on the backyard cesspool, around the corner of the garage from the basketball hoop" (209, 208). Harry ends this fight by physically beating Skeeter until he becomes another object in the living room: "His enemy is cringing on the floor, the carpet that cost them eleven dollars a yard and was supposed to wear longer than the softer loop for fifteen that Janice wanted...cringing expertly, knees tucked under chin and hands over head and head tucked under the sofa as far as it will go" (211).

But Skeeter and Jill never remain objects or furniture in Harry's house, and their mere presence is enough to disrupt his expectations, making his act of utilitarian hospitality into an act of critical hospitality. Harry's kindness, much like his antagonism, relies on his homeowner status, a position revoked by his neighbors, as the residents of Penn Villas burn down the Angstrom house with a fire that kills Jill and sends Skeeter on the run from the police. As his sister Mim blithely summarizes, all Harry's goodness earned him was "a burned-down house" (358). When the neighbors' fire destroys his house, the possession from which he derives his identity, Harry has been rendered homeless and his sense of self forever altered: he might make his coveted move to Penn Park in *Rabbit Is Rich*, but he remains keenly aware that the house belongs not to him, but to his bitter mother-in-law and increasingly independent wife, an independence she secures by becoming a successful realtor in *Rabbit at Rest* and "Rabbit Remembered." The strongest indication that Harry has fundamentally changed occurs late in *Redux*, when he admits to Janice "I feel so guilty...About everything" (406). Harry's admission sharply contradicts his refusal during his daughter's funeral at the end of *Run*—"Don't look at *me*...I didn't kill her."—and indicates "that Rabbit has been led back to a place where he may start a life in which claims of the outside world interact with the imperatives of his inner reality" (311; Campbell 132). As a decentering, potentially destructive force, the neighbor in *Redux* recalls Levinas, for whom guilt and interrupted subjectivity are the inevitable result of encounters with the other. Much of Levinas' narrative of the self and other mirrors Harry's interactions with Skeeter and Jill: from his normative perspective, Harry allows Skeeter and Jill to enter his house, their stay includes a series of teach-ins (according to Levinas, "The first teaching of the teacher is his very presence as teacher from which representation comes"), they gratify their egoism to a point of gross impropriety, and this indulgence results in the destruction of the house and the loss of Harry's centrism, forcing him to recognize his responsibility toward those around him. (*Totality* 100). Furthermore, this similarity helps address the quandary that Skeeter poses for readers. A self-styled "Black Jesus" who peppers his apocalyptic prophecies with snippets of American history and inner-city slang, Skeeter is arguably the most controversial figure in Updike's oeuvre[20]; Skeeter has a certain redemptive power for Harry in that he "teaches" him of things beyond the simple perceptions of centrism that marked his earlier behavior, challenging his assumptions about the Viet Nam war and forcing him to read Douglass and Fanon until these writers "penetrated Rabbit's consciousness" (Prosser "Updike, race" 79). Some have interpreted Harry's acquiescence as an inert passivity, but Harry does in fact engage with his guests: he contradicts Skeeter's rants and Jill's proclamations, and responds to arguments he finds distasteful. To the extent that they alter Harry's beliefs about things that occur outside his door, Skeeter and Jill redeem and restore him.

Skeeter's full redemptive power manifests in both his historical lectures and through the impropriety that undoes any claims to morality that Harry might make. This impropriety climaxes in a scene in which Skeeter goads Jill into having sex with him in front of Harry, convincing the trio to perform a scenario discussed during their teach-ins. "You is a big black man sittin' right there. You is chained to that chair," Skeeter tells Harry, "And I, I is white as snow." Likewise, Jill assumes the role of an "ebony virgin torn from the valley of the river Niger" (296). Mimicking the subjegating behavior of a slave trader at auction, Skeeter directs the action:

"Now," he sings, and his voice has become golden hoops spinning forward, an auctioneer who is a juggler, "we will have a demon-stray-shun of o-bee-deeyance, from this little coal-black lady, who has been broken in by expert traders working out of Nashville, Tennessee, and who is guaranteed by them ab-so-lutily to give no trouble in the kitchen, hallway, stable or bedroom!" Another soft slap, and the white clay dwindles; Jill is kneeling, while Skeeter still stands. (297)

The scene is all carnivalesque excess, in which the three conspirators entertain their basest desires while simultaneously being mastered by the other participants. Skeeter is sexually dominant, forcing Jill to perform for him and intimidating Rabbit into non-participation; but by portraying a lecherous slave owner, he re-enacts the history of exploitation he claims to deplore. Jill is both a victim of male power and a manipulator, who initiated the sessions and complies with its dark turn to secure drugs and shelter from the two men. Equally enamored with Skeeter's body as he is of Jill's, Harry gains a vicarious thrill by simply watching the two copulate, but he gets the opportunity only by becoming the enslaved, a piece of property within his own house. The actors then are both dominating and dominated, excited by the chance to gratify their egos and frightened by the disturbing lengths to which they will sink.

In Levinasian terms, the participants "enjoy" the act, which is a prerequisite for encountering the absolute other. Levinas argues that the enjoying perceiver, perusing his or her own desires, is shocked by the sight of the other's face, which demands a response: the face of a neighbor "signifies for me an unexceptionable responsibility, preceding every free consent, every pact, every contract" (*Otherwise* 88). Accordingly, the teach-in gone bad ends when Jill sees a face peering at them through a window, an exposure that transforms the trio's relationship to one another and begins to undo Harry's power as a homeowner. Where he once dominated over Jill and Skeeter, he now finds himself excluded: he tries to watch Skeeter inject Jill with heroin, who refuses his request, commanding, "You go upstairs, Chuck. I don't want you to see this"; later, when Jill comes to bed and Harry attempts to reclaim his role as protector by taking her to a doctor, Jill shrugs him off, saying, "It's too late for you to try to love me" (300–301). In fact, the face in the window literally becomes the means for Harry's unhousing, as it belongs to the son of Mahlon Showalter, who already came to the Angstrom house with fellow homeowner Eddie Brumbach to demand that Harry eject Skeeter from the neighborhood.

Despite his attempts to assert his homeowner's rights—"I'll keep my kid from looking in your windows, and you keep yours from looking in mine" and "He goes when he stops being my guest" (289–290)—Harry cannot prevent Showalter and Brumbach from returning and burning down his house. His property made him the incarnation of American values, but Harry's relation to his neighbors has left him homeless and property-less, a suspect in the eyes of others.

Strengthening the metaphorical conflation between property and subjectivity, Updike illustrates a change in Harry with two scenes at the novel's end, which tie his altered self to the loss of his home. The first scene finds homeless Harry forced to return to his parents' house in Mt. Judge—the place he had heretofore abandoned and avoided—sitting in his childhood bedroom and trying to imagine a suitable object for his masturbatory fantasies. Although he conjures several possibilities—his most recent sex partner Peggy Fosnacht, his most consistent partner Janice, and even a grotesque "Negress" from the depths of his id—their otherness evades his speculative grasp. He can only climax when an image of Mim and Charlie Stavros collapses into an all-consuming nothingness, and even then, the feeling he once called "a spaceflight" amounts to little more than "rocks thrown at a boarded window" (380). Amidst this failure, an unbeckoned chimera of Jill visits him, at once phantasmal and corporeal: "The minor details of her person that slightly repelled him, the hairlines between her teeth, her doughy legs, the apple smoothness of her valentine bottom, the something prim and above-it-all about her flaky-dry mouth, the unwashed white dress she kept wearing, now return and become the body of his memory" (380). Like his previous dream girls, Jill denies Harry's comprehension: he tries to touch her, but she disappears; he tries to recreate their near-orgy with Skeeter, casting himself as a more active participant, but she refuses. Updike repeats the word "presence" throughout the passage, highlighting her vicinity to him; but it is a receding presence, one that rebuffs any attempts to control or assimilate her. The simple splitting of strangers and representative enemies that once determined Harry's interactions with Jill have been forever altered. She and, in fact, all of the people Harry held within his objectifying gaze are now unknowable others. The experience strips Harry of his ontological confidence and forces him to reconstitute his selfhood in relation to those he encounters, starting with his wife Janice. Updike foregrounds Harry's shattered ego by setting their reunion first at the remains of their destroyed house and then in the quintessential property-less space—a roadside motel. Throughout the scene, the couple plays with their identities: neither one directly asserts a persona, but each slowly constructs their selves in relation to the other. When Harry checks into the motel and fills out the registry, he characterizes both their title—"Mr. and Mrs. Harold Angstrom"—and their address, their defining space in Penn Villas, as "lie[s]" (400). When Janice asks, "Who do you think you are?" Harry can only answer "Nobody" and admits his great guilt, which encompasses more than regret for his behavior's effect on Jill, Nelson, and Janice; it extends to everyone he meets, even the motel clerk—"He does, he *does* care," Harry repeatedly insists (405, 406).

Updike narrates these movements with the cosmic metaphors that filled the book, portraying Harry and Janice's rustling on a motel mattress as a celestial dance: "The slither of sheets as she rotates her body is a silver music, sheets of pale noise extending outward unresisted by space" and later, "The space they are in, the motel room long and secret as a burrow, becomes all interior space" (406). But Harry is no satellite hurling across the sky, nor a rocket following a single directive; he is responsive, making his moves in relation to those of Janice, filling and recreating the area between their bodies. The imagery highlights what has been an important theme throughout the novel: Harry shares his spaces with other people, who reject his egoistic domination and disrupt his assumptions; if he is to continue living among them, he cannot simply—as he declared in *Rabbit, Run*—"have the guts to be yourself" and make other people "pay your price" (157). Rather, he must respond to those who are present, to the neighbors who remain outside of his understanding.

Like so many other suburban fictions, *Rabbit Redux* ends with homelessness, but as I have demonstrated, the change in Harry's subjectivity helps explain the prevalence of this theme. As a property owner, Harry was combative, egoistic, and alone; he was a self-interested agent exercising his rights and hiding his affairs from the hostility outside his door. In short, he was the manifestation of all the unethical behavior invited by traditional theories of property. But once he was rendered homeless, Harry's relations shift to something more ethical and complex. When Harry's house is destroyed by fellow homeowners, or when Delaney becomes an aggressor in Cándido's tent, or when Eliot loses the happiness of his home, we see authors groping toward a redefinition of relations between property owner and neighbor. Like the narratives that reject the solipsistic identities dictated by neighborhood contracts, these novels reimagine the suburbs as a place for interdependent selves authentically relating to one another.

By removing the rights of the property owner, either by violence or by choice, the dependence on the neighbor becomes more clear. The neighbor is no longer someone who comes to steal, who comes to harm or to destroy, who disrupts the development of one's consciousness. Rather, as indicated most vividly by Cándido's outstretched hand, grabbing that of the drowning Delaney, the neighbor is someone necessary, who should be welcomed and defended.

## NOTES

1. For an informative discussion of Hoover's housing policies, see the articles "Herbert Hoover, Housing, and Socioeconomic Planning" by Fred J. Bjornstad and "No Place Like Home" by Regina Lee Blasczyk, both in the collection *Uncommon Americans: The Lives and Legacies of Herbert and Lou Henry Hoover*, edited by Timothy Walch.
2. "What one must stress is that the right to property was an unquestioned assumption of the American revolutionaries. To assert this is merely to assert that they were eighteenth-century men. But one must go on to say that they did not defend property as an end in itself but rather as one of the bases of republican government" (Katz 469–470).
3. A particularly pointed contradiction to Locke appears in Kant's description of the development of land. Where Locke believes that cultivation or development of a piece of land is the event that changes that land from the common to the proper, Kant claims that "developing land is nothing more than an external sign of taking possession, for which many other signs that cost less effort can be substituted." He continues: "Furthermore, may one party interfere with another in its *act* of taking possession, so that neither enjoys the right of priority and the land remains always free, belonging to no one? Not *entirely*, since one party can prevent another from taking possession only by being on adjacent land where itself can be prevented from being, *absolute* hindrance would be a contradiction. But *with respect to* a certain piece of land (lying between the two), leaving it unused, as *neutral* territory to separate the two parties, would still be consistent with the right of taking control. In that case, however, this land really belongs to both in common and is not something *belonging to no one (res nullius)*, just because it is *used* by both to keep them apart." (52–53, emphasis original)
4. Thoreau's *Walden*, Harriet Jacobs's *Incidents in the Life of a Slave Girl*, Kate Chopin's *The Awakening*, Upton Sinclair's *The Jungle*, Gertrude Stein's *Three Lives*, Willa Cather's frontier novels, Fitzgerald's *The Great Gatsby*, Hurston's *Their Eyes Were Watching God*, Sandra Cisnero's *The House on Mango Street*, Tim O'Brien's *The Nuclear Age* and *In the Lake of*

the *Woods*, Marilynne Robinson's *Housekeeping* and *Home*, John Edgar Wideman's Homewood Trilogy, and numerous works by Steinbeck, Faulkner, Morrison, and August Wilson.

5. Although less openly satirical than most of Boyle's work, at least in the chapters focused on Cándido, *The Tortilla Curtain*'s themes are not unusual for the author. His 1987 work *World's End* conflates land tenure in colonial America with predatory consumption, 1984s *Budding Prospects* features a group of environmentalists who battle for land to cultivate, and in 1990s *East Is East*, a group of Asian immigrants search for land to settle.

6. The egoism here is not unique to Kant's political philosophy. In *An Essay Concerning Human Understanding*, Locke describes identity as the coherence formed by one's self-reflection: the ideas of identity and diversity are not formed by comparing. We do not compare the self to others but "we compare it with itself existing at another time" (296).

7. The name "José Navidad" is a direct reference to Joe Christmas from Faulkner's *Light in August*, another liminal character whose external characteristics trouble his belonging in a racist society. For more, see Hicks, "On Whiteness in T.C. Boyle's *The Tortilla Curtain*."

8. As Kathy Knapp observes, the gated community represented in *The Tortilla Curtain* "embodies in miniature the nation's schizophrenic relationship with its undocumented immigrants since homeowner associations typically hire immigrants to maintain shared amenities such as pools, tennis courts, and playgrounds and individual homeowners require personal gardeners, house-cleaners, and nannies" ("Ain't No Friend" 122).

9. Updike acknowledged his debt to the "golden name" of John Cheever in a series of tributes written for elder authors, admitting, "my debt to him was real" (112). Chang-rae Lee makes a similar observation about Cheever's suburbia in *A Gesture Life*. Lee uses protagonist Doc Hata's habit of swimming laps in his pool as a metaphor for stagnation, leading to a scene in which, after one of his sessions is interrupted by a moment of existential angst, Hata recalls "The Swimmer" and contrasts his own dissatisfying adherence to social norms to Neddy Merril's authentic impropriety.

10. See Burhans, "John Cheever and the Grave of Social Coherence," and Andersson, "Burglary in Shady Hill and Sarsaparilla: The Politics of Community in White and Cheever." Collins wrote several insightful pieces on Cheever in the 1980s, but the article quoted here—"From Subject to Object and Back Again: Individual Identity in John Cheever's Fiction"—is particularly negative about *Bullet Park*.

11. "Each time we talk about things that can be experienced only in privacy or intimacy, we bring them out into a sphere where they will assume a kind of

reality which, their intensity notwithstanding, they never could have had before. The presence of others who see what we see and hear what we hear assures us of the reality of the world and ourselves, and while the intimacy of a fully developed private life, such as had never been known before the rise of the modern age and the concomitant decline of the public realm, will always greatly intensify and enrich the whole scale of subjective emotions and private feelings, this intensification will always come to pass at the expense of the assurance of the reality of the world and men." (Arendt 50)

12. The necessity of dwelling has been refigured by other thinkers, including Gaston Bachelard and Peter King. Bachelard's best-known work *The Poetics of Space* features a series of "day dreams," in which he traverses the house, expounding on the meaning of the corners, the dressers, and the walls. These meditations emphasize the home's sense of seclusion and security; against Heidegger, Bachelard claims that "[b]efore he is 'cast into the world,' as claimed by certain hasty metaphysics, man is laid in the cradle of the house" (7). The "day dream" terminology Bachelard employs underscores both the particularly subjective elements of home life and the ability to sleep, to be in repose, while exploring the relation between space and identity. For Bachelard, home is the point from which all reality extends: "For our house is our corner of the world. As has often been said, it is our first universe, a real cosmos in every sense of the word...all really inhabited space bears the essence of the notion of home" (4–5). Similarly, Peter King's books *In Dwelling* and *On Private Dwelling* explore the necessity of homes for identity construction. Like Bachelard and Arendt, King emphasizes the protection offered by the house—against the uncontrollable plurality of the exterior, the house is stable, knowable, and secure. In particular, it becomes a way to regulate relation and choose those with whom one shares intimacy. As in Arendt and Heidegger, Bachelard and King foreground the labor of intimacy and the way property owners exercise control over the house to construct a self.

13. In an interview with *Der Spiegel*, Heidegger emphasizes the importance of home related to an ethos: "According to our human experience and history, at least as far as I see it," Heidegger claimed, "I know that everything essential and everything great originated from the fact that man had a home and was rooted in a tradition" (*The Heidegger Controversy* 106).

14. See Waldron, *The Right to Private Property*.

15. It is important to note here that the essays by Reinhardt and Santer come from a collection entitled *The Neighbor: Three Essays in Political Theology*. Although Santer, with his focus on Benjamin and Rosenzweig, acknowledges a congruence with Levinas, both Reinhard and Slavoj Žižek make distinction between his ethics and their theories. Reinhard emphasizes the political nature of his own theory, despite Levinas's insistence that, "there

can be *no relationship* between ethics and politics" (48). Žižek is more critical of Levinas, as he has been in other writings like *Welcome to the Desert of the Real* or "Smashing the Neighbor's Face." Where, in the latter two works, his primary point of contention was the asymmetrical relationship Levinas posits, insisting that the neighbor's proximity can be overbearing to the Self, Žižek shifts his critique in his essay from *The Neighbor:* "In a properly dialectical paradox, what Levinas (with all his celebration of Otherness) fails to take into account is not some underlying Sameness of all humans but the radical, 'inhuman' Otherness itself: the Otherness of a human being reduced to inhumanity, the Otherness exemplified by the terrifying figure of the *Muselmann*, the 'living dead' in the concentration camps. This is why, although Levinas is often perceived as the thinker who endeavored to articulate the experience of the *Shoah*, one thing is self-evident apropos his questioning of one's own right to be and his emphasis on one's unconditional asymmetrical responsibility: this is not how a survivor of the *Shoah*, one who effectively experienced the ethical abyss of the *Shoah*, thinks and writes. This is how those think who feel guilty for observing the catastrophe from a minimal safe distance" (160).

16. As Seán Hand observes, "Levinas then develops this contrast, by pitting the notions of labour and possession which he associates with Heideggarian dwelling, against a vision of the home as a place of enjoyment, of familiarity and intimacy, of welcome and respite. The home can act as an invitation rather than as a protective exclusion. The contrast is mildly extreme, but it is really designed to operate an ethical vision. Heideggarian metaphors of building and dwelling contain within in them, in Levinas's view, a philosophy of anonymous reality and solitary self-establishment and possession; whereas for Levinas, reality from the beginning involves a welcoming of the other. In Levinas's social and ethical vision, then, dwelling and language, are not about imposing, grasping, or founding." (41)

17. Without a doubt, Updike and Levinas are an odd pairing, and one that no critic outside of John Neary (*Something and Nothingness: The Fiction of John Updike and John Fowles*) has made. This seeming incomparability stems partially from Kierkegaard's influence on Updike, a philosopher who, Levinas believed, "philosophized with a hammer." However, there are compelling points of convergence between the two thinkers, particularly their shared deference for the infinite identity and for the idea that truth is a struggle and not a triumph. For more, see the edited collection *Kierkegaard and Levinas: Ethics, Politics, and Religion* edited by J. Aaron Simmons and David Wood, particularly Jeffery Dudiak's article "The Greatest Commandment? Religion and/or Ethics in Kierkegaard and Levinas."

18. Harry's initial escape in *Run* is not away from Brewer, but to a new house across town; in *Rich*, Harry feels emasculated because he lives in a house owned by his mother-in-law; and Janice asserts her independence in *Rest* and *Remembered* by becoming a successful realtor. Additionally, several of the series' characters retell an Angstrom family legend about a squabble between Harry's father and a neighbor, who leave a strip of grass between their yards unmowed because both refuse to take responsibility for it.

19. This position is best summarized by Matthew Wilson's article "The Rabbit Tetralogy: From Solitude to Society to Solitude Again," in which Wilson argues that the tetralogy executes "a complicated interplay between these two 'extreme antagonisms' [of solitude and society]. Moving from the solitude of the fleeing young man to the solitude of the death-saturated older man, the sequence tacks between solitude and society (and achieves a momentary balance in *Rabbit is Rich*), only to have that moment inevitably destroyed by Rabbit's dwindling toward death. Within this interplay, the sequence also reveals an increasing awareness of history, which becomes a subject, almost obsessively, in the guise of contemporary events, and which is transformed in the final novel into a historical consciousness within Harry Angstrom" (6).

20. Some, like George Hunt, dismiss him as nothing more than "a despicable character," whose only traits are "irresponsibility, cruelty, moral weakness, schizophrenia, and cowardice," while Joyce B. Markle believes that, in the novel's terms, he is the "real Jesus, the Black Jesus" because he is "the only one with beliefs deep enough and a vision of America strong enough to be a priest and life-giver" (Hunt 179; Markle 150). Updike himself subscribed to the latter explanation, saying that "no one's given serious consideration to that the idea that Skeeter, the angry black, might be Jesus. He says he is. I think he probably might be." (*Picked-up Pieces* 510).

## CHAPTER 3

# Domesticated Strangers: Fissures Within the Nuclear Family

Although suburban communities were certainly designed around notions of similarity and property ownership, the model for the ideal community was the family. For thinkers from Aristotle to Arendt, the family is the cornerstone of Western society, but the version enforced in the postwar period—the so-called "traditional" family—was quite different from those practiced even in the decades directly preceding World War II. Unlike the assumed communities examined in Chaps. 1 and 2, the marital couple is a smaller, more intimate union, founded on vows exchanged by two members, who then create the other members as extensions of their selves. The supposed stability of the family was particularly important in the decade following World War II, when the fear of a Soviet conflict and the resurgent economy compelled young people to find security by redefining marriage according to strictly demarcated gender roles. Even now, 60 years after the establishment of this "traditional" marriage, pundits, politicians, and philosophers invoke the model as a means to a more safe and structured society.

Others, however, have been less eager to praise the nuclear family. In their landmark work *Anti-Oedipus*, French philosophers Gilles Deleuze and Felix Guattari claim that capitalism deploys the nuclear family as an agent of social production that inscribes itself "into the recording process of desire, clutching at everything," and performing "a vast appropriation of the productive forces; it displaces and reorganizes in its own fashion the entirety of the connections and the hiatuses that characterize the machines

© The Author(s) 2016

J. George, *Postmodern Suburban Spaces*,

DOI 10.1007/978-3-319-41006-7_4

of desire…reorganizes them all along the lines of the universal castration that conditions the family itself…but it also redistributes these breaks in accordance with its own laws and the requirements of social production" (124). In this way, the family "follows the pattern of its triangles" and distinguishes "what belongs to the family from what does not"; it directs desire—for example, modeling sexual attraction through the mother/father—and sets out restrictions, as in the incest taboo (125). This model reduces the members' infinite potential to a mere point in an Oedipal triangle, a variation of "mommy/daddy/me." Within this structure, the child's ultimate end is to mimic mommy or daddy, to follow the pattern set by the parents and repeat the bondage on his or her own children. But even as they recognize the growing strength of these arrangements, Deleuze and Guattari also claim that the triangle is not perfect, that no market force can fully determine the subject: "the family is by nature eccentric, decentered. We are told fusional, divisive, tubular, and foreclosing families…Families are filled with gaps and transected by breaks that are not familial: the Commune, the Dreyfus Affair, religion and atheism, the Spanish Civil War, the rise of fascism, Stalinism, the Vietnam war, May '68—all these things form the complexes of the unconscious, more effective than everlasting Oedipus" (97). Accordingly, the members of the family remain fundamentally unknowable—and therefore unsafe—to each other.[1] The unassailable difference between parent and offspring breeds an anxiety that is sublimated into stories about family, variously portraying it as a means for security or a tool of oppression.

The 1982 horror movie *Poltergeist* mines this tension for scares. The film focuses on the Freelings, an upper middle-class family whose youngest daughter Carol Anne (Heather O'Rourke) has an innocence that makes her a target for malevolent demons. Carol Anne comes to the spirits' attention when the Freelings occupy a suburban home, the finest in a modern planned community clandestinely built upon an old graveyard. Some of the movie's most horrific images—a closet transformed into a gaping maw, skeletons emerging from an unfinished swimming pool, a tree from the front yard attacking the kids' bedroom—alter the seemingly benign neighborhood into a hazardous place. This risk contradicts the sales pitches made by Freeling patriarch and star real estate agent Stephen (Craig T. Nelson), whose firm developed the subdivision; far from the "whole generation of security" his employers promised, the suburb's increasing perilousness directly implicates Stephen, who used his family's contentment as a selling point to potential buyers. The film also makes Carol Anne just as responsible as Stephen, as she is the first to witness and communicate with the ghosts. The horror of *Poltergeist*, then, rests on two, possibly divergent postulates: the Freeling family is in danger, exposed to malicious forces lurking in their suburban neighborhood, and the Freeling family is the danger, whose daily activities call the monsters forth.

These concerns are hardly unique to fright films like *Poltergeist*. While suburbanites expect blood ties and vows to safeguard the familial relationship—rendering it a more stable community than those formed with neighbors and fellow property owners—the members' inherent difference denies such pretensions, making these domestic strangers a favorite topic for writers of suburban fiction. This chapter locates portrayals of critical hospitality within families, examining stories that reject the limiting "traditional" form of wedlock and extreme focus on child safety often associated with suburban living, as well as the egoistic "free love" evoked in adultery tales. Each of these novels address the topic from a clearly bourgeois perspective, and while each is critical about the way family is practiced in middle-class suburban America, it focuses not on issues of class but those of responsibility. The first two novels I read in this chapter—Tom Perrotta's *Little Children* and John Irving's *The World According to Garp*—deal explicitly with these twin concerns: the former equates the impossible expectations of traditional marriage to pornographic fantasies, while the latter frames extreme defense of one's children as fundamentally self-centered. Like many of the works examined in this book, these novels tie acts of critical hospitality to the presence of death in the suburbs; however, they stand out from those previously discussed in their treatment of fantasy. Where texts such as *Rabbit Redux* or *Revolutionary Road* took a Heideggarian approach that preferences the present and factual over the expected, Perrotta and Irving advance a more nuanced approach, retaining some element of the unreal as a means for self-expression even within the ethical. Drawing from Jean-Luc Nancy's writings on love and obligation, I find this tension between the fantastic and the ethical in the Gladneys in Don DeLillo's *White Noise*. Foregoing the demanding constraints of the contract marriage and (eventually) the unrealistic expectation of safety, the Gladneys are a *bricoluer* family, constructed from the pieces of previous relationships, who bind themselves to each other while still recognizing the other's unknowable infinity, making explicit the obligated responsibility implied by Perrotta and Irving. By illustrating the critical hospitality members demand from one another, these novels reimagine the family as a contingent community, enacting an identity that one chooses while still deferring to the needs to care for the others to whom one is yoked. These stories portray suburbia not as a place where individuals are subsumed into a stringent family dynamic, but as a space in which proximity enhances the members' Deluzian alterity, a ground for ethical community.

## THE CONTRACT(ING) MARRIAGE

The center of the modern suburban family is the marital couple, a figure of contest in the popular and literary imagination. Perhaps one of the most paradigmatic examples is Ira Levin's 1974 conspiracy novel *The Stepford Wives*, and its better known, campy TV adaptation from the following year. At the narrative's climax, protagonist Joanna Eberhart learns that members of the Stepford Men's Association have been replacing their spouses with servile and sexually pliant clones, and that she is the next target. During her escape, Joanna encounters her own doppelgänger—an unassertive and impersonal, but more physically attractive, version of herself—and, in a moment of terrifying double-consciousness, sees herself as her husband Walter wishes to see her: a simple, thoughtless pleasure machine, designed to limit her own potential to become an unquestioning helpmate for her spouse. Like Levin's other well-known novel *Rosemary's Baby*, *The Stepford Wives* invokes a particularly communal form of terror, the fear of being the subject of a conspiracy. But the real horror of *The Stepford Wives* is the revelation that Walter, who heretofore professed allegiance to the women's liberation movement and supported Joanna's career plans, had orchestrated his wife's replacement since the beginning of the novel. The most basic union—the one on which all other communities rely, particularly in a suburb like Stepford—has been undone; Joanna's husband was not the man he promised to be.

The liberal politics and frank sex talk of *The Stepford Wives* might reflect its 1970s setting, but its ideologies are more rooted in the era of Eisenhower than that of Jimmy Carter. The titular clones are exaggerations of the stereotypical 1950s housewife, as marketed by Madison Avenue advertisements and memorialized in early sitcoms: the woman who spent her day tending to the house and children to make a safe haven for her husband, who worked outside of the home earning the family wage. For Walter, reverting Joanna back to the 1950s model allowed him to reap the benefits of that era's gender norms, in which he the breadwinner expected to return to a clean house, well-behaved children, and a sexually available wife. *The Stepford Wives* is hardly the only story to critique these expectations, and in fact, the 1950s marriage remains a powerful image that recurs in a number of contexts, valorized in *Leave It to Beaver* or satirized in *Desperate Housewives*, derided as a symbol of repression and socially sanctioned sexism or heralded as a defense of family values and stability. But despite being a prominent imaginary figure and a political flashpoint, historians contend that the 1950s marriage was in fact an anomaly, both unprecedented and relatively short-lived. According to historian Elaine Tyler May, the affluence of the 1920s and the austerity of the 1930s began the redefinition of gender norms that culminated in the 1960s and 1970s; it was "the generation in between—with its strong domestic ideology, pervasive consensus politics, and peculiar demographic behavior—that stands out as different" (9). The destruction witnessed during World War II, coupled with the oncoming threat of the Cold War, spurred Americans to look for security where they could find it, namely in a retroactively designated "traditional" wedlock. The loose sexual mores of the 1920s and 1930s, May explains, became considered not only immoral but also a threat to national security. As popular media, from screwball comedies like *His Girl Friday* to hardboiled Mickey Spillane novels, retold stories about liberated women wreaking havoc in the workplace and aiding Communist saboteurs, young Americans sought security through what May calls "domestic containment"—using the home space to establish a sexually demarcated set of American ideals. As Jessica Wiess notes, this ideology "was rooted in widely accepted gender roles that defined men as breadwinners and women as mothers. Many believed that a violation of these roles would cause sexual and familial chaos and weaken the country's moral fiber" (117). And while some young women were reluctant to forego the rights and pleasures their mothers have earned—to say nothing of the men who shuddered at the prospect of the long hours and emotional isolation required by a strict separation of spheres—many considered the stakes too great. The omnipresence of death and war made all other pursuits seem frivolous.

But whatever the power of these social forces, Weiss insists, the 1950s marriage was constructed by willing participants. In addition to the sense of security it provided, this compact also allowed individuals to express their sexual identities and achieve personal goals. The marriage pact assured each member a partner for their endeavors, and while that did of course require one to relinquish some potential goals, many young marrieds determined that the good outweighed the bad, at least initially. This emphasis on the companionate union, in which two free individuals

come together to make a pact, forced couples to rethink their relationship from a form of socially supported duty—in which external forces like
the state, the church, and the extended family came to aid and direct the
new couple—to the actions of two solitary agents. As a result, marriage
became considered an individual's work, the manifestation of independent choices. The stereotypical 1950s marriages of Harriet Nelson or June
Cleaver "obscures the fact that the decade encompasses only a single stage
in the family cycle of that first generation to form families after the war—
the parents of the baby boomers. Their children, the boomers, grew up
and went to school, then off to college and independent lives, and parents'
lives evolved with these changes and historical circumstances" (Weiss 2).[2]
Against May, then, Stephanie Coontz argues that this focus on work and
personal happiness makes the 1950s marriage not an anomaly, but rather
the culmination of a process that began with the nineteenth-century development of the middle class. Pre-Romantic Period coupling was largely an
economic and social function, designed to determine the "rights and obligations connected to sexuality, gender roles, relationships with in-laws,
and the legitimacy of children" and to define the "participants' specific
rights and roles within the larger society. It usually defines the mutual
duties of husband and wife and often the duties of their respective families
toward each other, and it makes those duties enforceable." (32). When
the middle class began to develop in the nineteenth century, attention
shifted to romance and individual fulfillment, and while this redefinition
was intended to make the duty of the marital rite more palatable to the
participants, it had an unintended consequence of prioritizing individual
choice and desires.[3] Consequently, Coontz contends, the 1950s marriage
was less a period of idealistic domination and rather a flawed reaction to a
continual unsettling of what was once a more overtly communal tradition.

These historians reveal a complexity within the seemingly stagnant and
oppressive nature of the Eisenhower-era marriage: whatever the inequalities
and abuses such a relationship entails, most Americans entered into it freely.
Though many recognized the limits they were putting on their freedom,
they accepted these burdens as means to another end, one that could not
be reached without the aid of the marital partner. This paradox is nothing
new, and in fact recalls the social contract theories discussed in earlier chapters, as best articulated by Rousseau—when fully formed and autonomous
individuals wish for an end they cannot accomplish themselves, they form
communities, thereby giving up some rights for the purpose of achieving
a particular goal. The postwar middle-class young adults wanted stability

and security in a dangerous time and therefore alienated their autonomy to establish it. But as so often happens, the contract becomes a contradiction, in which individuals perform their freedom by foregoing it.

Like the agreements discussed in the previous chapters, the contract marriage assumes that individuals are self-interested agents, fully conscious of the arrangements into which they enter. As the foundational community in most Western societies, marriage has received attention from most liberal social contract thinkers; however, where the agreements that govern property laws or the formation of civilizations have fairly narrow aims— society must be established to give security, property must be protected to honor an individual's labor, and so on—philosophers have struggled to articulate the role of marriage. Most notably, both Kant and Hegel, who come to radically different conclusions about the role of property, describe childbirth as the purpose of marriage, and therefore frame the pact as a supernatural bond that supersedes individual desires.[4] The inescapable social imperative implicit in this contract has, as Foucault puts it, made marriage the most public of private societies: it receives "the most intense focus of constraints; it was spoken of more than anything else; more than any other relation, it was required to give a detailed accounting of itself" (37). But for many feminist thinkers, the public nature of the marital contract undermines the possibilities of autonomy that Weiss and Coontz found. The root of the problem, Carole Pateman argues, is that the social contract assumes, and thereby covers over, a sexual contract, which insists that women remain enclosed in the home and servile under the male head[5]:

> Sexual difference is political difference; sexual difference is the difference between freedom and subjection. Women are not party to the original contract through which men transform their natural freedom into the security of civil freedom. Women are the subject of the contract. The (sexual) contract is the vehicle through which men transform their natural right over women into the security of civil patriarchal right. (6)

Pateman's position echoes the genealogy of femininity that Simone de Beauvoir outlines in *The Second Sex*. Where marriage pretends to be "a union freely entered upon by the consent of two independent persons," it remains "a very different thing for man and for woman," as the latter are barred from "making exchanges and contracts with the male caste upon a footing of equality" (425–426). The asymmetry between genders undermines the basic premises of the marital and social contracts, and thereby corrupts the community hoped to be formed by the central couple. They become a society in which the members "have lost their independence without escaping loneliness; they are statically united, they are the 'one,' instead of maintaining a dynamic and living relation"; as a result, the free autonomy espoused by contract theorists falls short, because the members "can give each other nothing, exchange nothing, whether in the realm of ideas or on the erotic plane. A thousand evenings of vague small talk, blank silences, yawning over the newspaper, retiring at bedtime!" (471).

It is no surprise that Beauvoir's argument resounded so strongly in the suburbs, particularly when articulated in Betty Friedan's 1963 bestseller *The Feminine Mystique*. After all, as part of the US government's attempts to continue World War II levels of patriotism against the oncoming Soviet threat, the suburb was specifically designed for nuclear families governed by these contracts. As May, Weiss, and other historians observe, a number of Federal mandates encouraged the space's continued growth and its imagery became a powerful rhetorical tool: when then-Vice President Nixon used suburbia as an example of the superiority of American capitalism over the socialism of Khrushchev's Soviet Union, he directly pointed to its advantages for women and families. For Nixon, and any number of American leaders after him, suburbia was built for the family home where "a man could display his success through the accumulation of consumer goods. Women, in turn, would reap rewards for domesticity by surrounding themselves with commodities" (May 164). Early pioneer of planned communities James Rouse articulated the connection in an interview with *Life Magazine*, explaining that urbanists have dealt with "highways, land uses, densities—even with crime, delinquency and disease, but it almost never begins with the simple question: 'How can we best provide for the happiness of a man, his wife, and family?'" (qtd. in Bloom 33). Scores of developers and real estate agents have followed Rouse's lead, making the suburbs the prime space to enact the conjugal contract, thereby forever linking suburbia and the 1950s marriage in the American imagination.

## CONTRACT AND EXPECTATION IN TOM PERROTTA'S *LITTLE CHILDREN*

The failure of the liberal marriage contract identified by Beauvoir and Pateman touches upon a conflict explored by a myriad of fiction writers, and critics have long associated the development of the novel with the advent of the modern companionate marriage.[6] Where the political unions suited early modern dramatists and courtly love was the subject for—and an invention of—the romantic poets, the novel's multivocal form effectively captured the tension between the earlier, more communal model of marriage and the changes wrought by post-Enlightenment individualism.[7] According to Tony Tanner, because marriage is, for bourgeois society, "the all-subsuming, all-organizing, all-containing contract," the bourgeois novelist "has no choice but to engage the subject of marriage in one way or another, at no matter what extreme of celebration or contestation," and will ultimately discover "that the bourgeois novel is coeval and coterminous with the power concentrated in the central structure of marriage" (15).

But while Leslie Fiedler agrees that love—"or more precisely, marriage and seduction"—is the "subject par excellence of the novel," he identifies a revulsion toward such couplings in its American version. Fiedler argues that American novelists, under influence of Puritan forbearers, have collapsed these impulses and thereby associate love in general, and women in particular, with death and damnation. As a result, the terror implicit in death and love is rarely directly addressed by American novelists, but is often sublimated into humor; American literature, then, resembles "a chamber of horrors disguised as an amusement park 'fun house,' where we pay to play at terror and are confronted in the innermost chamber with a series of inter-reflecting mirrors which present us with a thousand versions of our own face" (27). Therefore, the great American novels tend to be boy's stories—"books that turn from society to nature or nightmare out of a desperate need to avoid the facts of wooing, marriage, and child-bearing" (25). For Fiedler, Rip Van Winkle represents the paradigmatic figure, who memorializes "however playfully, the flight of the dreamer from the drab duties of home and town toward the good companions and the magic keg of Holland's gin," the first of many who run from civilization, "which is to say, the confrontation of a man and woman which leads to the fall, to sex, marriage, and responsibility" (26). Judith Fetterly considers Irving's story far less playful, identifying it as "one of the first American books in which man, nature, and beast...are sacrosanctly linked and woman is seen as the agent of civilization that seeks to repress this holy trinity" (5). Conversely, Rip, who sleeps long enough to evade his wife and her nagging, rejoins society as a philosopher king and a hero who successfully defeated "civilization and the imperatives of adulthood" (6). Fiedler and Fetterly's approaches have been troubled in the following decades by the recovery of domestic fiction performed by critics who restage the marriage plot as a form of female agency and influence on the political, as discussed in the previous chapter, but the central tension remains cogent: American writers often frame the "responsibility" inherent to marriage as something limiting, something to be feared and avoided.

Given the aforementioned connection between suburbia and the 1950s marriage—and, of course, the importance of contractual thought to the framers of the modern suburb—it is not surprising that some of the most compelling explorations occur in suburban fiction. In fact, nearly every suburban fiction focuses on married characters, making the marriage pact an important element, if not the exact focal point of these stories.[8] Some, such as Wilson's *The Man in the Grey Flannel Suit* or Cheever's *Bullet Park* portray the relationship as an intimate respite from the demanding outside world, while others deconstruct the restrictive nature of contracts and gender role, portraying it as a vice trapping both men and women. Outside of some more pointed portrayals, most depictions contain both elements, longing for the companionship and support marriage promises while simultaneously begrudging the restrictions imposed by long-term obligations. Like the stories in Chaps. 1 and 2, these fictions problematize the rigidity of the contractual model and seek an association based on obligation and interaction in which the members exhibit a care for one another that exceeds the limits of contract. They try to uncover the infinitely human nature of a long-term relationship between two people that is often buried under social expectations and economic concerns.

Tom Perrotta, a satirist in the vein of T.C. Boyle or Tom Robbins, addresses the oddities of these contracts in his 2004 novel *Little Children*. The novel lampoons the fantasies enacted by a group of suburbanites living on Blueberry Court, focusing largely on the extra-marital affair between feminist-turned-housewife Sarah and handsome stay-at-home dad Todd and on the campaign disgraced police officer Larry Moon launches against Ronnie McGorvey, a child molester and alleged child murderer who has returned from prison to live with his mother. As the book's title suggests, Perrotta frames these various pursuits as ultimately juvenile, based on an unreal set of desires that create ethical problems for others. The Moon/McGorvey plotline most clearly captures this viewpoint, as Moon's personal failings—he loses his job and wife after erroneously shooting an unarmed black teenager—drive his vendetta against McGorvey as much as a concern for the neighborhood children; the novel does not forgive McGorvey's horrid behavior, making it clear that he did murder a young girl he molested, but it also portrays Larry's behavior as a strategy to ingratiate himself to his neighbors by playing on the neighbor-hood's desire for security. *Little Children* portrays the affair pursued by Sarah and Todd as equally utilitarian, as they use one another as a means for indulging in fantasies about a perfect marriage while ignoring the facts of their current unions. In this way, the novel is more interested in mar-riage than in cheating; the main characters commit adultery not for the thrill of transgression, but for the chance to reset their marriages and to form a couple that maintains the static roles promised in their vows; in the same way Updike's *Marry Me: A Romance* is a story about adultery wrapped around a marriage plot, then, Perrotta embeds a marriage plot within an adultery narrative. The shift allows Perrotta to widen his criti-cal aim, mocking not only the absurdities of the middle-aged adulterers, but also the conjugal contract's attempts to lock infinite individuals into predetermined and unchanging identities.

Of the four people involved in the Todd/Sarah affair plot, Sarah's hus-band Richard Pierce receives the least attention and sympathy. An adver-tising executive with more money but less self-awareness than the other characters, Richard seems to embody all of the attributes typically mocked by suburban fictions: a member of the managerial class, a materialist of the highest order with one ex-wife and one unhappy current wife. Perrotta does little to flesh out this broad figure, but he does use him to lampoon some of the central assumptions of the contract marriage, particularly in a scene in which Richard meditates on the subject while looking at Internet pornography in his home office. As he ogles the digital images, Richard reflects on his hasty engagement to first wife Peggy and his deteriorating relationship to Sarah, describing marriage in terms that recall other literary husbands such as Frank Wheeler and Harry Angstrom. Richard considers himself constrained by his marriage and resents his wives for shackling him with "the burden of parenthood" and "imprisoning him in a suburban cage," sensing the end of his second marriage when he feels "a familiar sense of claustrophobia and resentment, as if he were once again a young man throwing away the best years of his youth" (117, 120). The fact that Richard frames his marriages as "wrong from the start" implies the pres-ence of a "right" marriage, or perhaps more accurately, a "true self" that is being violated by his marriages. In fact, the accounts he gives of both of his marriages—the "silence and passivity" into which he, prompted by an unwanted surprise pregnancy, married Peggy or how he "completely...mis-read his own needs" when throwing himself into his union with Sarah—rely on an authenticity that, despite the agreements into which he entered, was violated by the coupling (116, 121). When he dismisses his newfound pornographic desires with maxims—"if there was one thing life had taught him, it was that it was ridiculous to be at war with your own desires" or "*we want what we want…and there's not much we can do about it*"—he calls on the language of authenticity, framing his connubial life as an offense to the contract he hoped to put forth (109, 111, emphasis in original).

This language of authenticity becomes Perrotta's satirical target, as he describes the cheap, tawdry means by which Richard asserts his selfhood: his "night school MBA," coining trademarks for fast-food products "The Cheese-Bomb Mini-Pizza™" and "The Double-Wide Burger™," and embarking on "a string of hotel flings, as well as a long-term affair with a client's receptionist," or trying to convince Sarah to join swingers' "house parties" (117, 121). More ironically, Richard finds his paragon of authenticity in the persona of "Slutty Kay," a middle-aged model who specializes in housewife-themed pornography: where he considers most pornography problematically fake—"greedy male businessmen speaking through the mouths of young women with big fake tits"—he is convinced by her combination of the "brazen (calling herself 'slutty') and the banal ('actively pursuing a swinging lifestyle'; 'my God-given sexuality')" (114). Richard is struck by Kay's "moral and intellectual clarity," and sees a "niceness [that] radiated from her face," so innocent and pure in Richard's estimation that her "sweet nature was unmistakable, even when she was performing unspeakable acts with a champagne bottle" (115). This combination foregrounds Richard's primary attraction to Kay, specifically the way she retains a fantastic element of sexuality within the context of an ideal marriage. Accordingly, throughout the scene, in which Richard employs a pair of "used" underwear purchased from Slutty Kay's website as a stimulant, he struggles to draw a distinction between his wife and Kay: "He was a married man, after all. If he wanted to get his hands on a pair of unwashed panties, he didn't have to look any farther than the bathroom hamper…For all he knew, [the underwear] could have been worn by any woman in the world, including Sarah" (110, 121). The fantasy requires him to believe that Kay is "a different sort of woman" from his wives, thereby framing the unhappiness in his marriages to a type of authenticity, which reduces all to types, not people performing actions (110).

Perrotta complicates Richard's glee by repeatedly drawing attention to the ridiculous, contradictory nature of his obsession. The narrator punctuates the scene with asides that undercut any clear sense of unified selfhood, noting that part of Richard was both a "responsible adult who disapproved on moral grounds and understood quite clearly that the porn industry exploited and violated young women" and "a horny teenager who just thought it was incredibly cool to see pictures of naked ladies doing crazy stuff," or accentuating the "uncomfortable fact that [Kay] existed for him solely as a digital image" (113, 116). Even while trying to become aroused by the underwear—which he purchased to "provide a connection to the actual woman and her actual body, liberating him from the sanitized stillness of a photograph"—Richard must ignore the possibility that the "real" underwear was, in fact, subcontracted out to "a sweatshop full of bored women—Chinese and Latina seamstresses—all of them wearing polka-dotted thongs as they worked their sewing machines" by repeating to himself "*These are Kay's panties...These panties belong to Kay*" (116, 122). This comically shocking juxtaposition renders Richard's notions of authenticity utterly risible, a predetermined agreement that has little to do with the present and factual in front of him. As a result, marriage, in Richard's mind, becomes little more than a series of fantastic agreements, barely related to facts of the other's existence and able to be abandoned when they fail to serve the self.

Though a relatively minor and fully unsympathetic character—even Todd's demanding wife Kathy gets a full arc and some reader empathy—Richard's theory of marriage reverberates throughout the novel, giving insight to the central affair plot. Kathy secretly resents Todd for his inability to pass the bar exam and become a lawyer because she "wanted to have it both ways—wanted to live the interesting life of an artist without accepting the unpleasant financial sacrifices that usually came along with the package," while Todd senses this bitterness and wishes she would allow him to be a househusband (161). For her part, Sarah wants to continue enjoying the fruits of Richard's economic success while also having him home to watch their daughter Lucy as she pursues her neglected academic and artistic interests. Each of the characters, then, applies a contractual approach to their relationships, not unlike those that motivated the 1950s marriage: they seek security and prosperity by holding one another into strict roles. If Kathy and Sarah want to be the artists or scholars they think they should be, they need their husbands to be economically prosperous; conversely, if Todd and Richard want to be the successful people they consider themselves to be—Todd a football star, Richard a marketing genius—then they need specific, often sexual, responses from their wives. Despite Richard's professed progressiveness, Sarah's feminist studies, Todd's interest in non-traditional gender roles, or Kathy's successful career making popular television documentaries, the couples invoke the promises of the 1950s marriage: they expect the husbands to be the primary breadwinners while the wives provide support and tend to domestic duties. The failure to embody the terms of the contract motivates the story's adultery plot.

And yet, in the same way Richard's scene underscores the novel's problems with contract marriage, it also sets up the critical hospitality that offers an alternative to such staid relationships. Midway through the scene, a bit of free indirect discourse reveals that Richard wishes to hurry through his act "so he could get back downstairs to his real life, where his wife and daughter were waiting for him, their impatience increasing by the minute" (75). More than a simple spatial designation, the narration draws a distinction between Richard's isolated world of fantasy and unmitigated desire and the "real life" where his wife waits for him to watch their daughter so that she can go on a walk with a friend. These walks had become "the highlight of Sarah's day...the one thing she looked forward to all day" and required Richard's participation—watching their daughter Lucy—to achieve (75, 78). Sarah's presence on the periphery of Richard's fantasy is a demand for hospitality, a face-to-face interruption—quite literally, as she does eventually barge in on Richard and catch him in the act—that renders his strict demarcations ridiculous and irresponsible. In his embarrassment, Richard remembers the history of his relationship with Sarah—now framed as "wrong from the start" for going contrary to his desires—but, in doing so, highlights the terms of his contract that he uses to hold her to a certain role. Richard first encounters Sarah shortly after the dissolution of his first marriage, when, after a period of self-loathing and porn addiction, Richard entered a "period of unusual physical and mental health" in which he "joined a gym, took some yoga classes, started reading books again" and "began paying closer attention to the flesh-and-blood women he encountered as he went about his day, including the sullen, but obviously very intelligent young woman who took his orders at Starbucks, and who, to his amazement, agreed to go out with him the very first time he asked" (114). As this litany suggests, Richard considers the "obviously very intelligent" Sarah to be part of his identity construction, and he is "drawn to her bitter sense of humor, her youthful body, and her enigmatic sexuality (she claimed to be "basically straight," but spoke frequently about the Korean woman she'd been in love with in college)" (119). For that reason, when he sees her after the birth of their daughter Lucy, "sitting at the kitchen table, expressing milk from her engorged left breast with a loud electric pump, looking pale and haggard as she flipped through the newspaper," the "emotion toward her that was a little like contempt" indicates a sense of anger at the way she violated their agreement, failing to remain the woman he married (121). In this way, Richard acts very much like Sarah and Todd, wishing to elide the failures of the first marriage by embarking a second, seemingly more exciting version. However, the repetition of these failures, both in Richard's experiences and in Todd and Sarah's relationship, suggests that it is not the people, but the model that fails. This prevalence seems to repeat, then, a familiar suburban critique: bourgeois marriage is a false and damaging construct that binds individuals.

But the novel's climax, which takes place on the playground where Todd and Sarah first met, complicates this familiar criticism by juxtaposing the role of fantasy next to the threat of death that underscores the Moon/McGorvey plot. The playground signifies both Sarah and Todd's entrapment in their suburban marriages, but also as the means of their escape, as they plan to "slip out of their respective houses, rendezvous at the Rayburn School playground, and head north for a few days at the seashore [before beginning] the difficult process of orienting themselves to a new alignment of the domestic planets" (297). But at the same time that Sarah arrives at their point of departure, she is met by not only Ronnie McGorvey, mad with grief after his mother's death and followed by a pursuing Larry Moon, but also fellow suburban mom Mary Ann Moser. Sarah considers all three of the characters despicable in different ways: Ronnie is a child molester, Larry boorish, and Mary Anne is "one of those depressing supermoms, a tiny, elaborately made-up woman who dressed in spandex workout clothes, drove an SUV the size of a UPS van, and listened to conservative talk radio all day," a woman Sarah found so infuriating that if she "had spoken out in favor of kindness to animals and small children, Sarah might have felt tempted to take up the cause of cruelty" (4, 28). But by joining her at the place intended to be the start of her new, perfect life, the novel shows Sarah becoming aware of the factual reality of her life that she ignored while chasing fantasies. Whatever she thought her suburb was, whatever she thought her life was, she comes to realize that it is filled with others that she may not want, and may even find dangerous.

As these characters all converge in the same space, the narration highlights the juxtaposition between the characters' desires and the people they encounter at the playground. Mary Ann, sneaking to the playground to smoke a clandestine cigarette and to contemplate her sad marriage, thinks of the place as the site where she watched Todd, "that ridiculously handsome man playing with that beautiful child in his jester's cap," and thought about the life she could have had with a different husband; "it was like they were taunting her with an image of what might have been, the life that had been snatched away from her and replaced by something decidedly inferior" (345). Ronnie arrives distraught and wanting to talk to someone, begging Sarah "Please...Don't run away from me" (347), while Larry runs after to apprehend him, indulging in his fantasy of catching the bad guy and actually excited to hear Ronnie confess to child murder. But despite their dislike of one another, the characters' shared presence prompts a different type of response, as Ronnie's face becomes the call for critical hospitality; "She'd been momentarily paralyzed by the sight of him," the narrator explains, ready to run until "her maternal instincts had kicked in" (346). But even though Ronnie was "*so* not the man Sarah wanted to be embracing right now," Sarah does embrace him; she responds to his need and cares for him. Moreover, the sadness Ronnie has for his mother leads her to recognize that her plans with Todd were drawing her attention away from the facts of her life: "*Poor girl*, Sarah thought, reaching out to brush a strand of hair away from Lucy's clammy cheek. *I'm all you have*" (353). Instead of becoming the place where she embarks on her dream marriage—"She was here because he said he'd run away with her, and she believed him," read the final lines; "believed, for a few brief, intensely sweet moments, that she was something special, one of the lucky ones, a character in a love story with a happy ending"—it becomes the spot where she recognizes the needs of those in proximity (355).

This revelation, combined with Richard's plot, seems to condemn fantasy for being inherently unethical, but the novel does not dispose of fantasy altogether; rather it refigures the role of fantasy. Todd is notably missing from the park meeting because he decides to skateboard with some youths he had admired. The scene ends comically, with Todd falling on the first jump and knocking himself out, which seems to parody the ridiculousness of his fantasy life. However, the "lesson" Todd learns seems no more likely; he too realizes the falseness of his affair plot, admitting that "he'd never actually wanted to start a new life with [Sarah] in the first place," and all she did was distract him from "his imperfect marriage and the tedious obligations of child care, supercharging the dull summer days with a sweet illicit thrill" (350). Similarly, Sarah may reject her dream marriage with Todd, but does so by constructing a new fantasy about her life with Lucy:

A vision came to her as her lips touched Lucy's skin, a sudden vivid aware-ness of the life they'd lead together from here on out, the hothouse intimacy of a single mother and her only child, the two of them sharing everything, breathing the same air, inflicting their moods on each other, best friends and bitter rivals, competing for attention, relying on each other for companion-ship and emotional support, forming the intense, convoluted, and probably unhealthy bond that for better and worse would become the center of both of their identities, fodder for years of therapy, if they could ever figure out a way to pay for it. It wasn't going to be an easy future, Sarah understood that, but it felt real to her—so palpable and close at hand, so in keeping with what she knew of her own life—that it almost seemed inevitable, the place they'd been heading all along. It was enough to make her wonder how she'd ever managed to believe in the alternate version, the one where the Prom King came and made everything better. (353–354)

In both cases, one fantasy is replaced with another, but there is a crucial difference between the two. The first fantasy moves away from obligation, and the second moves toward those who are present and have helped the characters construct their identities. Todd comes to realize the falsehood of his behavior and the obligation he has toward Kathy by listening to her complain that instead of "spend[ing her] days at the pool, holding hands with some cute guy [she] just met yesterday" like Todd has done, she had to spend time "in a smelly VA Hospital, listening to old men explain how they lost their legs?" (334). Similarly, it is the recognition of the various people in her suburb that pushes Sarah back toward Lucy to embark on their new relationship.

The novel ends in a strange fashion, simultaneously denouncing the various misreadings suburbanites had engaged in, most wistfully in the form of Sarah's "lost fairy tale," while still suggesting that the married couples will continue indulging in different fantasies. I do not read this as a contradiction, but a rethinking of the marriage contract. Where the tra-ditional marriage pact holds participants to unreal expectations of same-ness—illustrated here by Richard's vision of Slutty Kay, the perpetually sexualized woman—the fantasies in which Sarah, Todd, and Mary Anne indulge are different, based on relation to the other person. This is under-scored by the spatial arrangement in this final scene, the place intended to be the starting point for Todd and Sarah's new life in a perfect marriage now marred by the presence of unwanted enemies. Much like the repu-diation of fence thinking described in Chap. 2, this presence—and, just as importantly, Sarah's reaction to her enemies—indicates a more ethical type of community, one based on care for the other. By reconstructing the marriage pact against this background, Perrotta begins to gesture toward a type of marital singularity, one that still expects the stability of obligation while allowing for the disruptions of difference.

## FEARFUL DREAMERS: THE ENDLESS ENEMIES OF *THE WORLD ACCORDING TO GARP*

The B-plot of *Little Children*, in which Larry Moon makes Ronnie McGorvey a scapegoat against whom he can re-establish his own sense of justice, reminds us that child safety narratives are central to the suburban experience. Stories about childhood have, of course, long been a favorite subject for novelists, as the bildungsroman was essential to the evolution of the form. According to Leslie Fiedler, American writers eschewed the social development plots favored by their European forerunners, associating any induction into a community with entropy and death.[9] Because the American writer's imagination focuses on the frontier—"the last horizon of an endlessly retreating vision of innocence...the margin where the theory of original goodness and the fact of original sin come face to face"—their adolescent adventures are driven by an abiding desire to maintain this innocence and to avoid the carnal mortality inherent to adulthood (27). The American bildungsroman, therefore, culminated not in the domestication of raging Jane Eyre or in the sudden nobility of Oliver Twist, but in the protagonist asserting his or her difference from others. Indeed, as R.W.B. Lewis famously argued, the paradigmatic American character was a variation of the Biblical Adam, and the plot was that of a figure moving from a pre-lapsarian state to one of Emersonian solitude within a crowd. The ultimate goal of this hero, then, is the establishment of an identity, of an ipsetic selfhood formed in isolation from others.

Given the preponderance of first-person narrators in the American bildungsroman, critics contend that the establishment of identity requires the destruction of the hero's privacy, "perversely refusing to acknowledge any off-limit zones even as the reader winces on his behalf" (Tolchin 10). Like the images of retreat and innocence that fill these narratives, this language of destruction suggests an inherent danger in the discourse of childhood, the recognition that youth fades as quickly as it is described. For this reason, writes Rachel McLennan, stories about childhood necessarily involve a distancing and a shortcoming: after all, they are the only narratives whose authors and readers can only speculate or approximate the subject.[10] According to McLennan, literary children are best imagined as "figurings" or "metaphors," something always obliquely approached, perpetually evading ontological stability. Nabokov best illustrates this difficulty, as Humbert Humbert spends much of the novel avoiding the fact that his Lolita is, at best, an approximation of the "real" Dolores Haze—that he could steal "the honey of a spasm without impairing the morals of minor" because his quarry is only a textual figure (62). To that end, any number of fictions throughout American literary history have featured children in distress, including some of the most important canonical texts of the nineteenth century: Huck on the run from drunken Pap, Melville's Pip tossed from the *Pequod*, or Stowe sacrificing little Eva St. Clare to spur right-feeling in her readers. The trend continued in post–Civil War texts, including Styron's *Sophie's Choice* and Morrison's *Beloved*, which use the parent's involvement in their offspring's death to drive their plots.[11]

Because the space is so inextricably tied to modern myth of innocent childhood, the child endangerment trope takes a unique twist when applied to suburbia. As opposed to the heightened language used to imbue the death of a character like Stowe's Eva with cosmic importance, death scenes in suburban fiction tend to highlight the banality of the situation, linking the calamity to a commonplace object or activity: a haunted television in *Poltergeist* or the killer bed in *A Nightmare on Elm Street*; *The Ice Storm*'s Mike Williams is electrocuted while playing on a road near his house; Paul Hammer abducts Tony Nailles from a garden party in *Bullet Park*; Henry Park of Chang-rae Lee's *Native Speaker* loses his son during "a stupid dogpile" in his front yard; Rebecca Angstrom of the *Rabbit* tetralogy drowns in a bathtub; the title character of David Gates' *Jernigan* stumbles upon a teenager who killed himself while watching VHS tapes; and, as we will see, DeLillo's *White Noise* closes with toddler Heinrich peddling out of his driveway and into oncoming traffic.[12] Proving the adage "most accidents happen at home," these stories suggest that, like the serial killer Michael Meyers of John Carpenter's *Halloween*, death lurks behind every cupboard and waits in every garage.

On the surface, the prevalence of this motif serves a basic horror story task by making the commonplace alien, subverting the dreams promised to suburban homeowners. More than a simple reversal of expectation, however, this juxtaposition of the horrific and the mundane reveals an anxiety on the part of the parent, an inability to mediate the hazards their children face. If the postwar revision of the American dream is to provide a better lifestyle for your children, and if suburbia is understood to be central to achieving that goal, then authors who refigure the space into a juvenile death trap upset that narrative: in these stories, parents who move their children to the suburbs do not evade the threat—they expose their young to it: *Little Children*'s Larry Moon rationalizes his vendetta against Ronnie McGorvey by appealing to the neighborhood's desire for safety; Charles Burns' *Big Baby* features a young boy who misidentifies molesters and wife beaters for aliens and mutants; William Cowling of Tim O'Brien's *The Nuclear Age* supplements his neighborhood securities with a bomb shelter in the backyard; the Weisses of Raymond Carver's "A Small, Good Thing" mistake a birthday cake baker for a malevolent stalker; the parents in Robert Coover's "The Babysitter" get drunk at a party while their young die at home. In each of these cases, the parents' efforts to safeguard their offspring in fact makes them vulnerable, rendering the adults not only powerless to save their young, but actually complicit in the child's death.[13]

T.S. Garp, the protagonist of John Irving's *The World According to Garp* (1978), spends much of the novel evading this complicity, going instead to extraordinary lengths to defend his progeny from what he considers an incessant stream of aggressors. Irving illustrates this attitude with Garp's response to the novel's most memorable scene, a car accident that leaves one child dead and another maimed for life. As the family convalesces at a seaside resort, Garp tells his wife Helen, "I don't blame you…I don't blame me either…It's the only way we can be whole" (427–428). Garp's aversion to responsibility resonates within the world of the novel, as several characters conflate wholeness with inviolability, from Garp's mother Jenny Fields—who advocates a fiercely anti-social brand of feminism ("In this dirty-minded world…you are either somebody's wife or somebody's whore")—to Garp's own pessimistic resilience ("In the world according to Garp, we are all terminal cases"), the major figures seek isolated self-sufficiency (179, 688). Readers have been quick to identify this inviolability ethos, arguing that the characters desire not "communal endurance and vulnerability but…solitary power and refuge" as primary modes of identity (Carton 57). But Garp's denial of guilt is puzzling and contradictory; after all, he actually did cause the accident when he turned out the headlights in the vehicle carrying his two sons and pulled into his driveway at full speed, unaware that the space was occupied by a car in which Helen was fellating her lover. Irving tempers the macabre imagery with a sense of cosmic justice: Helen's lover Michael, an unlikable college student who forces Helen into sexual compliance, loses his penis; Garp, a writer who struggled to replicate his early work, shatters his jaw and must communicate through short notes; Helen atones for her indiscretion with a broken arm and a renewed commitment to motherhood; Duncan, the elder son whose eye is gouged out by an errant stick shift, becomes a visual artist; and Walt, the sickly and doted-upon younger son, is killed and lost forever. While one might argue that the seemingly firm relationship between crime and punishment operates according to a Calvinist moral equilibrium, the accident's grotesque mayhem suggests an order more complex than mere cause and effect, and the punishments reverberate far beyond the actions of the individual offender to affect even the most inno-cent bystander. So while the world according to Garp is a Hobbesian war of all against all, *Garp*'s world according to Irving is one in which obses-sive paranoia makes enemies out of everyone around, transforming the fretful parent into the inescapable threat.

The world according to Garp is one of incessant violence, beginning with its very first scene: the young nurse Jenny Fields wards off a sexually aggressive young man by slicing him with a scalpel. Similar incidents occur in the chapters that follow, and several of them are directed at children. As a boy, Garp nearly falls to his death off the roof of a boarding school, and later he loses most of his ear in a dog attack. As a young adult, Garp gains a certain degree of notoriety after encountering a 10-year-old rape victim while jogging in the park and apprehending her attacker. Outside of the grizzly fate reserved for Garp's own sons, Duncan and Walt, the most prominent example of child violence is that of Ellen James, the young girl who has her tongue removed by her rapists, inspiring a group of women who call themselves the Ellen Jamesians and remove their own tongues to protest women's violence. As we will see in *White Noise*, death is ever present in suburban fiction, and does not spare children.

The potential danger for children remains ever present in Garp's mind, rendering him ambivalent about the prospects for familial safety. As the car crash scene demonstrates, Garp's own family provides no safety, a point underscored by the prevalence of extra-marital affairs between him and Helen. In fact, no family comes out looking par-ticularly stable: like the Garps, academic friends the Fletchers pursue in their own affairs—including one between wife Alice and Garp—that erupt into arguments and accusations. Helen was raised by her wrestling coach father after her mother abandoned them, leaving her, as a little girl, "forever on the lookout for nurses because she was forever on the lookout for her disappeared mother" (81). Though seemingly reliable,

Jenny's family fares no better, as she becomes the black sheep when she refuses to marry and has Garp out of wedlock. And while Jenny certainly treats Garp with more kindness than that, her devotion to his individuality—she repeatedly tells people that "Garp" is "his own name"—leads her to also put him under suspicion.

As this example demonstrates, the violent world of *The World According to Garp* is a Hobbesian state where all is against all. This is the central thesis of Jenny Fields' autobiography-turned-feminist manifesto, *The Sexual Suspect*: in her autobiography, Jenny wrote: "I wanted a job and I wanted to live alone. That made me A Sexual Suspect. Then I wanted a baby, but I didn't want to have to share my body or my life to have one. That made me A Sexual Suspect, too." (15). While this phrasing seems to position Jenny as a perpetual victim, Garp is quick to note his own mother's antagonism; "My mother seemed to need an enemy," Garp writes, "Real or imagined...helped her see the way she should behave, and how she should instruct me" (64). This play of victim/victimizer designations is another key aspect of this central theme, as those who would try to do good and protect others frequently find themselves implicated by the violence that envelops them. This is particularly true of the sexual violence that pervades the novel, leading Garp to write "my life has come in contact with so much rape," which "disgusted him with himself—with his own very male instincts, which were otherwise so unassailable. He never felt like raping anyone; but rape, Garp thought, made men feel guilt by association" (209). In this passage, Garp connects his seduction of a young college girl he remembers only by the nickname "Little Squab Bones" to "a rapelike situation," but that is far from the only charge against Garp's treatment of women; in addition to his numerous affairs and his solicitation of a prostitute, Garp frequently indulges in the lust about which his mother writes. The novel repeatedly underscores this point with several scenes in which Garp is confused for an attacker. This constant implication directly contradicts the lack of blame Garp claims after the accident: he must blame himself because he was involved in his children's lives. More importantly, it complicates his own insistence on enemies, particularly those who would threaten his children.

By his own admission, Garp is a "fearful dreamer" who interprets everything from a stuffy nose to immature babysitters as a direct assault on his offspring (311–312). As a writer whose considers the world "unnecessarily perilous" for both children and adults—"If Garp could have been granted one vast and naive wish, it would have been that he could make the world *safe*"—Garp confronts his anxieties through his fiction, which Irving often includes in part or in whole as embedded narratives within the novel (279). In particular, the story "Vigilance" directly addresses the effect the fear for his children has on his relationships with his neighbors, giving a first-person account of a suburban vigilante who tirelessly trains to defend his family from the dangerous speeders blasting down his neighborhood's streets. The narrator's indefatigable diligence often invites him to divide the world into simple types, identifying most in his "neighborhood full of children" as utterly helpless, but singling out reckless drivers as lethally careless and taking the role of defender for himself. Accordingly, he describes himself as a type of superhero whose impropriety—"I can travel across lawns, over porches, through swing sets and the children's wading pools; I can burst through hedges, or hurdle them"—represents heroic exceptionalism, a right afforded him because he is a father: the offending speeders are "almost always intimidated by my parenthood," which "sobers them, almost every time" (323). The logic of the story, then, eerily recalls Carl Schmitt's political theology, because the presence of children implies the presence of danger, and the father's role *qua* father necessarily puts him into eternal antagonism against the ever-present potential enemy.

In "Vigilance," as in Schmitt, the difference between friend and enemy is quite clear: the story's primary villain is a particularly belligerent young man in a "blood red" truck, while the hero's willingness to protect a laudatory little old lady justifies violent behavior. But contrary to this clarity and resolution, the narrator imagines his suburb as both a type of refuge from the more dangerous outer world—"in my neighborhood, the car is not king; not yet" —and as a perilous trap; "In my neighborhood there is no place to run," he explains in the opening lines, because "the sidewalks are threatened by dogs, festooned with the playthings of children, intermittently splashed with lawn sprinklers…just when there's some running room, there's an elderly person taking up the whole sidewalk, precarious on crutches or armed with quacking canes" (322). So when the narrator claims that "it's the suburbs [he's] training for," he means not only that he prepares himself to defend the people within the neighborhood, but also that these people themselves present a type of inescapable danger, always already in proximity. Simply put, suburbs are not safe because there are people in them. Accordingly, the narrator does occasionally forgo his firm distinctions and count himself among the dangerous suburbanites, recognizing that his actions often escalate the situation. "I should stop this crusade against speeders," he confesses to readers—"I go too far with them, but they make me so angry—with their carelessness, their dangerous, sloppy way of life, which I view as so directly threatening to my own life and the lives of my children." Similarly, when the little old lady asks what the neighborhood would be like without him, he must admit that, "[w]ithout me...this neighborhood would probably be peaceful. Perhaps deadlier, but peaceful" (331).

This admission, even at its most fleeting, complicates Garp's understanding of the world as inherently threatening toward his children: in the same way that Garp's own "filthy lust" implicates him in the sexual, gendered violence that permeates the novel, so also does his own presence and fear of violence create its own violence, often for his own children.[14] He is another one of the barbarians within the gates, endangering the children who share his space. Appropriately, this problem is illustrated most vividly in an episode from Garp's own life, in which he chases down a speeder who turns out to be "Mrs. Ralph," the recently divorced mother of one of Duncan's friends. As foregrounded by her awkward and nondescript title—none of the Garps know her first or last name, and only speak of her as the mother of Duncan's friend Ralph—Mrs. Ralph is ultimately an unknown to Garp, to whom he assigns an arbitrary signifier. Yet despite this capriciousness, Garp maintains his mistrust; his fear is only magnified when, after reluctantly allowing Duncan to have a sleepover at her house, Garp sees "a glow on the suburban horizon, which he imagined was the dreaded house of Ralph—in flames" and resolves to retrieve him from her clutches (262). While relating Garp's twilight rescue, Irving reiterates the porous divisions between potential danger and real banality, beginning with Mrs. Ralph's derisive greeting, "You're too late...Both boys are dead. I should never have let them play with that bomb" (282). Although the two clearly dislike and distrust each other, the narrator describes them as "a married couple" when they clean up after the boys together, underscoring an ontological inconsistency that only compounds when Mrs. Ralph asks Garp to eject an unidentified young man from her bedroom (283). Where Garp, like the vigilante from his short story, tries to enforce civility and moral and physical posturing, the other characters undermine his certainty by playing with identities: Mrs. Ralph tries to bolster Garp's position by insisting that he is her husband, while the lover asserts his rights as a guest by reminding them "she asked me in...[i]t was her idea" (286). The slippery nature of identity is underscored by Mrs. Ralph's behavior throughout their interactions, sometimes flirtatious and other times resentful, leading to the climax of the rescue, in which the drunk, despondent, and mostly naked Mrs. Ralph demands that Garp "prove" that he finds her attractive by showing her his erection. More than an innocent tease, the command attempts to force all the players to show their selves: heretofore, the philandering Garp had attempted to obfuscate his very real physical attraction to Mrs. Ralph by framing his compliments as mere self-esteem boosters, but when Mrs. Ralph insists "[s]how me your hard-on and I'll believe you like me," she dismisses the vagaries of falsehoods and playfulness and compels Garp to reveal himself and his intentions (290). Likewise, when Garp assents and lowers his shorts, he chooses to quite literally expose himself—to present himself as neither a dangerous invader nor an antagonistic father, but as a potential lover, aroused by her presence.

The fact that Garp consents to Mrs. Ralph's conditions against some powerful deterrents—Mrs. Ralph's clear instability, the sleeping children downstairs, Garp's vows to his wife—highlights the fact that Garp has made a decision regarding his relationship to Mrs. Ralph. The importance of decision, of identifying the other person's identity and acting accordingly, underscores the entire scene, particularly in regard to potential dangers. The need for decision has been present from his first encounter with Mrs. Ralph when, in spite of her speeding and her disheveled appearance, she repeatedly assures Garp, "Your kid's safe with me...Don't worry, I'm quite harmless—with children" (256). But the very notion of the decision requires a certain degree of ontological surety, which Irving repeatedly denies Garp, forcing him to admit that he knew little about Mrs. Ralph and "simply disliked her, on sight" (242). Moreover, Irving highlights the arbitrary nature of Garp's decision, explaining that poor Mrs. Ralph "was not the only victim perhaps slandered by his paranoid assumptions," but that "Garp suspected most people to whom his wife and children were drawn; he had an urgent need to protect the few people he loved from what he imagined 'everyone else' was like" (243).

This confusion between Garp's love for his family and his mistrust of all in proximity anticipates Michael Hardt and Antonio Negri's reinterpretation of Deleuze and Guattari. They consider the need to excessively defend one's children an unavoidable side effect of the nuclear family, a practice that corrupts the forms of love beneficial to the common and "unleashes some of the most extreme forms of narcissism and individualism" (161). According to Hardt and Negri, the family has restricted all alternative forms of affinity and relation, thereby transforming communal love into egoistic paranoia:

It is remarkable, in fact, how strongly people believe that acting in the interests of their family is a kind of altruism when it is really the blindest egotism. When school decisions pose the good of their child against that of others or the community as a whole, for example, many parents launch the most ferociously antisocial arguments under a halo of virtue, doing all that is necessary in the name of their child, often with the strange narcissism of seeing the child as an extension or reproduction of themselves. Political discourse that justifies interest in the future through a logic of family continuity—how many times have you heard that some public policy is necessary for the good of your children?—reduces the common to a kind of projected individualism via one's progeny and betrays an extraordinary incapacity to conceive the future in broader social terms. (*Commonwealth* 161)

But *Garp* upsets the antagonistic aspect of the Oedipal triangle by refusing to endorse its title character's fears, and in fact repeatedly collapses the distinction between safety and danger. Because Garp decides to retrieve Duncan on a whim and goes to Mrs. Ralph's house wearing only jogging shorts in the middle of the night, the narration positions Garp as a threat who does not belong. When Garp creeps through the shrubs and fences, the narrator likens him to "a gunman hunting his victim, [or] the child molester the parent dreads" (279). The other people who see Garp sneaking around wearing only running shorts share this suspicion, such as the young woman who "thinks he is a would-be exhibitionist" and "cries out and wobbles her bike around him," or the police officers who stop Garp on the way home and demand identification, which he cannot provide (280). Of course, as Garp protests throughout, all of his actions stem from his love for his children, but the story never backs this position, portraying the hero's fears as themselves frightening.

Irving himself admits to this conflation in the novel's afterword, in which he explains that the book is ultimately about "a father's fears." So while *Garp* "is and isn't 'autobiographical,'" Irving admits, it is based in his real worry for his children. "I'm just a father with a good imagination," Irving tells readers who express solidarity or condolences for his loss; "In my imagination, I lose my children every day" (xvi). Notice the active agent in these phrases: *I* lose my children, *I* imagine their deaths. Even as a father whose children live relatively safe and healthy lives in the real world, Irving confesses that he—not the myriad forces that could kill them all—orchestrates their ends; it is for his sake, not for theirs, that he fights to defend them. Accordingly, T.S. Garp, a ridiculous character in an absurdly dangerous world, can be seen as a parodic attempt to assuage this guilt and fear, an exaggeration of the Oedipal triangle that bears down on Irving and makes him worry for his young. No more is this apparent than in the novel Garp writes after the accident, a pulpy crime thriller called *The World According to Bensenhaver* that is so offensive that, despite Garp's literary reputation, only a pornographic magazine dares to publish it. Irving foregrounds the relationship between Garp and himself by including the entire first chapter of *Bensenhaver* within *Garp*, a lurid story about a suburban housewife who, to save her toddler, allows herself to be abducted and raped before gutting her attacker with a hunting knife. The bleak and merciless world of Adrian Bensenhaver, written by Irving as Garp, reflects the outlooks of both the fictional and the actual author: it is his imagination that has made the world into his enemies, focusing on grisly deaths instead of potential lives.

## A Cradle of Misinformation: Marriage and Obligation in DeLillo's *White Noise*

Each of the novels in this chapter—in fact, most of those in this study—position the presence of death as a key element of critical hospitality. But few novels address the topic as directly as Don DeLillo's 1985 *White Noise*, a sometimes farcical, sometimes sincere study in suburban anxiety. Easily DeLillo's most popular and one of his most commented-upon novels, *White Noise* has received a great deal of attention for its portrayal of death and belief in the era of late capitalism and increased media exposure. As Arno Heller puts it, part of the novel's draw is the reader's fear that "the ubiquitous predominance of a technologically and electronically generated hyper-reality may increasingly encroach upon the human identity, eventually leading to a numbing of the senses, to self-alienation and ultimately to an all-pervasive fear of death and non-existence" (37). At same time, some have noted that *White Noise* is perhaps DeLillo's "warmest" novel, in which warmth "is the definition of literary accessibility" and "family oriented writing [is] the direct route to lucidity" (Lentricchia 12). The notable exception here is Thomas J. Ferraro, who declares not only that *White Noise* is "Don DeLillo's stinging appreciation of the contemporary American family," but also that it is his "strongest contribution to our understanding of suburban domesticity." (15, 19). For others, suburbia exists largely as another example of the consumer culture and mass society the novel satirizes, a form of crowd mentality that "become[s] seductive, the collective mundane that nullifies the self, makes irrelevant the discovery of identity, and suppresses the inclination to reflect" (Dewey 80).

The novel's concerns with death, crowds, and selfhood all converge in the suburban neighborhood where main characters Jack and Babette Gladney enjoy a life of constancy: new students come every fall to the College-on-the-Hill where Jack teaches, television and radio commercials constantly float through the air, and the family members enjoy idiosyncratic diversions such as pen-pal chess games.[15] Initially, this familiarity seems to provide an ongoing assurance for Jack, so strong that he can pretend to shrug off a vague "airborne toxic event" that threatens his neighborhood and insist that such panic is better suited to "people who live in mobile homes out in the scrubby parts of the county, where the fish hatcheries are" (117). But this bravado is more posture than actual confidence, as Jack and Babette are in fact deeply afraid of death. Their conversations with one another repeatedly turn to the subject, even before Jack becomes exposed to the event and learns from doctors that he may die in 15 to 30 years. Of course, the diagnosis actually reveals nothing—Jack was always going to die eventually—but its comic rendering underscores the novel's central point: death remains ever present, despite humanity's many attempts to ignore it.

To illustrate this idea, the novel features characters deploying a number of evasion strategies to make sense of death, from religious dogmas to consumer goods to experimental drugs. Jack locates the purest form of security in the body of his wife, which becomes, as he puts it, "the agency of my resolve, my silence…I drew courage from her breasts, her warm mouth, her browsing hands, from the skimming tips of her fingers on my back" (172).[16] The protective element of their union leads Jack to call family "the cradle of the world's misinformation," in which the "[o]ver-closeness, the noise and heat of being…generates factual error." He and Murray Jay Susklind, the novel's gonzo voice of reason, debate the issue in a key passage:

> Murray says we are fragile creatures surrounded by a world of hostile facts. Facts threaten our happiness and security. The deeper we delve into the nature of things, the looser our structure may seem to become. The family process works toward sealing off the world. Small errors grow heads, fictions proliferate. I tell Murray that ignorance and confusion can't possibly be the driving forces behind family solidarity. What an idea, what a subversion. He asks me why the strongest family units exist in the least developed societies. Not to know is a weapon of survival, he says. Magic and superstition become entrenched as the powerful orthodoxy of the clan. The family is strongest where objective reality is most likely to be misinterpreted. What a heartless theory, I say. But Murray insists it's true. (81–82)

It may be heartless to Jack, but Murray's analysis quite succinctly characterizes his and Babette's marriage. They are overwhelmed by facts, and while they do discuss them—the two have numerous debates about who should die first—they also profess a literally absurd devotion to one another. At times, their conversations recall the silly repartee of love-struck teenagers—when Babette claims "I want to make you happy," Jack insists, "I'm happy when I'm pleasing you"; other times, it mirrors the connection between mother and child (28). Apropos of Heidegger, the couple remains resolute in their understanding of their world—they know that youngest son Wilder keeps running off, that the commercials invading their consciousness are lies, that there is no way to make sense of the end of life—and this knowledge pushes them back toward the factual reality of one another. In response to the unknowns, they form a community of two, sharing space.

The Gladneys' devotion is, of course, absurd and unreal.[17] The family here, like the pervasive media influence, "absorbs and metabolizes information from the larger atmosphere" (Veggian 59). In the same way "the 'white noise' of consumer culture is saying something far more compelling than that our minds have been colonized by the static of late capitalism," I argue that the Gladneys' union is not a simple lie to distract them from this possibility, but a Heideggerian response to it (Bonca 27). So where Jack might call the family "the cradle of the world's misinformation," the novel suggests that the falseness of marriage stems from "something even deeper, like the need to survive." Accordingly, I read the story's correlation between family and ignorance as not a heartless theory, but an optimistic portrayal of the obligated freedom to which *Little Children* and *The World According to Garp* allude, one that recalls Jean-Luc Nancy's contention that "I love you" is a promise both to the real person in proximity and to the unforeseeable possibilities he or she might pursue (81–82). The fictional family, and the marital pact in particular, though itself a construct or fantasy, provides a schematic of interaction in deadly times, forcing people to recognize their dependence on one another.

The importance of unreality and promise is clearly spelled out by a group of German nuns who appear toward the end of the novel to help Jack convalesce after a gun fight with "Mr. Gray" a.k.a. Willie Mink, a medical researcher who took sexual advantage of Babette. As the nuns tend to his wounds, Jack finds himself charmed by the sisters' quaint faith; but when he inquires further about the Church's teaching, he is sternly rebuffed with the question, "You would have a head so dumb to believe this?" (318).

Instead of ethereal dogmas about "angels, [and] saints, all the traditional things" that Jack had expected, the nun offers only pragmatic selflessness: "Our pretense is a dedication...Someone must appear to believe" (317, 319). Their faux-belief is a fiction into which they willingly enter, aware of both its shortcomings and its importance for other people; "It is for others," she tells him—"[t]he others who spend their lives believing that we still believe" (319, 318). The performance then is an act of hospitality, through which they take responsibility for those in proximity, regardless of their own desires. The nun demonstrates this hospitality at the start of the scene, when Jack, attempting to charm the nuns, tries to communicating with them in his rudimentary German. The four of them were "charmingly engaged in a childlike dialogue," but their speech never transcends "count[ing] to ten together" or doing "colors, items of clothing, parts of the body" (317). The nuns' participation and apparent enjoyment of the activity—"A smile appeared on her seamed face"—contradicts the pragmatic attitude they demonstrate later, revealing their acquiescence to Jack's games to be part of their devotion to other people.

Despite their playful indulgence with Jack's language games, the nuns never diminish their roles, but insist that they have taken "[s]erious vows" and live "a serious life" (319). The invocation of "vows" here and the serious implications they contain connects the nuns' behavior to the Gladneys' suburban marriage, and helps explain the outrageous promises Jack and Babette make to one another. In the same way the nuns have committed to an unreal performance for the sake of those in their care, the Gladneys' promises are an aspect of their devotion to one another. So while their family may very much be a "cradle of misinformation," it is not ignorant or distracting, but focused on the other in immediate proximity: the spouse. The facts that, Murray insists, "threaten our happiness and security" become, for Jack and Babette, the means for connection and devotion, as demonstrated by their many conversations about who should die first. Although Jack reveals to the reader that, despite telling Babette the opposite, he actually does not want to die first, that given "a choice between loneliness and death, it would take me a fraction of a second to decide," the prospect of loneliness is the prime motivating factor. Babette makes this point when she contends that Jack's death "would leave a bigger hole in her life than her death would leave in [his]" (101). This talk of gaps and absences underscores the prominence of presence for the construction of one another's lives, a point felt more keenly for the Gladneys because of—not in spite of—their knowledge of death; Jack's unascribed "prayer" may first demand "Don't let us die," but it also cries "Let us both live forever in sickness and health, feebleminded, doddering, toothless, liver-spotted, dim-sighted, hallucinating." (103). Jack and Babette do certainly cling to one another to look away from the reality of death, but DeLillo never frames this as an ignorance of or escape from death; the fear of death is "deep and real" for these characters, but it never paralyzes them—"We manage to function," largely because of the relationships to one another. When Jack asks "How is it no one sees how deeply afraid we were, last night, this morning?" he once again acts like, to use the nun's phrase, a "stupid head," neglecting his own knowledge of Babette's deep fears, and her knowledge of his (103). Like the nun's performances, the aversion Jack makes is part of his obligation to her, not an enclosing determining factor.

The demands and responses in Jack and Babette's dialogue illustrate the dialectic of obligation and ethics that Jean-Luc Nancy outlines in his essay "Shattered Love." Nancy identifies a "reticence" among philosophers when it comes to the topic of love, which he associates with the overwhelming potentiality of the subject. This potentiality suggests that "all the loves possible are in fact the possibilities of love...impossible to confuse and yet ineluctably entangled." But where his observation that love "in its singularity, when it is grasped absolutely, is itself perhaps nothing but the indefinite abundance of all possible loves" might, like Deleuze and Guattari, prioritize pure desire and potential, Nancy also emphasizes the role of promise and obligation (83).[18] In fact, not only is love the potential for all loves, but it is also not based in the identity of the lover or beloved, who requires a particular set of responses from his or her partner. So while this description of potentiality through desire clearly rejects the stagnant terms of the marital contract, Nancy does not concur with Deleuze/Guattari or Hardt/Negri's defense of potentiality through pure desire. Potentiality through desire does not create the love that reaffirms the common, Nancy argues, because desire is not love:

> Desire lacks its object—which is the subject—and lacks it while appropriating it to itself (or rather, it appropriates it to itself a lacking). Desire—I mean that which philosophy has thought as desire: will, appetite, conatus, libido—is foreign to love because it sublates, be it negatively, the logic of fulfillment. Desire is self extending towards its end—but love does not extend, nor does it extend itself toward an end. If it is extended, is buying upheaval of the other in me. (98)

Love cannot be pure desire because such desire ultimately leads to an egoism that reduces the object of one's love into exactly that: an object, a thing. In the same way that Levinas insists that enjoyment results in an interruption by the other, Nancy describes love as the upheaval of all terms and objects, the constant disruption of one's desires and intentions. Love, then, must be both an assertion of obligation and the acceptance of the beloved's refusal of these terms.

The coexistence of obligation and freedom is, of course, a contradiction; but, for Nancy, the contradiction is an inescapable element of the inexhaustible nature of love: "This nature is thus neither simple nor contradictory: it is the contradiction of contradiction and of noncontradiction…[t]he contradiction of the contradiction and of the noncontradiction organizes love infinitely and in each of its meanings" (87). If love is an unfulfillable faux-dialectic between the obligation imposed by the lover and the beloved's refusal to be reduced to these terms, then the phrase "I love you" must be more than simply a description of a current state: it must be a promise that "neither prescribes nor performs. It does nothing and thus is always in vain" (100). The promise of love cannot be the terms of a contract because they are inherently limited, but neither can it be the means of self-actualization because that limits the beloved to an event in the self's process of becoming. The ethical, reticent love that Nancy describes "is the promise and its keeping, the one independent of the other," that is committed to the inescapable infinity of the other because "one does not know what one says when one says 'I love you,' and one does not say anything, but one knows that one says it and that it is law, absolutely: instantly, one is shared and traversed by that which does not fix itself in any subject or in any signification" (100–101). Consequently, love is a law that imposes obligation on the self toward the other to whom one owes the potential through which the self is constructed.[19]

Accordingly, DeLillo repeatedly reminds readers that the presence and dependence the Gladneys enjoy comes with obligations. But in the same way the nuns' responsibility to unbelieving others puts restraints on their lives, they are not determining; the nuns' performances do not exhaust their potentiality, but rather display a critical hospitality that both performs and disrupts the other's expectations as a form of care and relation. So also do Jack and Babette allow for difference in their marriage, an element essential to their composition as a family. Though many times divorced and the veterans of several previous relationships, the Gladneys do not fit the orchid/wasp alternative to contractual marriage. Although Stacey

Olster argues that *White Noise* features crowds that offer a "sense of union" that "no longer depends on physical proximity," the shared space of the Gladney household remains a locus of identity construction (83). Jack and Babette have formed a patchwork family, pieced together from the elements of these previous relationships; their family tree is a twisted mess of grafted branches, despite the fact that "all the Gladneys 'interact' by any standard criteria, extremely well with one another, cooperatively and in concert, with admirable degrees of both mutual insight and self-irony" (Forraro 17–18). And while such anti-arboreal arrangements might recall Deleuze and Guattari, neither Jack nor Babette advocates the pure desire valorized by those thinkers, practicing instead a type of obligated freedom. They remain relatively friendly toward one another's former spouses, treating past relationships not (like Richard, Todd, and Sarah of *Little Children*) as mistakes from which they must repent, but as layers of experience that inform their current selves. The former marriages, and in fact all of their experiences, become the material of their selves; Babette and Jack "tell each other everything" because "marriages accumulate"; they become the material of identity, for which the other partner is a key and inescapable element (30). The logic here contradicts that of the contract or the affair. In the former, partners diminish their potential by embodying—and imposing—predetermined roles; in the latter, the individual lives by his or her desires, regardless of the needs of others. When the Gladneys turn one another's "lives for each other's thoughtful regard," they demonstrate something different, in which the self is a reaction to one's prior experience, one's desires, and one's obligations. This openness does not trivialize the Gladneys' marriage, but gives it substance.

So when Jack discovers that Babette has not only been secretly taking Dylar—an experimental drug designed to remove one's fear of death—but also procuring it by agreeing to clandestine sexual liaisons with Mr. Gray, he is hurt by both her infidelity and the fact that she has violated the identity she formed with him. But where Garp or Sarah Pierce would have deemed this transgression an irreparable breach of contract, Jack instead increases his devotion to Babette. Initially, this devotion appears to be the same unreality and falseness that troubles other marriages, as evident in the scene in which Babette confesses her indiscretions; while she explains what she has done, Jack reiterates his anger and disappointment by defining her: "All this without my knowing. The whole point of Babette is that she speaks to me, she reveals and confides," he complains—"Is this why I married Babette? So she would conceal the truth from me, conceal objects from me, join in a sexual conspiracy at my expense?" (199). These declarations may seem no different than the static expectations found in the traditional marriage contract or in the egoism of the adulterer, but two important elements differentiate Jack's demands. First, Jack does wish to remind Babette of her obligation to him, but this is not simply the irresponsible terms of a contract, formed without relation to the real and infinite person. Rather, it is based on his and Babette's factual experience, on the fiction of security they constructed together. Babette tries to make the problem solely hers—"Dylar was my mistake. I won't let you make it yours as well"—but Jack's insistence reminds her that they both had equal stakes in the relationship they formed (225). Because he was just as much a part of her identity as she was of his, Jack absolutely has the right to make certain demands of Babette, but they must be responsible demands, based in the facticity of the infinite other in the relationship, and this responsibility is the second difference from the other forms of relation. So when Babette insists on complicating Jack's simple narrative about betrayal and abdication of the family—"This is not a story about your disappointment at my silence. The theme of this story is my pain and my attempts to end it" (192)—she calls for a redefinition of her and Jack's marital identities in relation to the current reality of their existence. Her liaisons with Mr. Gray have become one more experience built into their identities and they need to respond to it, not simply demand that Babette be a particular type of person. And, indeed, Jack comes to accept this redefinition, as indicated by the openness of his new promise to Babette: he begins by asserting his embodied presence—"I'm right here"—and then shifts to an open-ended promise made to an unknowable and infinite other: "Whatever you want or need, however difficult, tell me and it's done" (199).

The tenderness exemplified in this scene is increased when placed in context of the phrase repeated throughout *White Noise*: "All plots tend to move deathward" (26). First introduced in a discussion of the plot to kill Hitler, the narrating Jack constantly returns to the idea, most prominently during his fight with Mink, in which he repeatedly reminds himself, "Here is my plan" (304). The same idea occurs earlier when Babette's father Vernon Dickey gives Jack the handgun he will eventually use to shoot Mink. With the gun in his possession, Jack accentuates the connection between plotting and death by reveling in his narrative sovereignty: a "concealed lethal weapon" is to him "a secret, it was a second life, a second self, a dream, a spell, a plot, a delirium"; he begins taking it to his classes, where it creates a "second reality" for him—reality he could "control, secretly dominate" over the unarmed people who came into his office (254, 297). In the process of delivering the handgun, so crucial for the novel's plot, Vernon briefly pontificates on the state of modern marriage. When Jack mentions that he and Babette consider him "too lawless for marriage," Vernon answers:

> The thing about marriage today is you don't have to go outside the home to get those little extras. You can get whatever you want in the recesses of the American home...Wives will do things. They want to do things. You don't have to drop little looks. It used to be the only thing available in the American home was the basic natural act. Now you get the options too. The action is thick, let me tell you. It's an amazing comment on our times that the more options you get in the home, the more prostitutes you see in the streets. (246)

This short pairing of the death-bringing gun and the wildness of marriage cannot be an accident, as it reveals the concept of marriage—of pledging yourself to another person—as itself a type of plotting, one that will also lead to death. In fact, the lead-up to the fight with Mink underscores this connection, as Babette initially refuses to tell Jack about "Mr. Gray's" identity because "You're a male. A male follows the path of homicidal rage." And although he denies it, Jack initially considers Mr. Gray—which, he learns, is name given to a group of several men involved in the Dylar experiments, not just Willie Mink—"The image was hazy, unfinished. The man was literally gray, giving off a visual buzz" (214). The decision to find Mink and kill him, then, can be understood as a way to finish Mr. Gray, to complete his story and provide surety. For his part, Mink performs his own bit of storytelling with his set of rules for behavior in the hotel in which he conducts his experiments, which he calls "room behavior." Room behavior is a contractual logic that positions Mink as the sovereign and those who enter his domain as his subjects:

> People behave one way in rooms, another way in streets, parks and airports. To enter a room is to agree to a certain kind of behavior. It follows that this would be the kind of behavior that takes place in rooms. This is the standard, as opposed to parking lots and beaches. It is the point of rooms. No one should enter a room not knowing the point. There is an unwritten agreement between the person who enters a room and the person whose room had been entered, as opposed to open-air theaters, outdoor pools. The purpose of a room derives from the special nature of a room. A room is inside. This is what people in rooms have to agree on, as differentiated from lawns, meadows, fields, orchards. (306)

In each of these cases, we see a strong correlation between not just a form of plotting that reduces others to pieces of your story, plot points to be finished, but also the way they hasten, not distract from death.

But these practices do not encompass all forms of storytelling in the novel, as many others are represented as, if not proper diversions, then at least reasonable responses to the presence of death, presenting storytelling as a means for comfort and intimacy. In the midst of the initial panic concerning the airborne toxic event, various characters turn to religious and scientific narratives to make sense of their situation: Heinrich lectures on the science of the event, while an unnamed Jehovah's Witness offers his own religious solace. Babette works as a volunteer reading to the blind, and she and Jack read erotica aloud to one another as part of their sexual relations. In these cases, storytelling becomes not simply a way to distract from reality, but a way to pull people closer. In most cases, those involved recognize the falsehood of their actions—recall the German nuns whose vows are for others—but they also recognize the way the performance of the story helps other people.

The novel neither fully endorses nor fully rejects the fantasy element, but instead dwells in a necessarily tenuous in-between state. Narratives distract one from death, cover over its randomness and ever-presence, but narratives also give meaning and make the actions one takes before death's coming worthwhile. The novel's closing image succinctly captures this in-between state, in which Jack and Babette sit under an overpass with their youngest child Wilder. In earlier scenes, the Gladneys describe Wilder as a symbol of pre-lapsarian innocence so pure that even a bout of full-day inconsolable crying becomes a form of comfort in which he says "nameless things in a way that touched [Jack] with its depth and richness," an exemplar of the fearless state Dylar promises to induce (78). But the final chapter opens with fearless Wilder riding his trike through the busy street, unaware of the vehicles careening by him until he reaches the other side, where "[s]tunned, he made the decision to cry. It took him a moment, mud and water everywhere, the tricycle on its side. The women began to call once more, each raising an arm to revoke the action. Boy in the water, they said. Look, help, drown. And he seemed, on his seat in the creek, profoundly howling, to have heard them for the first time, looking up over the earthen mound and into the trees across the expressway" (323). The overpass, then, represents a loss of innocence, the one last Gladney not haunted by death comes to realize his mortality. And yet, the novel closes with the trio sitting there watching it all. The image reminds us that not just plots—everything leads toward death. In the same way Jack was dying before he was exposed to the event, so also are all people always already exposed and vulnerable. The final image reminds us that not only do the stories we tell give life meaning, but so also do the people we live with, particularly the family. The family, then, is not simply a cradle of misinformation, but a way of making sense of the time before death, to construct an identity. So while *White Noise* certainly illustrates the ethical problems that arise when one person uses another for their own ends, it also demonstrates the necessity of making myths with that other person.

As the aforementioned historians argued, the traditional contract marriage and the nuclear family are, ultimately, security strategies, particularly suited to suburbia's own history of domestic stability. But each of the three novels examined here insist that death and dissolution can occur anywhere, even within the most calm suburb. Because of this inescapable presence, each of the novels emphasize authentic relation to the present and factual elements of one's life, namely the people with whom one shares space. In many cases, the person with whom one shares most space are members of one's family, and as such, *Little Children*, *The World According to Garp*, and *White Noise* imagine the family as a construct in which one practices obligated freedom, recognizing the false nature of the marital vow and the unknowability of children, while still expecting a degree of obligation from those who help shape one's identity. In this way, the novels do not imagine family as a respite from death, but a way of making life both meaningful and ethical.

## NOTES

1. Deleuze and Guattari are hardly the first to insist on the difference between the child and its parents. Indeed, at the end of *The Eumenides*, the final play of Aeschylus's *Oresteia* trilogy, Apollo decides that Orestes is not guilty of matricide, despite killing his mother Clytemnestra, because he is unrelated to her since the mother is a stranger to her child, serving as merely a receptacle for the man's reproductive material.
2. Weiss reminds readers that "Harriet Nelson, the actress, was a working mother with an accomplished career, even if Harriet Nelson, the character, played second fiddle to Ozzie on the show. Middle-class women, whose lives on the surface conformed with the June Cleaver stereotype, were in fact at the forefront of significant gender change in the postwar years." (7)
3. The emphasis on the individual ultimately clashed with the separation of spheres "by making men and women depend upon each other and insisting

that each gender was incomplete without marriage. It justified women's confinement to the home without having to rely on patriarchal assertions about men's right to rule. Women would not aspire to public roles beyond the home because they could exercise their moral sway over their husbands and through them over society at large. Men were protecting women, not dominating them, by reserving political and economic roles for themselves." (176)

4. This problem is particularly apparent in Kant, who includes the marital contract as a subpoint of his discussion of property in *The Metaphysics of Morals*. In typical fashion, Kant portrays the relationship as a burden one imposes on another, granting "the reciprocal use that one human being makes of the sexual organs and capacities of another," thereby giving each other "lifelong possession of each other's sexual attributes" (61–62). But because the contract prohibits the free use of one's own body, Kant sees the restriction as different from those against murder or stealing; the restriction, in effect, "makes [the individual] into a thing" and therefore "conflicts with the right of humanity in his own person." Kant solves this conundrum by introducing a third element—the child a couple creates through intercourse. By making procreation the ultimate end of marriage, Kant reframes the agreement as not just a contract decided by two unencumbered agents, but also a law implemented for the good of the human race: "Even if it is supposed that their end is the pleasure of using each other's sexual attributes, the marriage contract is not up to their discretion but is a contract that is necessary by the law of humanity, that is, if a man and a woman want to enjoy each other's sexual attributes they MUST necessarily marry, and this is necessary in accordance with pure reason's laws of right" (62). Hegel, who tried to reject Kant's contractual model and posit marriage as an ethical good—the form through which an individual manifests his or her desires in society—runs into a similar wall in *The Philosophy of Right*. Foregrounding the communal nature of the nuptial bond, Hegel argues that not only the act transforms the two into one, but also that procreation transforms the one into the many. Because the relationship forms a single person, it cannot be beholden to the individualism esteemed by Romantics or allowed by Kant. But despite his attempts to separate himself from Kant and discover a spiritual, intersubjective element in the conjugal pact, Hegel still ultimately falls back on contractual thinking, arguing that individuals gain social respect by entering into an association that reinforces strict divisions of spheres and gender roles: "Man therefore has his actual substantial life in the state, in learning [ *Wissenschaft* ], etc., and otherwise in work and struggle with the external world and with himself, so that it is only through his division that he fights his way to self-sufficient unity with himself. In the family he has a peaceful intuition of this

unity, and an emotive [*empfindend*] and subjective ethical life. Woman, however, has her substantial vocation [*Bestimmung*] in the family, and her ethical disposition consists in this [family] *piety*." (166)

5. Pateman describes Hegel's omission of the sexual contract in terms that recount his master/slave dialectic: "Hegel's story of the development of universal freedom requires that men recognize each other as equals: the day of the master and slave is past. But men's self-consciousness is not purely the consciousness of free civil equals (the story of the social contract)—it is also the consciousness of patriarchal masters (the story of the sexual contract). The ostensible universalism of Hegel's public world (just like that of the classic contract theorists) gains its meaning when men look from the public world to the private domestic sphere and the subjection of wives. The family (private) and civil society/state (public) are separate and inseparable; civil society is a patriarchal order. As a husband, a man cannot receive acknowledgment as an equal from his wife. But a husband is not engaged in relations with other men, his equals: he is married to a woman, his natural subordinate. Wives do not stand to husbands precisely as slaves, but a wife cannot be an 'individual' or a citizen, able to participate in the public world. If the family is, simultaneously, to be part of the state and separate from it, constituted through a unique contract, and if patriarchal right is not to be undermined, women's acknowledgment of men cannot be the same as men's acknowledgment of their fellow men. Men cease to be masters and slaves, but Hegel's social order demands a sexually differentiated consciousness (his discussion of ethico-legal love notwithstanding). The recognition that a husband obtains from a wife is precisely what is required in modern patriarchy; recognition as a patriarchal master, which only a woman can provide." (178–179)

6. See Watt, *The Rise of the Novel; Armstrong, Desire and Domestic Fiction: A Political History of the Novel; McKeon, The Secret History of Domesticity.*

7. See C.S. Lewis, *Allegories of Love.*

8. There are, of course, some notable exceptions, such as homosexual characters like Shit and White Willie from Gaynor's *Linden Hills* or the Davids from Jane Smiley's *Good Faith.* Also, divorced or singles occasionally appear in these stories—Updike's Rabbit Angstrom or Barthelme's Peter Wexler, or Lee's Doc Hata and widower Jerry Battle. These characters are strong outliers, and usually either serve to provide guidance for other couples or to be marked as uncoupled. See Dines, *Gay Suburban Narratives in American and British Culture: Homecoming Queens.*

9. In *The Writer in America*, Van Wyck Brooks argues that the American novelist remains inherently childish because he/she has no mature models: "The important thing is that they should transcend the juvenile roles they so often perform—the role of the playboy, the tough guy, the groping

adolescent—in which they perpetually repeat themselves and exploit their personalities until they are as tired of themselves as we are tired of them. Only the right models, rightly chosen to fit their special aptitudes, can jog them out of these roles into which they settle, models whom they cannot 'knock out of the ring' because they are a sort of superior selves, of the same nature with them but enlarged and ripened" (85).

10. See Honeyman, *Elusive Childhood: Impossible Representations in Modern Fiction*; Pifer, *Demon or Doll: Images of the Child in Contemporary Writing and Culture*; Rose, *The Case of Peter Pan, or the Impossibility of Children's Fiction*.

11. Edna Pontellier of Chopin's *The Awakening* is a notable exception to this trope—as she swims away from the shore at the end of the story, she imagines her "children appear[ing] before her like antagonists who had overcome her; who had overpowered and sought to drag her into the soul's slavery for the rest of her days" (108).

12. Richard Ford's *Independence Day* certainly belongs to this set of stories, as Bascombe becomes responsible only when his son Paul is gravely injured. However, unlike other characters, Paul harms himself when he walks into the path of a fastball. Furthermore, the injury occurs away from suburban Haddam, taking place at the Baseball Hall of Fame in Cooperstown, New York. And yet, the basic theme is the same: the father's failure results in the near death of the son.

13. Most often, the character who either feels responsible for endangering the children or at least receives blame from the story perspective is the father.

14. Several critics have questioned Irving's decision to align the feminist movement with, at best, the curmudgeonly Jenny Fields or, at worst, the violent and delusional Ellen Jamesians. See Doane, "Women in *The World According to Garp*."

15. Although he refers here to the novel's overall treatment of time and space, Peter Boxall's observation certainly recalls suburbia's reputation as a "geography of nowhere": "But in *White Noise*, we are thrown into a narrative time with no co-ordinates, with no assigned beginning or end… *White Noise* is set in an eternal present which fails, eternally, to become present" (111).

16. Midway through the novel, Jack sees Babette on the television and, in the same way their infant son Wilder cannot distinguish between his real mother and the image of her he sees in photographs, the appearance of her on the screen reduces Jack to an infant state: "[H]er appearance on the screen made me think of her as some distant figure from the past, some ex-wife and absentee mother, a walker in the mists of the dead. If she was not dead, was I? A two-syllable infantile cry, *ba-ba*, issued from the deeps of my soul." (104)

17. According to John Frow, "*White Noise* is obsessed with one of the classical aims of the realist novel: the construction of typicality. What this used to mean was a continuous process of extrapolation from the particular to the general, a process rooted in the existence of broad social taxonomies, general structures of human and historical destiny. Social typicality precedes the literary type—which is to say that the type is laid down in the social world; it is prior to and has a different kind of reality from secondary representations of it. First there is life, and then there is art. In *White Noise*, however, it's the other way round: social taxonomies are a function not of historical necessity but of style." (420)

18. Nancy makes a much clearer rejection of the libidinous philosophy of Delueze/Guattari and Hardt/Negri and their emphasis on potentiality: "But love is not 'polymorphous,' and it does not take on a series of disguises. It does not withhold its identity behind its shatters: it *is* itself the eruption of their multiplicity, it *is* itself their multiplication in one single act of love, it is the trembling of emotion in a brothel, and the distress of a desire within a fraternity. Love does not simply cut across, it cuts itself across itself, it arrives and arrives at itself as that by which nothing arrives, except that there is 'arriving,' arrival and departure: of the other, always of the other, so much *other* that it is never *made*, or *done* (one makes love, because it is never *made*) and so much *other* that it is never *my* love (if I say to the other 'my love,' it is of the other, precisely, that I speak, and nothing is 'mine')." (102)

19. For Nancy, the joy of interruption allowed by love requires the presence of an other: "It is the question of a presence: to joy is an extremity of presence, self exposed, presence of self joying outside itself, in a presence that no present absorbs and that does not (re)present, but that offers itself endlessly."

CHAPTER 4

# Assimilation and Appropriation: Contest and Collaboration in Global Suburbia

In his conclusion to *The Crabgrass Frontier*—still the most frequently cited history of suburbia—Kenneth T. Jackson claims that reasonable people in 1985 could "debate whether the United States was a racist nation, an imperialist nation, or a religious nation [but] scarcely anyone could quarrel with its designation as a suburban nation" (284). Although Jackson does adeptly capture the contentious nature of the country under Reagan, the USA earned that designation long before the final years of the Cold War. Most notably, Vice President Richard Nixon made a similar and more spectacular claim in July of 1959, when he and Soviet Premier Nikita Khrushchev held their famous "Kitchen Debate." Initially intended to be a friendly public relations meeting at the American National Exhibit in Moscow's Skolniki Park, the two men used the opportunity to contrast the virtues of their respective economic models. Insisting that it would be "better to compete in the relative merits of washing machines than in the strengths of rockets," Nixon took the lead by praising American televisions and appliances as evidence of his country's superiority (Perlstein 95). The centerpiece of Nixon's argument was a model suburban house, nicknamed "Splitnik" because "it had a path cut through the middle to allow crowds to walk through the interior" (Safire).[1] According to Nixon, the significance of the house lay not just in its marvelous modern conveniences—accoutrements that Khrushchev dismissed as "gimmicks"—but also in its egalitarian nature.

© The Author(s) 2016
J. George, *Postmodern Suburban Spaces*,
DOI 10.1007/978-3-319-41006-7_5

This was the "typical American home," not a mansion reserved for the East Coast elite or for the glamorous Hollywood set, but a luxury available to even "any steel worker" (Perlstein 92).

Nixon's claims were, of course, false—a bit of exaggerated showmanship from a politician better remembered for his lack of televisual flair[2]—because no American could afford Splitnik: it was not a home at all, but a show, a simulacrum. Despite this inauthenticity, Nixon's invocation of the suburbs powerfully realized a claim implicit in the arguments of the Levitts and of Senator McCarthy, not to mention hundreds of advertisements and *Home Beautiful* articles: to be suburban is to be American. But where the message had heretofore been directed at other Americans, who believed the model manifested Hoover's redefinition of the American Dream, Nixon's performance turned the message outward, making suburbia "the center of the postwar global discourse" (Beauregard 170). The maneuver was more successful than the Vice President could have imagined: in the decades that followed, suburbia has become one of the USA's most powerful ideological exports, to the point that similar neighborhoods in cities from London to Cape Town to Tokyo are still considered faux-American.[3] The suburbs put a physical face on the American Dream—a face that looked outward to the rest of the world.

Nixon's insertion of suburbia into a global order anticipates the identitarian conflicts that would play out within the space, a battle that has been both anticipated and refigured by the fictions examined in the preceding chapters. The contingent communities imagined by these stories become of greater import in the period of global late capitalism, with some key differences: where societies consisting of homeowners and married couples are practical and personal, Nixon's rhetoric links suburban living to a single, cohesive American identity—an imagined community held together by an ideological bond. In the increasingly global post–Cold War era, this implication is felt most keenly not by the middle-class whites to whom it was initially extended, but by those who, despite living within the nation's borders, have been excluded from its promises. For these outcasts, the suburbs take on a greater symbolic meaning, as inclusion in the local imagined community of suburbanites means entry into the larger imagined community of Americans, even if legal and systematic obstacles still remain.[4] But as the rhetoric and reality of the American dream clash on Elm Streets across the country—from the race-based riots in 1960s and 1970s Detroit and St. Louis to more recent post-9/11 violence against

Sikhs and Muslims—writers of suburban fiction have questioned not only the possibility of attaining an American character through suburbia, but also the entire notion of cohesive national identities. Such conflicts are central to the American Dream myths retold by authors like Philip Roth, Jhumpa Lahiri, and Gish Jen, whose stories of contest and rejection position the space as the prime relational nexus in the period of late capitalism.

These authors perform this work by addressing the communal aspects of the American Dream, which have been present since the phrase was popularized in 1931. Although it first appeared in journalist Walter Lippmann's 1914 book *Drift and Mastery*, the concept was best articulated in James Trunslow Adams's *The Epic of America*, who repeatedly referred to

> that American dream of a better, richer, and happier life for all our citizens of every rank, which is the greatest contribution we have made to the thought and welfare of the world. That dream or hope has been present from the start. Ever since we became an independent nation, each generation has seen an uprising of ordinary Americans to save that dream from the forces which appeared to be overwhelming it. (qtd. in White and Hanson 3)

The phrase almost immediately captured the public imagination, effectively articulating an ethos of achievement implicit in the Constitution, the work of Romantics like Emerson and Thoreau, the Western pioneers, the Beats, and Civil Rights crusaders.[5] While the notion is most often associated with the protestant belief in individual achievement through hard work that observers like Tocqueville and Weber considered inherent to Americans, historian Jim Cullen argues that the dream has acted as a type of "shared ground...binding together people who may have otherwise little in common and may even be hostile to one another"; it is a "kind of lingua franca, an idiom that everyone—from corporate executives to hip-hop artists—can presumably understand" (189, 6). Against Cullen's lofty language, the American Dream has cast a dark shadow, implying an exceptionalism that some have invoked as an excuse for racism and jingoism. Furthermore, the physical and metaphysical elements of the American Dream rhetoric—"the spiritualization of property and consumption, the investment of joy and dignity in consumption and property ownership"—can amount to little more than glorified consumerism (Kimmage 28). Yet despite these shortcomings—or perhaps because of them—the disenfranchised have called upon the Dream to assert their rights, using that "lingua franca" to speak in a manner the nation would understand. In doing so, they assume the existence of a great community of Americans and demand inclusion into it.

As Cullen observes, the modern American Dream might greatly differ from the "nation of yeoman farmers" imagined by founders like Jefferson, but "the suburbanization of the United States realized a Jeffersonian vision of small stakeholders" (151). Whatever its vagaries, the Dream has always been one of property, which, since the mid-1940s, is most often realized within a suburban context—a point made by nearly every historian chronicling the rise of suburbia.[6] More strikingly, the conflation between the Dream and suburban living has been a central part of ad campaigns launched by hundreds of real estate companies; for example, the Fannie May company—the government-sponsored lender christened by *The Financial Times* as "Savior of the Suburbs"—declared, "We are in the American Dream business." Even those who foretell the downfall of the suburban model couch their invectives in the language of the American Dream: Kenneth Jackson predicts the end of suburbia because the model has put the American Dream out of the average homebuyer's reach; the environmentalist Sierra Club famously distributed a pamphlet that labeled sprawl the "Downside of the American Dream"; Andres Duany, Elizabeth Plater-Zyberk, and Jeff Speck's oft-cited New Urbanist handbook claims that current practices have resulted in the "Decline of the American Dream"; Douglas Morris employs much more vivid language to insist that the suburbs have "paved over the American Dream" and "twisted it into a nightmare" (12, 82). Within all this doom and gloom, the message is clear: the suburbs should be a manifestation of the American Dream, a way to claim an American identity.

This assumption continues to have the most significance among those who have been excluded from the Dream, those who see a house and a yard not only as a good in itself, but also as a means for inclusion in a perceived community heretofore unavailable to them. Certainly, some suburbanites considered their neighborhoods the ideal space to welcome these others, such as sociologist Herbert J. Gans, who insisted that the homogeneity so closely associated with suburbia "violates the American Dream of a 'balanced' community where people of diverse age, class, race and religion live together" (165). Historically, however, Gans' position has been decidedly in the minority, as racial covenants, HOA pressures, and outright violence have conspired to keep African Americans, Jews, and immigrants out of their subdivisions.[7] But as figures like Nixon used suburbia to crystallize "Americans' sense of themselves as capable, prosperous, and free" and made it into a symbol that "stood for achievement at home—the realization of the American Dream—and American exceptionalism in the world," strict exclusion grew increasingly untenable (Beauregard 159, 145). In recent decades, not only have suburbs become more integrated—sometimes peacefully, sometimes violently—but variations of what geographer Jon C. Teaford calls "lifestyle suburbs" have cropped up, devoted to specific ethnic groups or peoples. Indeed, instances of "black flight," in which affluent African Americans escape the inner cities for suburbs, to say nothing of ethnic and immigrant communities, are increasing every day, replacing the ghettos of the twentieth century.[8]

Unsurprisingly, this tension between political reality and ideological pretensions informs literary fiction. Long before Adams defined the American Dream, the desire for autonomy and freedom was dramatized by Huck Finn's escape to Indian Territory, by Frederick Douglass' act of autonomy, and by James Gatz's Gatsby persona.[9] In the postwar era, American dream stories have taken a decidedly suburban turn: Tom Rath of *The Man in the Grey Flannel Suit* and Updike's Harry Angstrom cement their financial success by moving to respectable subdivisions, David Gates' Jernigan considers his home a sign of independence, and the Lamberts of Jonathan Franzen's *The Corrections* treat their childhood in St. Jude as a badge of privilege. More recent suburban fiction features people using suburbs, whether as an act of contestation or redefinition, to perform Americanness. Gloria Naylor's *Linden Hills* does the former, suggesting that the adoption of white, patriarchal practices will only result in a hell of self-loathing and irresponsibility. John Edgar Wideman's Homewood trilogy, on the other hand, focuses on an exceptional neighborhood, a place of care and historical roots largely divorced from the exploitative power structures in nearby Pittsburgh. Suburban immigrant stories tend to spotlight those who use their homes as a form of assimilation, such as the Iranian family in Andre Dubus III's *House of Sand and Fog* or the protagonists of Chang-rae Lee's first three novels. Whatever be their differences, each of these stories accept suburbia's role as manifestation of the American Dream and try to claim these promises for themselves. But unlike the Lamberts or the Raths, the characters in Wideman, Lee, and Dubus find antagonism instead of acceptance in their neighborhoods, pressures that force them to rethink their place in the American imagination.

## JEWISH GODS AND NEMESES IN PHILIP ROTH'S WEEQUAHIC NOVELS

A surprising source of fiction about the international suburban experience can be found in the work of Philip Roth. Although his literary reputation has been firmly cemented alongside American straight white male writers such as Updike and Irving, Roth remains an author whose "natural subject is the self-conscious Jew, newly formed middle-class, the Jew whose 'identity,' though never in doubt, is a problem to himself" (Kazin 106). And in Roth's work, the place for those newly formed middle-class Jews is Newark, New Jersey in general, and the suburb Weequahic in particular. Mark Shechner puts it best: "As the Jews once lamented Jerusalem, Roth laments Newark... Not just the Weequahic section, that Mesopotamia of Roth's civilization, but the Italian neighborhood, Down Neck, where immigrant families from Naples did piecework in tenement workshops" (144).

Philip Roth has made this conflation between suburbia and the American persona a central concern of his work, informing everything from the central novella of his first book, 1959s *Goodbye, Columbus*, to his final novel, 2010s *Nemesis*. *Columbus* protagonist Neil Klugman best encapsulates this equivocation when, amazed by the edenic abundance and material success promised in the American Dream, he describes the affluent suburb Short Hills as a place where "[f]ruit grew in their refrigerator and sporting goods dropped from their trees" (43). But as Timothy Parrish notes, "it is impossible to talk about Roth's Americanness without also addressing his Jewishness"; furthermore, although Roth has always defined himself as an American writer, "his work cannot be fully understood without addressing how Roth engages a sense of Jewish history that cannot be understood to be equivalent with his perspective as an American writer" (127). And so when Jewish characters of Roth's later work create their own suburb in Weequahic, where they can enjoy the privileges of citizenship while protecting their ethnicities, it is very much a transnational event. We can see that cosmopolitan nature even in the following Norman Rockwell-esque description of the neighborhood : a "grid of locust-tree lined streets into which the Lyons farm had been partitioned during the boom years of the early twenties, [where] the first postimmigrant generation of Newarks Jews had regrouped into a community that took its inspiration more from the mainstream of American life than from the Polish shtetl their Yiddish-speaking parents had re-created around Prince Street in the impoverished Third Ward"; storytellers rhapsodize about local kids playing baseball together, local shopkeepers taking time to chat with their customers, and religious holidays being celebrated with family members (*Pastoral* 10). But Roth troubles these pleasing images by foregrounding the narrators' unreliability, employing those who no longer live in Weequahic and can only imagine their neighborhood through a thick nostalgic glaze. In fact, these stories often reject outright the very possibility of the American Dream, focusing on the failure or dissolution of the subdivision instead of its material success or cultural homogeny. International concerns, far exceeding any zoning board limits, bear down on residents, forcing them to redefine their national identity projects according to the realities of those in proximity; negating not only the possibility of an ethnically pure enclave, but even the very notion of a cohesive Jewish or American persona.[10]

This unreliable narration is particularly pronounced in Roth's best-known work, the 1998 Pulitzer Prize winner *American Pastoral*, which serves as the middle section of his Newark trilogy. *Pastoral* and the other entries in the trilogy, *I Married a Communist* and *The Human Stain*, "might be read as parables about ethnic and racial identity and the seductive pastoral dream of 'passing' in American society" (Brauner 157). The novel describes the downfall of Seymour "The Swede" Levov, the much-loved local athletic star and son of a self-made businessman, whose integration into larger American society fails when his daughter becomes a domestic terrorist. With his movie star looks and athletic prowess, the "household Apollo of the Weequahic Jews" is adored not only for his talents, but also for his gentile acceptability: he represents not just the best the neighborhood has to offer, but also "a boy as close to a goy as [Weequahic Jews] were going to get" (4, 10). The Swede was proof that the residents can enjoy status as Jews and Americans, and the more "Anglicized" he seems to become—leaving Weequahic for the rural New England town of Old Rimrock and marrying a Catholic beauty queen—the more he is respected by his home community. The novel is narrated by one such admirer: Nathan Zuckerman, a writer who idolized the Swede as a boy and is charged with telling his hero's life story. Although the story focuses on Levov, Zuckerman reveals at various points that he had fairly limited interaction with his subject, rendering *American Pastoral* "more of a narrative on Nathan Zuckerman and the ways in which he constructs reality and less of an explanatory tale of the enigmatic Swede" (Royal 199). As such, Zuckerman's story is a communal myth delineating the dangers of (con)fusing two disparate national identities, as indicated by the headings of the three main sections—"Paradise Remembered," "The Fall," and "Paradise Lost"—and by the monstrous daughter sprung from the Jewish/Catholic union, who threatens to destroy the structural pillars of the USA.

While Zuckerman's memoir might seem to condone an exclusionary approach to communal life—suggesting that the Swede would have been happier had he never left Weequahic—Arnold Mesnikoff, the narrator of *Nemesis*, brings his story to a very different conclusion. Like Zuckerman, Arnold retells the life of his childhood hero: Bucky Cantor, who ran a volunteer boy's athletic association during a polio outbreak in the last days of World War II. Although he shares the Swede's athleticism and communal respect, Bucky is decidedly more rooted than his counterpart, as only the opportunity to fight Nazis tempts him to leave. When his poor eyesight precludes him from service in any branch of the military, Bucky devotes himself to the neighborhood youth, serving the community by training young Jewish men. But as the title suggests, *Nemesis* is less interested in the way common good forms a community, and focuses instead on the unity afforded by the presence of a common enemy. Accordingly, Roth emphasizes antagonistic solidarity, from the birth of Weequahic as a refuge from oppression to Bucky's own sense of responsibility, the desire to teach his charges "toughness and determination, to be physically brave and physically fit and never to allow themselves to be pushed around or, just because they knew how to use their brains, to be defamed as Jewish weaklings and sissies" (28).[11] The narrating Arnold understands this antagonism as central to his community's ethos and frames it as a motivating factor in the early days of the breakout, when the disease infected all of the Newark suburbs except Weequahic, to the worst days of the plague, in which the Jewish community suffers the highest concentration of polio cases. Arnold's story, then, is organized according to the various enemies who could potentially be the cause: teens from an Italian neighborhood who spit on a playground to "spread some polio," a mentally disabled man who regularly defecates in public, a hot dog vendor frequented by the victims, and even Bucky himself (14). But because "nobody then knew the source of the contagion," Arnold admits, "it was possible to grow suspicious of almost anything," making his story less the account of a community, and instead that of a mob, never united against anything but shadows and sounds (5).

Arnold's dichotomies are undone by the novel's closing revelation that Bucky himself was the carrier, thereby contradicting any *American Pastoral*-like racial purity plot. Where the Swede's downfall occurs when he forsakes Weequahic for the WASP countryside, Bucky never tries to be anything but pure, devoted to his people and his neighbors—even when he flees the neighborhood, he still goes to a Jewish summer camp, where he can serve a different set of young Jewish men—and is "punished" for his fidelity. The twist mirrors Roberto Esposito's contrast between *communitas* and *immunitas*, in which the former—the latter to protect one from the wound and exposure inherent to being with others—constricts and undoes the community. Furthermore, the international aspect of these neighborhoods recalls Wai Chee Dimock's notion of "deep time," that "crisscrossing set of pathways, open-ended and ever multiplying, weaving in and out of other geographies, other languages and cultures" inherent to national identities (3). For Dimock, deep time contradicts the "standardization" of modern nationalism by positing an indebtedness that exceeds any historical dates and legal borders, making a national persona a mix of cultural influences instead of a legal designation. To be sure, the Jews of Weequahic experience this type of exceedance: they are troubled by the actions of Hitler; they think of their relatives captured in Poland and their sons fighting in France; they remember their grandparents living in Russia and their roots in the Middle East; they perform this remembrance in New Jersey, in an America that exterminated the Natives, that persecuted non-Christians, and that provided an economic system and infrastructure that allows them to flourish. In that sense, the neighborhood of Weequahic is not simply a residential model, but the nexus of diverse peoples and remnants of empires.

But authors like Roth never treat suburbia as a tidy place to collect these vast histories; rather, they choose a suburban setting because the place is filled with people—people who draw on deep time to give imminence to their lives, and people who live these lives in the presence of others. However impressive, honorable, and meaningful cultural histories might be, they ultimately exist to be used by individuals, and these individuals clash and respond to one another.[12] The lack of immunity on display in *Nemesis*, then, is not just the infection by the disease, but also the infection of identity. The Jewish-ness of the Weequahic residents transcends their borders, becoming entangled with the nearby Italians, with the lost Native Americans evoked at Indian Hill summer camp, with the anti-Semites in the state capital. In the same way Bucky's persona is informed both by his grandfather, who taught him cultural traditions, and by the bullies who threatened him and inspired him to be an athlete and a mentor, so also are these ethnic identities created by individuals making use of culture and by others rejecting and refracting the performance.

## JHUMPA LAHIRI'S COSMOPOLITAN SUBURBS: THE BIRTHPLACE OF VAGRANTS

Like the Weequahic Jews, the Ganguli family of Juhmpa Lahiri's 2003 novel *The Namesake* understand their suburban home to be a place of transition, the locus of their inability to establish themselves in only one place. A scene midway through the novel best illustrates this condition, when the family returns to their house on Pemberton Road in Providence, Rhode Island, following an eight-month sabbatical in India. The days after the return, the narrator explains, the family feels out of place, neither fully at home in the Pemberton Road house in which they currently live, nor in the Bengali city where father Ashoke and mother Ashima were born. Back in the American suburbs, the Gangulis feel "disconcerted by the space, by the uncompromising silence that surrounds them," still "somehow in transit, still disconnected from their lives, bound up in an alternate schedule, an intimacy only the four of them share" (87). The family only re-establishes itself when neighbors come to check on them, enacting rituals that other writers in this study associate with suburban WASPs: "But by the end of the week, after his mother's friends come to admire her new gold and saris, after the eight suitcases have been aired out on the sun deck and put away, after the chanachur is poured into Tupperware and the smuggled mangoes eaten for breakfast with cereal and tea, it's as if they've never been gone." As the passage closes, the narrator seems to repeat negative stereotypes common to suburbia's critiques, emphasizing the loss of family cohesion within a morass of mass market goods:

> They retreat to their three rooms, to their three separate beds, to their thick mattresses and pillows and fitted sheets. After a single trip to the supermarket, the refrigerator and the cupboards fill with familiar labels: Skippy, Hood, Bumble Bee, Land O' Lakes. His mother enters the kitchen and prepares their meals once again; his father drives the car and mows the lawn and returns to the university. Gogol and Sonia sleep for as long as they want, watch television, make themselves peanut butter and jelly sandwiches at any time of day. Once again they are free to quarrel, to tease each other, to shout and holler and say shut up. They take hot showers, speak to each other in English, ride their bicycles around the neighborhood. They call up their American friends, who are happy enough to see them but ask them nothing about where they've been. And so the eight months are put behind them, quickly shed, quickly forgotten, like clothes worn for a special occasion, or for a season that has passed, suddenly cumbersome, irrelevant to their lives. (87)

Some observers may read this description as an assimilation narrative in miniature, as if American culture has eroded the ethnic identity and cohesion the Gangulis recovered in Bengal; however, much of the novel undermines such a reading. *The Namesake* certainly illustrates a tension between American immigrants assimilating into their new surroundings and losing aspects of their native culture, but the novel never suggests that suburbia erases that former identity. Rather, Lahiri presents a multivalent process of identity construction, in which characters understand themselves to be cosmopolitans, hybrid citizens of the world by inviting all manner of others into their suburban home.

The aforementioned passage powerfully illustrates a recurring theme in *The Namesake*: Lahiri's characters establish themselves as true citizens of the world, as members of not one nation, but of many. Many of Lahiri's readers have commented on her unique approach to diaspora and global hybridity, one that blurs the distinction between insider/outsider. Sufficient focus has certainly been given to the role the novel's A-plot, the "anxiety of influence" narrative between Ashoke and his son Gogol that gives the book its name, but critics have also noted that the B-plot concerning Ashima's home life refigures these anxieties. For instance, for Madhurima Chakraborty, *The Namesake* not only represents "migrant life as a dialogic arena that, though the product of the interaction between home and host, is a distinct space with features unique to the contingencies of migrant life," but also "characterizes this space as being fairly fixed and consistent, thus complicating the typical association of heterogeneous identities with shifting or mobile ones" ("Allegiances" 611).

Most critics have commented upon the way in which Ashima's story dovetails with "the trope of isolated motherhood and insular cultural reproduction [which] define her experience of assimilation: (Bhalla 120). More so than any of the characters in the novel, Ashima acutely feels the role her home space plays in her identity construction. According to Chakraborty, Lahiri is "interested in elaborating what happens to a people when it cannot produce earthly proof of its presence on the landscape of American life, namely, in the shape of markers like graves and reliquary legacies to commemorate names," and while she rightly notes that the Pemberton Road house becomes occupied by strangers after the Gangulis leave it for other destinations, the house still serves as a vibrant space of identity ("Leaving" 815). For authors such as Lahiri, "social maladies no longer lie in public spheres for unrecognized subjectivities, but in private homes that become the 'uncanny sites' of social conflict or personal trauma. Their concerns have moved beyond outmoded cultural translation of identity politics to reconstruct new cultures of their own by creative writing" (Chui 161). Accordingly, the "architecture of old American houses" that appear in Lahiri's fiction illustrates "the emotional spaces between the people who live in those houses"; where American-born writers tend to understand domesticity as a space from which one must escape to establish a selfhood, "Lahiri's rooms and houses are filled with people who must find the imaginary space that will enable them to live with one another, and whether or not they succeed in doing so depends on their abilities to create their own imaginary societies with their own rules" (Ceasar 52, 67).

As incisive as these readings certainly are, they fail to sufficiently emphasize the role suburbia plays in this development. In fact, Ashima's transition from immigrant to cosmopolitan occurs precisely along the lines of her acceptance within her suburb. As the narrator explains, Ashima found that "migrating to the suburbs feels more drastic, more distressing than the move from Calcutta to Cambridge had been." She comes to believe that "being a foreigner...is a sort of lifelong pregnancy" because both states elicit "the same curiosity from strangers, the same combination of pity and respect" (49). Ashima's attitudes shift when she discovers connections to Bengal within her the suburbs of New England, in which the countrymen she and Ashoke met as he earned his PhD in Cambridge, Massachusetts "moved to places like Dedham and Framingham and Lexington and Winchester, to houses with backyards and driveways" (62). But while the Gangulis and their friends certainly perform the rituals they brought with them to the USA, they are presented in a particularly suburban manner. The narrator's descriptions of Saturday evenings that "consist of a single, repeated scene" could almost be those found in any other story examined in this study: "thirty-odd people in a three-bedroom suburban house, the children watching television or playing board games in a basement, the parents eating and conversing in the Bengali their children don't speak among themselves" (63). Lahiri's narrator repeatedly makes observations such as these to comment on the way the Gangulis have translated American suburbs into a Bengali lifestyle. To the casual observer, the narrator claims, the Gangulis, "apart from the name on their mailbox, apart from the issues of India Abroad and Sangbad Bichitra that are delivered there, appear no different from their neighbors," a point the narrator proves by enacting a "keeping up with the Joneses" style litany of consumer goods: "Their garage, like every other, contains shovels and pruning shears and a sled. They purchase a barbecue for tandoori on the porch in summer." And yet, at no point does this come to be a full assimilation, but rather a cosmopolitan act, often made in "consultation with Bengali friends" (65). In fact, much of the novel's early descriptions refer to this strange mix of Bengali tradition and American style, from "the worship of Durga and Saraswati" occurring in "a high school or a

Knights of Columbus hall overtaken by Bengalis" to dual birthdays for Gogol, an American one with "with pizzas that his father picked up on his way home from work, a baseball game watched together on television, some Ping-Pong in the den" and a Bengali one with "lamb curry with lots of potatoes, luchis, thick channa dal with swollen brown raisins, pineapple chutney, sandeshes molded out of saffron-tinted ricotta cheese" (64, 72). In each of these cases, the Bengali/American identity fashioned by the Gangulis occurs not in opposition to the suburb in which they live, but in relation to it. Without the walls of the house to hold the partygoers, the neighbors living in proximity, or the lawn on which they gather, the family's process of identity construction would be very different.

Which is not at all to suggest that Lahiri portrays the Ganguli's suburban experience as something devoid of conflict. Gogol resents "having to tell people that it doesn't mean anything 'in Indian'" or dealing with graffiti on his mailbox that shortens his last name "to GANG, with the word GREEN scrawled in pencil following it" or the awareness of "cashiers smirking at his parents' accents, and of salesmen who prefer to direct their conversation to Gogol" (76, 67–68). In fact, the novel's titular A-plot is predicated, in part, by an act of American privilege, as the doctor who delivers Gogol insists that his parents forego their tradition—that the child be named by the maternal grandmother—and adhere to American custom by naming the child now. Because the grandmother's poor health and eventual death prevents the proper name from coming, a pet name Ashoke gives his son becomes Gogol's only game.

The inescapable power structure of American normativity in both Gogol's nomenclature and in Ashima's American suburban experience highlights the way that both plots foreground the hybridity of their identity construction. According to Ruediger Heinze, Nikolai Gogol's short story "The Overcoat," which is so beloved by Ashoke that he chooses to name his son after the author, serves as a metaphor for the complex influences that shape our identity. "The image of the overcoat, if taken as a metaphor for personal and cultural identity, represents the continuously changing subject positions that we don, our 'identity choices' and cultural affiliations made in communicating with our surroundings," Heinze states, "It could also serve as an ambivalent metaphor for immigration, where the target country's culture is donned—individually and communally—over the home country's traditions and values, suggestive of both the old and the new culture" (197–198). As much as Ashima tries initially to avoid assimilation into American culture generally, and the suburbs in particular, she eventually finds the experience central to her identity.

Again, the distinction here is not violent, per se, but definitely accusa-
tory. The various interlocutors put the Gangulis into question, prompting them to give an answer for themselves. While the power differences
between the Gangulis and their Euro-American neighbors do certainly
take on the quality of the interactions described by W.E.B. DuBois, with
their implicit question, "How does it feel to be a problem?"; however,
the family's socioeconomic position and role as members of the model
minority mitigate the level of oppression they face, making the questioning more akin to the models of interactions described by Judith Butler
in *Giving an Account of One's Self*. Drawing from Levinas, Foucault, and
Adorno, Butler argues that the self is constructed in a series of moments in
which an interlocutor asks an other to give an account of itself:

> An encounter with an other effects a transformation of the self from which
> there is no return. What is recognized about a self in the course of this
> exchange is that the self is the sort of being for whom staying inside itself
> proves impossible. One is compelled and comported outside oneself; one
> finds that the only way to know oneself is through a mediation that takes
> place outside of oneself, exterior to oneself, by virtue of a convention or
> a norm that one did not make, in which one cannot discern oneself as an
> author or an agent of one's own making. (28)

Crucially for our discussion, Butler insists that this demand for explanation
occurs within "the social conditions of its emergence" (8). For Ashima,
then, the expectations and interactions of others—as uncomfortable as
they may be, like Gogol's ill-fitting Russian/Indian/American overcoat—
become the space in which "any of us start to narrate ourselves, or find
that, for urgent reasons, we must become self-narrating beings" (11).

This notion of self-narrating via relationships appears most literally in
*The Namesake* in the sections describing Ashima's life after Ashoke has
died and her children have moved out. Ashima's solitary behavior in this
section echoes that of the first chapters. Once again, she is gripped with
loneliness, filled with dread at the thought of "returning in the evenings
to a dark, empty house, going to sleep on one side of the bed and wak-
ing up on another" (160). But while she initially credits Ashoke's distant
behavior at the end of his life as the phenomenon that shaped her new
identity—"He was teaching me how to live alone," she tells people—the
narration once again emphasizes the role of the home in establishing her
new selfhood (183). She initially deals with her loneliness by establishing

her space, "cleaning out closets and scrubbing the insides of kitchen cupboards and scraping the shelves of the refrigerator, rinsing out the vegetable bins" (160).

But as is often the case, the novel refuses to treat the house as a good unto itself. Rather, it understands the house as a space to be shared, a tool of hospitality in which individuals can interact with one another. The narrator's descriptions of the space not only highlight the stereotypical accoutrements of suburban life—mailboxes in uniform design, Christmas lights outlining windows—but also indicate the other people who occupy that space. The novel, in fact, ends with descriptions of the final two parties Ashima hosts in her suburban home: the first a funeral for Ashoke, and the second a sort of going away. The image of "friends [Gogol's] parents have collected for almost thirty years are in attendance, to pay their respects, cars from six different states lining the whole of Pemberton Road" provides a useful image of the novel's understanding of suburban life (181). The figures share space and give space to give an account of one another, sometimes uncomfortably, but always in a manner necessary for building selfhood. So when the narrator observes that Ashima, at the end of the novel, "still does not feel fully at home within these walls on Pemberton Road," she can still recognize it as "home nevertheless—the world for which she is responsible, which she has created" (280). This creation, *The Namesake* repeatedly demonstrates, happens not alone, but in relation to others in proximity. They have established an American dream within the suburban space.

## AMERICAN MEANS BEING WHATEVER YOU WANT

Even more than Roth and Lahiri, Gish Jen has made this suburban rejection and refraction a centerpiece of her fiction, in which cultural personas are repeatedly adopted and adapted by unlikely individuals. From her first novel *Typical American* to her recent *World and Town*, Jen's characters live on the fault lines of ethnic markers, forced to negotiate their subjectivities according to relationships with those nearby. Like the Weequahic tales, Jen's 1997 novel *Mona in the Promised Land* chooses a largely Jewish suburb as the setting for this contest of identities, in which Mona Chang, daughter of Chinese immigrants, decides to "switch" from Chinese to Jewish, a right she demands as an American. While Jen does not shy away from the conflicts raised by Mona's decision, particularly the betrayal her mother Helen feels, her comic tone emphasizes the playful and contingent aspect of selfhood construction, making even the most tense contentions a part of one's selfhood. Furthermore, Jen rejects the isolationism desired by the Weequahic residents in Roth's novels, insisting that the residential essence of suburbia precludes any notion of exclusions, that culture supersedes the limits of walls and borders when used by relational human beings. Instead of a mere contest, then, Jen's stories model a form of community that demands response through difference.

This creation is most pronounced in the way the various suburbanites enact—and insist others respect—their American Dreams. Mona's entire plan to switch, in fact, stems from her understanding of her rights as an American: "Jewish is American," she tells her mother; "American means being whatever you want, and I happened to pick being Jewish" (43). As her frank, matter-of-fact tone indicates, Mona sees no irony in her desire: her embrace of Jewish culture does not negate her Chinese heritage, and both roles are manifestations of her American rights. Furthermore, while Mona receives the most teasing or resentment for her decision, nearly all of Jen's characters have similarly fluid selfhoods, including a liberal teenager who seeks a cosmopolitanism that rejects ethnicity, an affluent family who gets plastic surgery to diminish their Jewish features, and a black cook who laments the rights denied him. Recalling the American Dream's function as social glue, Jen links these figures via the appeals made to others around them, focusing on the tension wrought by such identity shifts, particularly those between Mona and her mother Helen. As an immigrant enjoying financial success in the USA, Helen is most vocal—and least self-aware—about this play of selfhoods. She admits that she has "signed up for her own house and garage," but she exploits her neighbors' Orientalist assumptions to construct her own version of Chinese-ness: she develops a personal history that enfolds the achievements of other cultures with her own—claiming that the Chinese people invented both paper and tomatoes—and valorizing her civilization over others: "We were wearing silk gowns with embroidery before the barbarians even thought maybe they should take a bath, get rid of their smell" (42, 38). As these insistences indicate, the personas adopted by these characters, as idiosyncratic as they may seem, are ultimately performances for and with other people.

Jen's attention to the conflicts and collaborations that spring out of Mona's act of autonomy models the intersubjective process of identity formation, similar to those found in novels such as Jeffery Euginides's *The Virgin Suicides*, *Independence Day*, and *Rabbit Redux*. But Jen gives these interactions a decidedly international flair, as each neighbor posits their own ideal version of "American-ness." Once again, Jen positions Helen, who "likes a lot of American things," as the most vocal combatant, angrily rebuking a Japanese exchange student's racist drawings and invocation of the Rape of Nanking by hissing "This is the U.S. of A., do you hear me!" but later denying Mona's desire for free speech by insisting "No America here! In this house, children listen to parents!" (42, 19, 183) The novel's main narrative centers on the stresses caused by Mona's desire to switch, which disturbs everyone from her Jewish neighbors to her African American coworkers. While some, such as the sympathetic Rabbi Horowitz, emphasize the performative nature of culture, assuring Mona that becoming Jewish is the "lesson of a lifetime," others find her decision insulting and unorthodox: for Helen, it is a rejection of her history; for some of her Jewish neighbors, it crosses a line that diminishes the significance of their culture (39). Jen offers a more pronounced example within African American Alfred, who, after being unfairly fired because of Helen's racism, dismisses Mona's desires as selfish and futile. Alfred's presence in the novel prevents the story from ever becoming an unproblematic tale of uplift, creating a contrast that signals Mona's acceptance and privilege, because African Americans like him—even those within the suburb—are "never going to have no big house or no big garage, either." No matter what they insist to call themselves, Alfred explains, "We're never going to be Jewish, see, even if we grow our nose like Miss Mona here is planning to do. We be black motherfuckers." (103)

The contrast between Alfred and Mona correctly identifies her position: she will always be Chinese, or at least Asian, in the eyes of her friends and neighbors, no matter what rituals she conducts, or even the physical changes she makes. And yet, her very desire for Jewish-ness forces people to redefine what they mean by "Jewish," in the same way it questions notions of "Chinese," "African American," and "American." These labels gain meaning through the interactions of those who claim them, through the responses and rejections of one's neighbors. As the narrator explains,

> Mona tries to imagine what it would be like to forget she's Chinese, which is easy and hard. It is easy because by her lonesome she in fact often does. Out in the world of other people, though, Mona has people like Miss Feeble to keep the subject shiny. So here's the question: Does the fact that Mona remembers all too well who she is make her more Jewish than, say, Barbara Gugelstein? (31)

More notably, Jen's narrative suggests that this none of these processes—not Mona's dream of becoming Jewish, not Helen's version of Americanness, not Alfred's critique of their attitudes—would be possible outside of the suburbs. Mona's proximity to models like Barbara Gugelstein and Rabbi Horowitz, Alfred's presence in Barbara's guest house, and Helen's sense of achievement by owning a home and sending her daughters to well-to-do schools, all influence Mona's potential life choices. So while she does experience pressure to conform and even a sense of exclusion, she does not simply subscribe to a binary of acceptance or rejection. Rather, Mona responds to those in proximity, even to their contentions.

The American Dream of *Mona in the Promised Land*—much like that of Roth's Weequahic Tales, of Ford's *Sportswriter* trilogy, of Updike's *Rabbit* tetralogy, of Lee's *A Gesture Life*, of Lahiri's *The Namesake*, and in fact of all the fictions in this study—is not so different from that of James Trunslow Adams or of even Richard Nixon: these characters want a "better, richer, and happier life"; to live where they want and be who they wish to be. But where Nixon and his fellow proponents of suburban living praised the model as the end of the American Dream, as a place where the chosen self can live securely and freely, these authors position the lack of safety or peace as the constituent element of the Dream. Mona discovers who she wishes to be only by relating with other people: the interactions are not often desired or pleasant, but they are necessary and made unavoidable by the mixture of proximity and autonomy in the suburbs. People do not simply pass through—they live together, and must necessarily engage with one another as they live their lives. For that reason, within the images of disruption, conflict, and difference found in these fictions, there is also, in every case, a desire for welcome and for hospitality. The potentially dangerous and wholly unknowable other has become the neighbor next door, who may not—and, statistics show, most likely will not—share one's beliefs and assumptions. But one's beliefs, one's sense of self, have no content without the interactions of others who respond to the performance, confirming and contradicting it. As these fictions suggest, the performance can never be made safe and static, but it can be made hospitable. And this dream of hospitality, of welcome and care for an unknowable, alterier neighbor, is perhaps the most enduring and necessary American Dream.

# NOTES

1. *New York Times* columnist William Safire, who attended the exhibit as an employee of the company that built Splitnik, recalls that the house was "not on the official tour," but was added as a stop when Nixon's handlers, sensing a rhetorical loss for the Vice President, were offered the chance to take Khrushchev to what they claimed was "the typical American house."
2. Throughout the debate, both Nixon and Khrushchev were keenly aware of their audience, not just those immediately present, but also those who would watch the argument on television. "We should hear you more on our televisions," Nixon even told Khrushchev, "You should hear us more on yours." (Perlstein 90).
3. Mark Clapson and Ray Hutchison, editors of *Suburbanization in Global Society*, lament the difficulty of examining the individual suburbs because "the Anglo-suburban idea of the good life has been appropriated for urban design in countries that were once British and European countries" (4).
4. See Singer, Hardwick, and Brettell, *Twenty-First Century Gateways: Immigrant Incorporation in Suburban America*; Tavernise and Gebeloff, "Immigrants Make Paths to Suburbia, Not Cities."
5. In the introduction to their essay collection *The American Dream in the 21st Century*, Sandra L. Hanson and John Kenneth White describe the wide range of definitions of the Dream, from "being able to get a high school education" to freedom to be "like Huck Finn; escape to the unknown; follow your dreams" (9, 8).
6. Several observers have noted the connection between suburbia and the American Dream. See Teaford, *The American Suburb*; Baxandall and Ewan, *Picture Windows*; Beauregard, *How American Became Suburban*; Hayden's introduction to *Building Suburbia*.
7. See Keating, *The Suburban Racial Dilemma*; Johnson, *Black Power in the Suburbs*; Loewen, "Dreaming in Black and White."
8. See Suro, Wilson, and Singer, "Immigration and Poverty in America's Suburbs"; Frey, "The New Great Migration" and "Melting Pot Cities and Suburbs."
9. A recent collection of essays, edited by Harold Bloom, surveys the literary history of American Dream narratives. J.A. Leo Lemay identifies Benjamin Franklin's *Autobiography* as "the definitive formulation of the American Dream," whose rags-to-riches story "is often commonly supposed to be the progenitor of the Horatio Alger success story of nineteenth-century American popular literature" (23).
10. This tension is hardly reserved to Roth's suburban stories. For example, the 2008 novel *Indignation* describes the fears of Newark resident Marcus Messner, who cannot shake the fear that he will be sent to war and will die in Korea.

# Conclusion: Changing the Suburban Myth

As has been demonstrated repeatedly in the preceding chapters, the modern American suburb is a highly mythological space. Even beyond the fiction we watch and read, the very act of buying a house, of interacting with neighbors, of understanding a national heritage is highly mediated and motivated by a variety of assumptions, beliefs, and expectations. Furthermore, many of the problems with suburbia put forth by this book stem from mythologies about race, property, family, and national identity. But the fictional intercessions examined in *Postmodern Suburban Spaces* suggest that these myths can be refigured, retold in a manner that emphasizes hospitality for others within suburbia. By way of conclusion, then, I would like to look at Jeffrey Eugenides' 1993 novel *The Virgin Suicides*. The characters in the novel clearly entertain assumptions not unlike those of T.S. Garp—that the suburb should be an antiseptic place for children perfectly safe—but find this belief disrupted and refigured after the death by suicide of five mysterious sisters. As the narrators reflect on life with and after the girls, they come to understand their lack of understanding not only of their crushes, but also of the space they shared together.

*The Virgin Suicides* takes place in a Detroit suburb in the mid-1970s, and its central characters—the five adolescent Lisbon sisters—shatter their neighborhood's pretensions to safety by killing themselves over the course of a year. After youngest girl Cecelia fails in her initial attempt, psychiatrist Dr. Hornicker asks, "What are you doing here, honey? You're not even old

© The Author(s) 2016

J. George, *Postmodern Suburban Spaces*,

DOI 10.1007/978-3-319-41006-7_6

enough to know how bad life gets" (5). A year later, after the remaining four sisters tried to kill themselves on the same night, an attempt that was successful for all but one, an exasperated neighbor sneers, "Shit...what have kids got to be worried about now? If they want trouble, they should go live in Bangladesh" (247). Despite the very different sentiments, both statements reveal a central assumption: suicide should not happen to these girls, in this place. The "should" statement this invokes, then, recalls the myth of the ideal childhood described by Stephanie Coontz and other historians, the assumption of perfect safety and tranquility that has motivated suburban development for generations. In rejecting the promise of suburban safety and success, *The Virgin Suicides* directly addresses the myths that motivate suburbia, reformulating it by making the girls tragic figures and positing a new form of responsibility.

As thinkers from Plato to Hegel to Heidegger have stated, myths are integral to community, providing individuals with a reason for being together. Like the liberal contractualism represented by CC&Rs or HOAs, communal myths provide a schematic of interaction and identity; they help members understand their place among each other. To that end, the nostalgic myth of suburban childhood gives imminence to the neighborhoods found in stories like *Garp*, *Native Speaker*, and *Little Children*. Jean-Luc Nancy explores this function when he explains that "[a]ll myths are primal scenes, all primal scenes are myths"; they are essentially "of and from the origin, [as] it relates back to a mythic foundation, and through this relation it founds itself (a consciousness, a people, a narrative)" (45). And yet, despite their necessity for community, Nancy warns, myths also run the risk of becoming "totalitarian," reducing real and infinite individuals into roles defined by these stories. In the same way, then, "myth and myth's force and foundation are essential to community and that there can be, therefore, no community outside of myth...[t]he interruption of myth is therefore also, necessarily, the interruption of community" (57). The interruption of myth draws attention to the its own shortcomings and prompts a new communal myth, a new coming together and rebuilding of a community in the gaps caused by interruption. Nearly every text in this study gestures toward this interruption, but it is central to Eugenides' *The Virgin Suicides*, a story about a neighborhood's reaction to ineffable grief, a tragedy that shatters the myth of suburban childhood and forces the survivors to re-evaluate their relations to each other.

Eugenides' narrative both illustrates and humanizes the process of myth making and breaking described in Nancy by portraying the different reactions to the death of the Lisbon girls. The initial culprit identified is Mr. and Mrs. Lisbon themselves, a conservative couple who grows more strict after Cecelia's death and nearly draconian after the girls try to rebel. Eugenides portrays the elder Lisbons as simultaneously graceless in their severity—which climaxes in a total cloistering of the girls, pulling them from school and non-Sunday church activities—and genuine in their love for their troubled daughters. When an elderly Mrs. Lisbon, reflecting on the events decades later, tells her interviewers, "None of my daughters lacked for any love. We had plenty of love in our house," Eugenides gives readers no reason to doubt her, but his descriptions of the house highlight the family's corrosive isolationism (84). After they lock themselves in, the house begins to show "signs of uncleanliness," where "[d]ust balls lined the steps" and a "half-eaten sandwich sat atop the landing where someone felt too sad to finish it"; later "the soft decay of the house began to show up more clearly" when the boys noticed "how tattered the curtains had become, then realized we weren't looking at curtains at all but at a film of dirt, with spy holes wiped clean" and how "the gutters sagged" (50, 160). When Mr. Lisbon, the last member of the family to continue interacting with his neighbors, hides away as well, the narrator exclaims "[n]ow the house truly died...becoming one big coffin" (163). As this final phrase suggests, the narrative conflates removal, no matter how reasonable, with death: like Deleuze and Guattari's Oedipal triangle, these expectations limit individuals and fail to respond to them as infinite others. So while the Lisbons act out of love and concern for their children, their restrictions were ultimately unethical, destroying the inherent potentiality of life.

Against the totalizing by the elder Lisbons, the rest of the neighborhood experiences a brief being-toward-death, shocked into authentic responsibility by Cecelia's demise. Like Nancy, Roberto Esposito argues that wounds are inherent to community, as the root word "munus" can be translated as "debt" or "wound." If the wound is necessary for association, then the "'immune' is not simply different from the 'common' but is its opposite, what empties it out until it has been completely left bare, not only of its effects but also of its own presupposition; just as the 'immunization' project of modernity isn't directed only against specific *munera* (class obligations, ecclesial bonds, free services that weigh on men in the earlier phase) but against the very same law of their associated coexistence" (12). Just such improper wound occurs in the novel when the neighborhood comes together to remove the fence on which Cecelia was impaled after she threw herself from the window. The narrators describe the project as "the greatest show of common effort we could remember in our neighborhood, all those lawyers, doctors, and mortgage bankers locked arm in arm in the trench, with our mothers bringing out orange Kool-Aid, and for a moment our century was noble again." Indeed, the entire act becomes transformative, changing their "paper-pushing" fathers into "Marines hoisting the flag on Iwo Jima" (53–54). In fact, the act transforms nearly all aspects of neighborhood interactions: although the removal offended a number of property rights and assumptions—it was on the Lisbons' property, but the men of the suburb had to intrude on the adjacent yard to pull it out—the neighbors forego their own desires to care for this family. They secured legal permission, procured the necessary tools, and performed the removal all without expecting payment or even consulting Mr. Lisbon—the need exceeded the confines of propriety. Eugenides highlights the emphasis of ethics over propriety with the neighborhood boys' reactions, amazed that the truck that pulled out the fence "gave Mr. Bates the worst lawn job we'd ever seen" and that "Mr. Bates didn't scream or try to get the truck's license plate, nor did Mrs. Bates, who had once wept when we set off firecrackers in her state-fair tulips—they said nothing, and our parents said nothing." Although the boys' summary of the events—"for all their caretaking and bitching about crab-grass they didn't give a damn about lawns"—reads like a naïve joke on the part of the observers, it reveals a greater order (55). Certainly, the suburbanites of *The Virgin Suicides*, like those of many other fictions addressed in this study, care deeply for their lawns, associating them with a form of ethical selfhood; however, Cecelia's death was so great, so offensive to their notions of decorum that it shocked them into responsibility. In the remains of the old myth of a safe, idyllic neighborhood, the residents form a new myth based on concern for their hurting neighbor.

Initially, this new myth functions according to the heightened fictionality Nancy describes, which prioritizes the infinity of individuals over the static nature of firm figures. Early in the proceedings, the neighbors insist that the girls' death involves something that exceeds the simple understanding of the childhood myth, as demonstrated by the note one leaves for Mrs. Lisbon: "I don't know what you're feeling. I won't even pretend" (46). But as the situation progresses—rebellious daughter Lux's behavior goes more wild and the other girls eventually commit suicide—the neighbors seek an answer, collapsing the girls' excessive otherness into neat caricatures: the local intellectual attributes the loss to the "spiritual bankruptcy" of late capitalism, while another claims that the girls carried "the 'bad genes' that caused cancer, depression, and other diseases" (231, 247). The most pronounced example is Ms. Perl, a reporter who writes about "[t]he tony suburb known more for debutante parties than for funerals of debutante-aged girls" and "[t]he bright bouncy girls show little sign of the recent tragedy." Ms. Perl weaves the girls' lives into a palatable, and ultimately forgettable, narrative of "suicide pacts" and obsession with the dark lyrics of a Goth pop group (92). As indicated by the narration, Ms. Perl and her fellow journalists reduce the girls to simple figures, exploring "less and less…why the girls had killed themselves" and instead "talked about the girls' hobbies and academic awards" and other irrelevant facts (219).

In short, the parents diminish the exceedance and otherness of the girls, treating them like knowable cyphers while framing their deaths as something exceptional and unlikely. As Nancy warns, their rebuilt totalizing narrative precludes further interruption and thereby inhibits community by removing potential for singularity, a development Eugenides illustrates when he describes "people [speaking] of the Lisbon girls in the past tense…with the veiled wish that she would hurry up and get it over with" (219). The explanations given by various characters might be sensible—"Unfortunately, we had problems of our own"—but they also reveal a certain selfishness, a need to return to normal at the cost of another person's suffering (44). After being thrust into something unknowable by the girl's death, they ultimately decide to recreate the myth again, dismissing the Lisbons as an exception that ultimately has little bearing on their lives.

Conversely, the Lisbon girls remain an irresistible mystery for the neighborhood boys who watched them as youths and continue to obsess about them as adults. The now-grown boys serve as narrators for the novel, mixing their memories with archival evidence and information gleaned from interviews conducted in the decades following the Lisbon girls' deaths. Eugenides uses a narrative trick to illustrate the boys' community, relating the story through a collective first-person "we" while still referring to individual members of the group. By switching between the collective "we" and the singular individuals—"Tim Winer compared the tree to the last speaker of Manx" (242) and so on—Eugenides reveals the boys to be the type of community described by Esposito and Nancy, simultaneously joined together and individualized. The myth that connects them is the Lisbon girls, but even as they tell and retell the story, each definition or comprehensive explanation they devise ultimately falls short. So while, for example, the boys' "own knowledge of Cecilia kept growing after her death," it rarely expands beyond coincidental interactions in the neighborhood: "We had stood in line with her for smallpox vaccinations, had held polio sugar cubes under our tongues with her, had taught her to jump rope, to light snakes, had stopped her from picking her scabs on numerous occasions, and had cautioned her against touching her mouth to the drinking fountain at Three Mile Park" (37).

To be certain, there is an exploitative and invasive element to the boy's interest—"I'm going to watch those girls taking their showers," one declares—from which Eugenides never turns away; but this bravado often falls short when the Lisbons resist and exceed these simple figures (8). This tragic resistance is most pronounced in Lux Lisbon's sexual rebellion, in which she invites various men and boys from the city and adjacent neighborhood to have sex with her on the roof of her parents' house. Even though the boys gawk and leer, Lux's ferociousness becomes frightening and alien, forcing them to resort to ridiculous malapropisms to describe the actions they see—"we spoke of 'yodeling in the canyon' and 'tying the tube,' of 'groaning in the pit,' 'slipping the turtle's head,' and 'chewing the stinkweed'"—revealing their boasting to be a type of ignorance, a conscious unknowing (141). Similarly, their interest at times takes on a surreal romanticism, in which they become enamored with their "new mysterious suffering, perfectly silent, visible in the blue puffiness beneath their eyes or the way they would sometimes stop in mid stride, look down, and shake their heads as though disagreeing with life" (49). The boys ascribe unreal properties to the girls, associating them with Catholic chastity after finding a laminated picture of the Virgin Mary among Cecelia's belongings, and later translating the Lisbons' defense of the neighborhood trees as a type of pagan earthiness. They pour over the girls' belongings, using any excuse to enter the house as a means to shoplift certain objects and imbue them with an almost mystical quality; after one boy sneaks into the bathroom, he returns to his compatriots to describe the "deodorants and perfumes and scouring pads for rubbing away dead skin, and we were surprised to learn that there were no douches anywhere because we had thought girls douched every night like brushing their teeth" (8).

And yet, every time the boys believe they have comprehended the Lisbons, that they have defined them to the point of knowable objects for their group, the girls reveal their confounding nature. They interrupt the myth, never more vividly than when, using Morse code and pop song messages, they lure the boys to the Lisbon house to witness their suicides. As the narrator summarizes, "We had never known her. They had brought us here to find that out" (215). As they do for the neighborhood parents, the girls' death shatters the myth that has developed around them. But for the narrating boys, it is a constantly interrupting myth, a story told and retold.

And so despite the unquestionably dark nature of *The Virgin Suicides*, it ultimately moves toward a type of belonging only gestured toward in other suburban fictions, one where people respond to and care for one another, even as they maintain an unknowability that resists conscription into stultifying roles. Such a community is possible within suburbia, these novels contend, but only when a nostalgic myth of a perfectly knowable and stable neighborhood is discarded for a new myth. Against the paranoid antagonism or fearful ostracizing invited by the rhetoric of authenticity and exclusion, conceptions of childhood that dominate American suburbs, this new myth, based on the unknowable alterity of those in proximity—even one's child—requires a new narrative and new relation. The fictions studied here help us tell these new narratives and imagine new relations, relations of responsibility that admits both the infinity of and the need to care for those in proximity.

# WORKS CITED

Appiah, K. Anthony. *The Ethics of Identity.* Princeton: Princeton UP, 2005.
———. *Cosmopolitanism: Ethics in a World of Strangers.* New York: W. W. Norton & Co., 2006.
Agnew, John. "Home Ownership and Identity in Capitalist Societies." *Housing and Identity: Cross-Cultural Perspectives.* Ed. James S. Duncan. New York: Holmes & Meier Publishers, Inc. 1982 (60–97).
Andersson, Lars. "Burglary in Shady Hill and Sarsaparilla: The Politics of Community in White and Cheever." *Australian Literary Studies* 22.4 (2006): 432–442.
Arendt, Hannah. *The Human Condition.* Chicago: U of Chicago P, 1998.
Armstrong, Nancy. *Desire and Domestic Fiction: A Political History of the Novel.* Oxford: Oxford UP, 1987.
Aubry, Timothy. John Cheever and the Management of Middlebrow Misery. *Iowa Journal of Cultural Studies* 3 (2003): 64–83.
Bachelard, Gaston. *The Poetics of Space.* Trans. Maria Jolas. Boston: Beacon Press, 1964.
Baxandall, Rosalyn and Elizabeth Ewen. *Picture Windows: How the Suburbs Happened.* New York: Basic Books, 2000.
Beauregard, Robert A. *When America Became Suburban.* Minneapolis: U of Minnesota Press, 2006.
Beuka, Robert. *Suburbia Nation: Reading Suburban Landscape in Twentieth-Century American Fiction and Film.* New York: Palgrave Macmillan, 2004.
Bell, Daniel A. "Residential Community Associations: Community or Disunity?" *The Essential Communitarian Reader.* Ed. Amitai Etzioni. Lanham: Rowman & Littlefield Publishers, 1988 (167–176).

© The Author(s) 2016                                                            191
J. George, *Postmodern Suburban Spaces,*
DOI 10.1007/978-3-319-41006-7

Bell, Jeannine. *Hate thy Neighbor: Move-In Violence and the Persistence of Racial Segregation in American Housing.* New York: New York University Press, 2013.

Berube, Alan and Elizabeth Kneebone. "America's Shifting Suburban Battlegrounds." *Brookings.edu,* 16 Aug. 2013. Web. 18 March 2014.

Boswell, Marshall. *John Updike's Rabbit Tetralogy.* Columbia: U of Missouri P, 2001.

de Beauvoir, Simone. *The Second Sex.* Trans. and Ed. H. M. Parshley. New York: Vintage Books, 1989.

Bonastia, Christopher. *Knocking on the Door: The Federal Government's Attempt to Desegregate the Suburbs.* Princeton: Princeton UP, 2006.

Bonca, Cornel. "Don DeLillo's *White Noise*: The Natural Language of the Species." *College Literature* 23.2 (1996): 25–44.

Boxall, Peter. *Don DeLillo: The Possibility of Fiction.* London: Routledge, 2006.

Brauner, David. *Philip Roth.* Manchester: Manchester UP, 2007.

Bouvier, Luke. "Reading in Black and White: Space and Race in Linden Hills." *Gloria Naylor: Critical Perspectives Past and Present.* Eds. Henry Louis Gates, Jr. and K. A. Appiah. New York: Amistad, 1993 (140–151).

Boyle, T. C. *World's End.* New York: Penguin Books, 1987.

———. *East is East.* New York: Penguin Books, 1990.

———. *The Tortilla Curtain.* New York: Penguin Books, 1995.

Brooks, Richard R. W. and Carol M. Rose. *Saving the Neighborhood: Racially Restrictive Covenants, Law, and Social Norms.* Harvard UP, 2013.

Brooks, Van Wyck. *The Writer in America.* New York: Dutton, 1953.

Bruegmann, Robert. *Sprawl: A Compact History.* Chicago: U of Chicago P, 2005.

Bull, Leif. "A Realism of Internal Others: Richard Yates' *Revolutionary Road.*" *Realism's Others.* Eds. Geoffrey Baker and Eva Aldea. Newcastle upon Tyne: Cambridge Scholars Publishing, 2010 (209–226).

Byrne, Michael D. "Split-Level Enigma: John Cheever's *Bullet Park.*" *Studies in American Fiction* 20.1 (1992): 85–97.

"Canterwood Homeowners Association." *canterwood.org.* Web. 18 March 2014.

Carman, Taylor. *Heidegger's Analytic: Interpretation, Discourse, and Authenticity in Being and Time.* Cambridge: Cambridge UP, 2007.

Carpenter, John, dir. *Halloween.* Compass International, 1978.

Carroll, Hamilton. "Traumatic Patriarchy: Reading Gendered Nationalisms in Chang-rae Lee's *A Gesture Life.*" *Modern Fiction Studies* 51.3 (Fall 2005): 592–616.

Carton, Evan. "The Politics of Selfhood: Bob Slocum, T.S. Garp and Auto-American-Biography." *Novel: A Forum on Fiction* 20.1 (1986): 41–61.

Carver, Raymond. *Where I'm Calling From: Selected Stories.* New York: Vintage Contemporaries, 1988.

Castronovo, David and Steven Goldleaf. *Richard Yates*. New York: Twayne Publishers, 1996.

Caesar, Judith. "American Spaces in the Fiction of Jhumpa Lahiri." *English Studies in Canada* 31.1 (2005): 50–68.

Celello, Kristin. *Making Marriage Work: A History of Marriage and Divorce in the Twentieth-Century United States*. Chapel Hill: U of North Carolina P, 2009.

Chakraborty, Madhurima. "Adaptation and the Shifting Allegiances of the Indian Diaspora: Jhumpa Lahiri's and Mira Nair's *The Namesake(s)*." *Literature Film Quarterly* 42.4 (2014): 609–621.

Chakraborty, Mridula Nath. "Leaving No Remains: Death Among the Bengalis in Jhumpa Lahiri's Fiction." *The South Atlantic Quarterly* 110.4 (2011): 813–829.

Cheever, John. *Bullet Park*. New York: Vintage International, 1991. [1967].

———. *The Stories of John Cheever*. New York: Vintage International, 2000.

Chen, Tina. *Double Agency: Acts of Impersonation in Asian American Literature and Culture*. Stanford: Stanford UP, 2005.

Chernecky, William G. "Nostalgia Isn't What It Used to Be:' Isolation and Alienation in the Frank Bascombe Novels." *Perspectives on Richard Ford*. Ed. Huey Guagliardo. Jackson: UP of Mississippi, 2000 (157–176).

Chiu, Tzuhsiu Beryl. "Cultural Translation of a Subject in Transit: A Transcultural Critique of Xiangyin Lai's "The Translator" and Jhumpa Lahiri's *Interpreter of Maladies*." *Comparative Literature Studies* 52.1 (2015): 160–177.

Christian, Barbara. "Naylor's Geography: Community, Class and Patriarchy in The Women of Brewster Place and Linden Hills." *Gloria Naylor: Critical Perspectives Past and Present*. Eds. Henery Louis Gates Jr. and K. Anthony Appiah. New York: Amistad, 1993 (106–125).

Collins, Robert G. "From Subject to Object and Back Again: Individual Identity in John Cheever's Fiction." *Twentieth -Century Literature* 28.1 (1982): 1–13.

Coontz, Stephanie. *The Way We Never Were: American Families and the Nostalgia Trap*. New York: Basic Books, 1992.

———. *Marriage, a History: How Love Conquered Marriage*. New York: Penguin Books, 2006.

Curnutt, Kirk. "Teenage Wasteland: Coming-of-Age Novels in the 1980s and 1990s." *Critique* 43.1 (2001): 93–111.

Dame, Frederick William. Jean-Jacques Rousseau in *American Literature: Traces, Influence, Transformation, 1760–1860*. Frankfurt am Main: Peter Lang, 1996.

Deleuze, Gilles and Félix Guattari. *Anti-Oedipus: Capitalism and Schizophrenia*. Trans. Robert Hurley, Mark Seem, and Helen R. Lane. New York: Penguin Books, 1977.

———. *A Thousand Plateaus: Capitalism and Schizophrenia*. Trans. Brian Massumi. Minneapolis: U of Minnesota Press, 1987.

DeLillo, Don. *White Noise*. New York: Penguin Books, 1985.

Dewey, Joseph. *Beyond Greif and Nothing: A Reading of Don DeLillo*. Columbia: U of South Carolina P, 2006.

Digler, Robert Jay. *Neighborhood Politics: Residential Community Associations in American Governance*. New York: New York UP, 1992.

Dimock, Wai Chee. *Through Other Continents: American Literature Across Deep Time*. Princeton: Princeton UP, 2006.

Dines, Martin. *Gay Suburban Narratives in American and British Culture: Homecoming Queens*. London: Hampshire: Palgrave Macmillan, 2010.

Doane, Janice. "Women in *The World According to Garp*." *Gender Studies: New Directions in Feminist Criticism*. Bowling Green: Popular Press, 1986.

Donaldson, Scott. *The Suburban Myth*. New York: Columbia UP, 1969.

———. "Supermarket and Superhighway: John Cheever's America." *Virginia Quarterly Review* 62.4 (1986): 654–668.

Dougherty, Conor and Robbie Whelan. "Cities Outpace Suburbs in Growth." *The Wall Street Journal* 28 June 2012. Web. 18 March 2014.

Dupuy, Edward. "The Confessions of an Ex-Suicide: Relenting and Recovering in Richard Ford's *The Sportswriter*." *Perspectives on Richard Ford*. Ed. Huey Guagliardo. Jackson: UP of Mississippi, 2000 (71–82).

Emerson, Ralph Waldo. "The Over-Soul." *Emerson's Prose and Poetry*. New York: W.W. Norton & Co., 2001 (163–174).

Esposito, Roberto. *Communitas: The Origin and Destiny of Community*. Trans. Timothy Campbell. Stanford: Stanford UP, 2010.

Eugenides, Jeffrey. *The Virgin Suicides*. New York: Warner Books, 1993.

Fass, Paula S. "The Child-Centered Family? New Rules in Postwar America." *Reinventing Childhood after World War II*. Eds. Paula Fass and Michael Grossberg. Philadelphia: University of Pennsylvania Press, 2012 (1–18).

Feidler, Leslie A. *Love and Death in the American Novel*. Champaign: Dalkey Archive Press, 1997. [1960].

Fetterly, Judith. *The Resisting Reader: A Feminist Approach to American Literature*. Bloomington: Indiana UP, 1978.

Fogelson, Robert M. *Bourgeois Nightmares: Suburbia, 1870–1930*. New Haven: Yale University Press, 2005.

Ford, Richard. *The Sportswriter*. New York: Vintage Contemporaries, 1986.

———. *Independence Day*. New York: Vintage Contemporaries, 1995.

———. *The Lay of the Land*. New York: Vintage Contemporaries, 2006.

Forraro, Thomas J. "Whole Families Shopping at Night!" *New Essays on White Noise*. Ed. Frank Lentricchia. Cambridge: Cambridge UP, 1991 (15–38).

Foucault, Michel. *The History of Sexuality, Volume 1: An Introduction*. Trans. Robert Hurley. New York: Vintage Books, 1998. [1979].

Friedan, Betty. *The Feminine Mystique*. New York: W.W. Norton & Co., 2001. [1963].

Frey, William H. "Melting Pot Cities and Suburbs: Racial and Ethnic Change in Metro America in the 2000s." Washington: Metropolitan Policy Program at Brookings Institute, 2011. Web. 11 Sept, 2011.

Freund, David M. P. *Colored Property: State Policy and White Racial Politics in Suburban America*. Chicago: U of Chicago P, 2007.

Frow, John. "The Last Things Before the Last: Notes on *White Noise*." *South Atlantic Quarterly* 89.2 (1990): 413–429.

Gans, Herbert J. *The Levittowners: Ways of Life and Politics in a New Suburban Community*. New York: Vintage Books, 1967.

Gauthier, David J. *Martin Heidegger and Emmanuel Levinas and the Politics of Dwelling*. Lanham: Lexington Books, 2011.

Gleason, Paul Wilson. *Understanding T. C. Boyle*. Columbia: U of South Carolina P, 2009.

Greiner, Donald J. *John Updike's Novels*. Columbus: Ohio State UP, 1984.

———. *Adultery in the American Novel: Updike, James, and Hawthorne*. Columbia: University of South Carolina Press, 1985.

Goddard, Joseph. *Being American on the Edge: Penurbia and the Metropolitan Mind, 1945–2010*. New York: Palgrave, 2012.

Goddu, Teresa. "Reconstructing History in *Linden Hills*." *Gloria Naylor: Critical Perspectives Past and Present*. Eds. Henry Louis Gates, Jr. and K. A. Appiah. New York: Amistad, 1993 (215–230).

Guagliardo, Huey. "The Marginal People in the Novels of Richard Ford." *Perspectives on Richard Ford*. Ed. Huey Guagliardo. Jackson: UP of Mississippi, 2000 (3–32).

Guignon, Charles. *On Being Authentic*. London: Routledge, 2004.

Guinn, Matthew. "Into the Suburbs: Richard Ford's Sportswriter Novels and the Place of Southern Fiction." *South to a New Place; Region, Literature, Culture*. Eds. Suzanne W. Jones and Sharon Monteith. Baton Rouge: Louisianna State UP, 2002 (196–207).

Hand, Seán. *Emmanuel Levinas*. New York: Routledge, 2009.

Hansberry, Lorraine. *A Raisin in the Sun*. New York: Vintage International, 1994. [1959].

Hardt, Michael and Antonio Negri. *Multitude: War and Democracy in the Age of Empire*. New York: Penguin Books, 2004.

———. *Commonwealth*. Cambridge: Belknap Press, 2009.

Hassan, Ihab. "The Idea of Adolescence in American Fiction." *American Quarterly* 10.3 (1958): 312–324.

Hayden, Delores. *Building Suburbia: Green Fields and Urban Growth, 1820–2000*. New York: Vintage International, 2004.

Hegel, Georg Wilhelm Friedrich. *Elements of the Philosophy of Right*. Trans. and Ed. Allen W. Wood. Cambridge: U of Cambridge P, 1991.

Heidegger, Martin. *Being and Time*. Trans. John Macquarrie and Edward Robinson. New York: Harper Perennial Modern Thought, 1962.

———. *Basic Writings*. Ed. David Farrell Krell. New York: Harper Perennial Modern Thought, 1977.

Heinze, Ruediger. "A Diasporic Overcoat? Naming and Affection in Jhumpa Lahiri's *The Namesake*." *Journal of Postcolonial Writing* 43.2 (2007): 191–202.

Heller, Arno. "Simulacrum vs. Death: An American Dilemma in Don DeLillo's *White Noise*." *Simulacrum America: The USA and the Popular Media*. Eds. Elisabeth Kraus and Carolin Auer. Rochester: Camden House, 2000 (37–48).

Henry, DeWitt and Geoffrey Clark. "An Interview with Richard Yates." *Ploughshares* 1.3 (1972): 65–78.

Hill, Greg. *Rousseau's Theory of Human Association: Transparent and Opaque Communities*. New York: Palgrave Macmillan, 2006.

Honeyman, Susan. *Elusive Childhood: Impossible Representations in Modern Fiction*. Columbus: The Ohio State University Press, 2005.

Hooper, Tobe, dir. *Poltergeist*. Metro-Goldwyn-Meyer, 1982. Film.

Irving, John. *The World According to Garp*. New York: Ballantine Books, 1976.

Jackson, Kenneth T. *Crabgrass Frontier: The Suburbanization of the United States*. New York: Oxford UP, 1985.

James, Henry. *The Turn of the Screw*. Ed. Anthony Curtis. New York: Penguin Classics, 2003.

Jacobs, Harriet. *Incidents in the Life of a Slave Girl*. New York: Dover Publications, 2001.

Jacobson, Kristen J. *Neodomestic Fiction*. Columbus: The Ohio State UP, 2010.

Jerng, Mark C. "Recognizing the Transracial Adoptee: Adoption Life Stories and Chang-rae Lee's *A Gesture Life*." *MELUS* 31.2 (Summer 2006): 41–67.

Jurca, Catherine. *White Diaspora: The Suburb and the Twentieth-Century American Novel*. Princeton: Princeton University Press, 2001.

Kamp, Allen R. "The History Behind *Hansberry v. Lee*." *U.C. Davis Law Review* 20.41 (1986): 484–499.

Kant, Immanuel. *The Metaphysics of Morals*. Ed. Mary Gregor. Cambridge: Cambridge UP, 1996.

———. "Toward Perpetual Peace: A Philosophical Sketch." *Toward Perpetual Peace and Other Writings on Politics, Peace, and History*. Ed. Pauline Kleignfeld. and Trans. David L. Colclasure. New Haven: Yale UP, 2006.

Katz, Stanley. "Thomas Jefferson and the Right to Property in Revolutionary America." *Property Rights in American History: From the Colonial Era to the Present*. New York: Garland Publishers, 1997.

Kazin, Alred. "The Earthly City of the Jews." *Critical Essays on Phillip Roth*. Ed. Sanford Pinsker. Boston: G.K. Hall & Co., 1982 (97–116).

Keats, John. *The Crack in the Picture Window*. Boston: Houghton Mifflin Co., 1956.

Keating, W. Dennis. *The Suburban Racial Dilemma: Housing and Neighborhoods.* Philadelphia: Temple UP, 1994.

Keenhagan, Eric. "Reading Emerson, in Other Times: On a Politics of Solitude and an Ethics of Risk." *The Other Emerson.* Eds. Branka Arsić and Cary Wolfe. Minneapolis: U of Minnesota P, 2010 (167–200).

Kimmage, Michael C. "The Politics of the American Dream, 1980 to 2008." *The American Dream in the 21st Century.* Eds. Sandra L. Hanson and John Kenneth White. Philadelphia: Temple UP, 2011 (27–40).

King, Peter. *Private Dwelling: Contemplating the Use of Housing.* London: Routledge, 2004.

———. *In Dwelling.* London: Routledge, 2008.

Kirkman, Robert. "Rousseau in the Suburbs: Geography, Environment, and the Philosophical Tradition." *Earth Ways: Framing Geographical Meanings.* Eds. Gary Backhaus and John Murungi. Lanham: Lexington Books, 2004 (43–58).

Knapp, Kathy. "'Ain't No Friend Of Mine': Immigration Policy The Gated Community, And The Problem With The Disposable Worker In T. C. Boyle's *Tortilla Curtain.*" *Atenea* 28.2 (2008): 121–134.

———. *American Unexceptionalism*: The Everyman and the Suburban Novel after 9/11. Iowa City: U of Iowa P, 2014.

Kneebone, Elizabeth and Alan Berube. *Confronting Suburban Poverty in America.* Washington: Brookings Institution Press, 2013.

Klinkowitz, Jerome. *The New American Novel of Manners: The Fiction of Richard Yates, Dan Wakefield, and Thomas McGuane.* Athens: The U of Georgia P, 1986.

Kushner, David. *Levittown: Two Families, One Tycoon, and the Fight for Civil Rights in America's Legendary Suburb.* New York: Walker & Co., 2009.

Kunstler, James Howard. *The Geography of Nowhere: The Rise and Decline of America's Man-made Landscape.* New York: Touchstone Books, 1993.

Lahiri, Jhumpa. *The Namesake.* Boston: Mariner Books, 2003.

Lamb, Charles M. *Housing Segregation in Suburban America Since 1960.* Cambridge: Cambridge UP, 2005.

LaBute, Neil, dir. *Lakeview Terrace.* Sony, 2008. Film.

Lee, Chang-rae. *Native Speaker.* New York: Riverhead Books, 1995.

———. *A Gesture Life.* New York: Riverhead Books, 1999.

———. *Aloft.* New York: Riverhead Books, 2004.

———. *The Surrendered.* New York: Riverhead Books, 2010.

Lee, Sue-Im. *A Body of Individuals: The Paradox of Community in Contemporary Fiction.* Columbus: The Ohio State University Press, 2009.

Leonard, John. "Evil Comes to Suburbia." *The New York Times* (April 29, 1969): 43.

Levin, Ira. *The Stepford Wives.* New York: HarperTouch, 2000. [1972].

Levinas, Emmanuel. *Totality and Infinity: An Essay on Exteriority*. Trans. Alphonso Lingis. Pittsburgh: Duquesne UP, 1969.

———. *Otherwise than Being, Or Beyond Essence*. Trans. Alphonso Lingis. Pittsburgh: Duquesne UP, 1993. [1974].

———. *Difficult Freedom: Essays on Judaism*. Trans. Seán Hand. Baltimore: Johns Hopkins UP, 1990.

Lewis, Sinclair. *Babbitt*. Mineola: Dover Thrift Editions, 2003. [1922].

Locke, John. *Second Treatise of Government*. Ed. C. B. Macpherson. Indianapolis: Hackett Publishing Inc., 1980. [1690].

———. *An Essay Concerning Human Understanding*. New York: Penguin Classics, 1997.

Loewen, James W. "Dreaming in Black and White." *The American Dream in the 21st Century*. Eds. Sandra L. Hanson and John Kenneth White. Philadelphia: Temple UP, 2011 (59–76).

Maltby, Paul. "The Romantic Metaphysics of Don DeLillo." *Contemporary Literature* 37.2 (1996): 258–278.

May, Elaine Tyler. *Homeward Bound: American Families in the Cold War Era*. New York: Basic Book Publishers, 1988.

McGinn, Daniel. *House Lust: America's Obsession With Our Homes*. New York: Doubleday, 2008.

McGuire, Ian. *Richard Ford and the Ends of Realism*. Iowa City: U of Iowa P, 2015.

McKenzie, Evan. *Privatopia: Homeowner Associations and the Rise of Private Government*. New Haven: Yale UP, 1996.

McKeon, Michael. *The Secret History of Domesticity*. Baltimore: Johns Hopkins UP, 2005.

McLennan, Rachael. *Adolescence, America, and Postwar Fiction: Developing Figures*. New York: Palgrave Macmillan, 2009.

Meisenhelder, Susan. "'The Whole Picture' in Gloria Naylor's Mama Day." *The Critical Response to Gloria Naylor*. Eds. Sharon Felton and Michelle C. Loris. Westport: Greenwood Press, 1997 (113–128).

Meyerson, Gregory. "*The Tortilla Curtain* and *The Ecology of Fear*." *Contracorriente: A Journal of Social History and Literature* 2.1 (2004): 67–91.

Miller, Chuck. "Dealing with Difficult People." *HOAPulse.com*. Web. 18 March 2014.

———. "Going Rogue." *HOAPulse.com*. Web. 18 March 2014.

Mintz, Stephen. "The Changing Face of Children's Culture." *Reinventing Childhood after World War II*. Eds. Paula Fass and Michael Grossberg. Philadelphia, University of Pennsylvania Press, 2012 (38–50).

Monahan, Michael. "The Person as Signatory: Contractarian Social Theory at Work in Suburbia." *Listening: Journal of Religion and Culture* 38.2 (2003): 116–135.

Moody, Rick. *The Ice Storm*. Boston: Back Bay Books, 1994.

Moraru, Christian. "The Other, the Namesake: Cosmopolitan Onomastics in Change-rae Lee's *A Gesture Life*." *Names* 55.1 (2007): 17–36.

Moreno, Michael P. "Consuming the Frontier Illusion: The Construction of Suburban Masculinity in Richard Yates's Revolutionary Road." *Iowa Journal of Cultural Studies* 3 (2003): 84–95.

Moyn, Samuel. *Origins of the Other: Emmanuel Levinas Between Revelation and Ethics*. Ithica: Cornell UP, 2005.

Murphy, Bernice M. *The Suburban Gothic in American Popular Culture*. New York: Palgrave Macmillan, 2009.

Nancy, Jean-Luc. *The Inoperative Community*. Ed. Peter Connor. Minneapolis: U of Minnesota P, 1991.

Nadel, Alan. *Containment Culture: American Narratives, Postmodernism, and the Atomic Age*. Durham: Duke University Press, 1995.

Naylor, Gloria. *Linden Hills*. New York: Penguin Books, 1985.

Naylor, Gloria and Toni Morrison. "A Conversation." *Conversations with Gloria Naylor*. Ed. Maxine Lavon Montgomery. University Press of Mississippi, 2004 (10–38).

Neary, John. *Something and Nothingness: The Fiction of John Updike and John Fowl*. Carbondale: Southern Illinois UP, 1992.

Nedelsky, Jennifer. *Private Property and the Limits of American Constitutionalism*. Chicago: U of Chicago P, 1990.

Olster, Stacey. *"White Noise." The Cambridge Companion to Don DeLillo*. Ed. John N. Duvall. Cambridge: Cambridge UP, 2008 (79–93).

Oliver, J. Eric. *Democracy in Suburbia*. Princeton: Princeton UP, 2001.

Parrish, Timothy. "Roth and Ethnic Identity." *The Cambridge Companion to Philip Roth*. Ed. Timothy Parrish. Cambridge: Cambridge UP, 2007 (127–141).

Pateman, Carole. *The Sexual Contract*. Stanford: Stanford UP, 1988.

Pifer, Ellen. *Demon or Doll: Images of the Child in Contemporary Writing and Culture*. Charlottesville: University Press of Virginia, 2000.

Plath, James. *Conversations with John Updike*. Jackson: University of Mississippi Press, 1994.

Purcell, Michael. *Levinas and Theology*. Cambridge: Cambridge UP, 2006.

Putnam, Robert D. *Bowling Alone: The Collapse and Revival of American Community*. New York: Simon & Schuster, 2000.

Robinson, Sally. "'Unyoung, Unpoor, Unblack': John Updike and the Construction of Middle American Masculinity." *Modern Fiction Studies* 44.2 (1998): 331–363.

Roediger, David R. *Working Toward Whiteness: How America's Immigrants Became White: The Strange Journey from Ellis Island to the Suburbs*. New York: Basic Books, 2006.

Romines, Ann. *The Home Plot: Women, Writing, and Domestic Ritual*. Amherst: U of Massachusetts P, 1992.

Ronald, Richard. *The Ideology of Home Ownership: Homeowner Societies and the Role of Housing*. New York: Palgrave Macmillan, 2008.

Rose, Jacqueline. *The Case of Peter Pan, or the Impossibility of Children's Fiction*. Philadelphia: University of Pennsylvania Press, 1993. [1984].

Roth, Philip. *Goodbye, Columbus and Five Short Stories*. New York: Vintage International, 1987. [1959].

———. *American Pastoral*. New York: Vintage International, 1997.

———. *Nemesis*. Boston: Houghton Mifflin Harcourt, 2010.

Rousseau, Jean-Jacques. *Émile: or, On Education*. Trans. Allan Bloom. New York: Basic Books, 1979.

———. "Discourse on the Origin of Inequality." *The Basic Political Writings*. Trans. and Ed. Donald A. Cress. Indianapolis: Hackett Publishing Company, 1987 (25–110).

———. "On the Social Contract." *The Basic Political Writings*. Trans. and Ed. Donald A. Cress. Indianapolis: Hackett Publishing Company, 1987 (141–227).

———. *Reveries of the Solitary Walker*. Trans. Russell Gouldbourne. Oxford: Oxford UP, 2011.

Royal, Derek Parker. "Pastoral Dreams and National Identity in *American Pastoral* and *I Married a Communist*." *Philip Roth: New Perspectives on an American Author*. Westport: Praeger Publishers, 2005 (185–208).

Rubenstein, Roberta. *Home Matters: Longing and Belonging, Nostalgia and Mourning in Women's Fiction*. New York: Palgrave, 2001.

Ruhlman, Michael. *House: A Memoir*. New York: Viking, 2005.

Rybczynski, Witold. *Home: A Short History of an Idea*. New York: Pocket Books, 2001.

Sandiford, Kieth. "Gothic and Intertextual Constructions in Linden Hills." *Gloria Naylor: Critical Perspectives Past and Present*. Eds. Henry Louis Gates, Jr. and K. A. Appiah. New York: Amistad, 1993 (195–214).

Seigan, Bernard H. *Property Rights: From the Magna Carta to the Fourteenth Amendment*. Piscataway: Transaction Publishers, 2001.

Schmitt, Carl. *The Concept of the Political*. Trans. George Schwab. Chicago: U of Chicago P, 1996.

Schultz, David Andrew. *Property, Power, and American Democracy*. New Brunswick: Transaction Publishers, 1992.

Schäfer-Wünsche, Elisabeth. "Borders and Catastrophes: T. C. Boyle's Californian Ecology." *Space in America: Theory, History, and Culture*. Eds. Klaus Benesch and Kerstin Schmidt. New York: Rodopi Press, 2005 (401–420).

Shain, Barry Alan. *The Myth of American Individualism: The Protestant Origins of American Political Thought*. Princeton: Princeton UP, 1994.

Shamir, Milette. *Inexpressible Privacy: The Interior Life of Antebellum American Culture*. Philadelphia: U of Penn Press, 2006.

"The Shelter." *The Twilight Zone*. *Season 3*. Writ. Rod Sterling. Dir. Lamont Johnson. CBS, 1961. DVD.

Simmons, J. *Aaron and David Wood. Kierkegaard and Levinas: Ethics, Politics, and Religion*. Bloomington: Indiana UP, 2008.

Singer, Audrey. "Twenty-First-Century Gateways: An Introduction." *Twenty-First-Century Gateways: Immigratant Incorporation in Suburban America*. Eds. Audrey Singer, Susan W. Hardwick, and Caroline B. Brettell. Washington: Brookings Institution Press, 2008.

Smith, Wendell. "The Life of the Writer: Lunch with Richard Ford." *Conversations with Richard Ford*. Ed. Huey Guagliardo. Jackson: UP of Mississippi, 2001 (49–57).

Spacks, Patricia Meyers. *The Adolescent Idea: Myths of Youth in the Adult Imagination*. New York: Basic Books, 1983.

Spigel, Lynn. *Welcome to the Dreamhouse: Popular Media and Postwar Suburbs*. Durham: Duke University Press, 2011.

Stein, Allen F. *After the Vows Were Spoken: Marriage in American Literary Realism*. Columbus: Ohio State UP, 1984.

Tanner, Tony. *Adultery in the Novel*. Baltimore: Johns Hopkins UP, 1979.

Tate, Claudia. *Domestic Allegories of Political Desire: The Black Heroine's Text at the Turn of the Century*. Oxford: Oxford UP, 1992.

Taylor, Charles. *Sources of the Self: The Making of the Modern Identity*. Cambridge: Harvard UP, 1989.

Teaford, Jon C. *The American Suburb: The Basics*. New York: Routledge, 2008.

Tolchin, Karen. R. *Part Blood, Part Ketchup: Coming of Age in American Literature and Film*. Lanham: Lexington Books, 2007.

Tompkins, Jane. *Sensational Designs: The Cultural Work of American Fiction, 1790–1860*. Oxford: Oxford UP, 1986.

Updike, John. *Rabbit, Run*. New York: Fawcett Books, 1960.

———. *Assorted Prose*. New York: Alfred A. Knopf, 1965.

———. *Couples*. New York: Fawcett Books, 1969.

———. *Rabbit Redux*. New York: Alfred A. Knopf, 1971.

———. *Rabbit is Rich*. New York: Fawcett Books, 1981.

———. *Rabbit at Rest*. New York: Alfred A. Knopf, 1990.

———. *Licks of Love*. New York: Alfred A. Knopf, 2000.

Vogel, Lawrence. *The Fragile "We": Ethical Implications of Heidegger's "Being and Time."* Evanston: Northwestern UP, 1994.

Waldron, Jeremy. *The Right to Private Property*. Oxford: Oxford UP, 1990.

———. "Who is my Neighbor? – Proximity and Humanity." *The Monist* 86 (2003): 333–354.

Walch, Timothy. *Uncommon Americans: The Lives and Legacies of Herbert and Lou Henry Hoover*. Westport: Greenwood Publishing Group, 2003.

Walker, Elinor Ann. *Richard Ford*. New York: Twayne Publishers, 2000.

Watt, Ian. *The Rise of the Novel: Studies in Defoe, Richardson, and Fielding*. Berkeley: U of California P, 1957.

Webb, Frank J. *The Garies and Their Friends*. Baltimore: Johns Hopkins UP, 1997.

Weiss, Jessica. *To Have and To Hold: Marriage, the Baby Boom, and Social Change*. Chicago: U of Chicago P, 2000.

Wihite, Keith. "John Cheever's Shady Hill, Or: How I Learned to Stop Worrying and Love the Suburbs." *Studies in American Fiction* 34.2 (2006): 215–239.

———. "Contested Terrain: The Suburbs as Region." *American Literature* 84.3 (2012): 617–644.

Williamson, Thad. *Sprawl, Justice, and Citizenship: The Civic Costs of the American Way of Life*. Oxford: Oxford UP, 2010.

White, John Kenneth and Sandra L. Hanson. "Introduction: The Making and Persistence of the American Dream." *The American Dream in the 21st Century*. Eds. Sandra L. Hanson and John Kenneth White. Philadelphia: Temple UP, 2011 (1–16).

Wilson, Matthew. "The Rabbit Tetralogy: From Solitude to Society to Solitude Again." *Modern Fiction Studies* 37.1 (Spring 1991): 3–24.

Wolin, Richard. *The Heidegger Controversy: A Critical Reader*. Boston: MIT Press, 1993.

Veggian, Henry. *Understanding Don DeLillo*. Columbia: U of South Carolina P, 2015.

Yates, Richard. *Revolutionary Road*. New York: Vintage Contemporaries, 2000. [1961].

"You Can't Miss the Bear." *Weeds: Season One*. Writ. Jenji Kohan. Dir. Brian Dannelly. Showtime, 2006. DVD.

Žižek, Slavoj. *The Desert of the Real*. London: Verso, 2002.

———. "Smashing the Neighbor's Face." lacan.com. 2005. Web. 05 Jan 2012.

———. "*Love Thy Neighbor? No Thanks!*" *The Essential Žižek: The Plague of Fantasies*. London: Verso, 2008 (55–106).

Žižek, Slavoj, Eric L. Santer, and Kenneth Reinhard. *The Neighbor: Three Inquiries in Political Theology*. Chicago: U of Chicago P, 2005.

# INDEX[1]

**A**

affairs, 56, 114, 122, 131–3, 136, 141, 142, 153. *See also* infidelity

Agamben, Gorgio, 28, 29

The American dream, 32, 37, 140, 164–9, 177, 178, 181n5

Appiah, Kwame Anthony, 18, 19, 40n13, 102

Arendt, Hannah, 36, 82, 98, 100, 103, 106, 117n11, 117n12, 121

authenticity, 4, 5, 13, 17–19, 27, 74, 93, 102, 131–3, 189. *See also* selfhood

*The Awakening*, 116n4, 160n11


**B**

Bangladesh, 184

Bengali. *See* Bangladesh

Beuka, Robert, 31

bildungsroman, 138

Blanchot, Maurice, 29, 40n18

Boyle, T. C., 36, 82, 87–92, 116n5, 116n7, 130

Brooks, Van Wyck, 160n9

Burns, Charles, 86, 140

Butler, Judith, 176


**C**

Carver, Raymond, 94, 103, 104, 107, 140

Cheever, John, 4, 36, 63, 64, 116n9, 117n10

  *Bullet Park*, 36, 92–103, 130

  *The Swimmer*, 63

civil rights, 35, 46, 51, 165

The Cold War, 2, 10, 31, 125, 163, 164

contracts, covenants, and regulations, 8, 10, 12–15, 46, 184

contractualism, 11, 15, 17, 22, 51, 58, 60, 61, 76, 81, 88, 89, 184

Coontz, Stephanie, 126, 127, 184

Coover, Robert, 86, 140

[1] Note: Page numbers with "n" denote notes.

© The Author(s) 2016

J. George, *Postmodern Suburban Spaces*,

DOI 10.1007/978-3-319-41006-7

cosmopolitanism, 23, 37, 40n13, 95, 168, 172–8
covenants, conditions, and restrictions (CC&Rs). *See* contracts, covenants, and regulations

**D**
de Beauvoir, Simone, 127
de Certeau, Michel, 27
Deleuze, Gilles, 28, 37, 121, 122, 145, 151, 153, 158n1, 185
DeLillo, Don, 5, 36, 123, 139, 147, 151, 152
Department of Housing and Urban Development (HUD), 47
Derrida, Jacques, 40n14
  "*On Hospitality*", 24, 25
  *The Politics of Friendship*, 28
Detroit, 47, 48, 164, 183
Dimock, Wai-Chee, 171
domesticity, 27, 125, 128, 147, 157, 174
DuBois, W.E.B., 176

**E**
Emerson, Ralph Waldo, 12, 138, 165
Esposito, Roberto, 29, 36, 39n7, 82, 171, 185
ethics, 19, 22, 24–6, 29, 34, 35, 37, 61, 62, 66, 82, 94, 101, 104–7, 114, 118n15, 151, 159n4, 159n5, 186
Euginides, Jeffery, 183, 184, 187, 188

**F**
Federal Highway Act, 6, 9
Federal Housing Administration, 8, 49
Fetterly, Judith, 129
Fiedler, Leslie, 129, 138

Ford, Richard, 5, 36, 45, 52–60, 76, 77n3, 77n4, 160n12, 180
Foucault, Michel, 127, 176
Franzen, Jonathan, 31, 94, 167
Friedan, Betty, 77n2, 128

**G**
Gans, Herbert J., 166
gated communities, 6, 33, 48, 116n8
ghost doctrines, 46, 47, 51
G.I. Bil. *See* 1944 Serviceman's Readjustment Act
Giuatari, Felix. *See* Deleuze, Gilles

**H**
*Halloween* (film), 86, 139
Hansberry, Lorraine, 45, 71
Hardt, Michael, 28, 29, 145, 151, 161n18
Hegel, G. F. W, 127, 158n4, 159n5, 184
Heidegger, Martin, 17, 18, 20, 25, 26, 36, 39n8, 39n9, 82, 98, 100, 103, 106, 117n12, 117n13, 149, 184
HOAs. *See* Home Owners Associations (HOAs)
Hobbes, Thomas, 12, 13, 85, 87, 141, 142
Home Owners Associations (HOAs), 9–11, 13, 14, 33, 38n3, 40n19, 45, 166, 184
hospitality, 5, 22–7, 29, 30, 33, 34, 39–40n11, 40n12, 40n14, 45, 46, 51, 53–5, 60, 65, 67, 68, 73, 82, 92, 94, 101, 103, 104, 106, 110, 123, 134, 136, 147, 150, 153, 177, 181, 183
The Housing and Community Development Act, 6
HUD. *See* Department of Housing and Urban Development (HUD)

**I**

infidelity, 72, 153. *See also* affairs
integration, 43, 44, 47, 48, 50, 60,
    69, 86, 169
Irving, John, 5, 36, 123, 140, 141,
    143–7, 160n14, 168

**J**

Jackson, Kenneth T, 8–10, 49, 83,
    163, 166
Jameson, Fredric, 27, 35
Jefferson, Thomas, 12, 85, 166
Jen, Gish, 4, 5, 37, 165, 178–80
Jewish identity, 50, 168–72, 178–80
Jurca, Catherine, 2, 9, 30–3, 86

**K**

Kant, Immanuel, 23, 24, 36, 40n12,
    40n13, 85–7, 90, 91, 103, 106,
    115n3, 116n6, 127, 158–9n4
Khrushchev, Nikita, 37, 128, 163
Kraemer, Shelley v., 44

**L**

Lahiri, Jhumpa, 165, 172–8, 180
*Lakeview Terrace* (film), 43, 44,
    77n1
Lee, Chang-rae, 5, 31, 36, 45, 51, 60,
    63, 64, 76–8n6, 77n5, 94,
    116n9, 160n8, 167, 180
Levinas, Emmanuel, 25–7, 29, 36,
    40n14–16, 56, 58, 64, 82, 89,
    105–7, 111, 112, 118–19n17,
    118n15, 118n16, 152, 176
Levittown, 6, 9, 50, 84
Levitt & Sons, 50, 84, 164
Lewis, Sinclair, 86
Locke, John, 12, 36, 85–8, 90, 91,
    103, 115n3, 116n6

**M**

Making Home Affordable Act, 6
Martin, Trayvon, 48, 76
McBride, Renisha, 48, 76
McCarthy, Eugene, 84–6, 164
Morrison, Toni, 16n4, 70, 73, 74, 139

**N**

Nancy, Jean-Luc, 28, 29, 37, 40n18,
    64, 123, 149, 151, 152, 161n18,
    161n19, 184–7
Naylor, Gloria, 4, 36, 38n4, 44, 51,
    69, 70, 72–4, 76, 78n8, 78n9,
    79n10, 167
Negri, Antonio. *See* Hardt, Michael
neighbor(s), 1, 4, 7, 8, 14, 15, 17, 19,
    22, 27, 28, 33, 36, 45, 46, 50, 51,
    53, 54, 60–3, 68, 76, 81–119, 171,
    172, 175, 176, 179–81, 183, 186
*A Nightmare on Elm Street* (film), 86,
    139
1944 Serviceman's Readjustment Act, 6
Nixon, Richard, 9, 10, 37, 128, 163,
    164, 166, 180

**O**

O'Brien, Tim, 116n4, 140

**P**

paranoia, 90, 141, 145, 189
Percy, Walker, 52
*Poltergeist*, 123, 139
pornography, 123, 131, 132, 147

**R**

racial covenants, 8, 35, 44, 46, 60, 166
Roediger, David, 7
Romney, George, 47, 48

Roth, Philip, 37, 165, 168–72, 178, 180, 182n10

Rousseau, Jean-Jacques, 12–15, 17, 29, 39n6, 39n7, 74, 85, 126

**S**

St. Louis, 164

Schmitt, Carl, 35, 44, 48–53, 61, 62, 64, 66, 90, 105, 143

selfhood(s), 11–13, 15, 17, 22, 23, 64, 73, 75, 76, 94, 109, 114, 132, 138, 148, 174, 177, 178, 186

singularity, 28–30, 92, 138, 151, 187

social contract theory, 10, 12–14, 16, 29, 39n6, 45, 51, 53, 82, 85, 101, 102, 126, 127, 159n5

stranger(s), 23, 24, 31, 40n11, 49, 60, 92–4, 104, 105, 113, 121–61, 174

**T**

Taylor, Charles, 18, 39n10

Thoreau, Henry David, 12, 116n4, 165

*The Twilight Zone*, 81

**U**

Updike, John, 2, 5, 36, 52, 82, 94, 107–9, 111, 113, 116n9, 118n17, 119n20

**W**

Wilson, Sloan, 2, 130

World War II, 9, 10, 46, 50, 64, 83, 121, 128, 170

**X**

xenophobia, 74

**Y**

Yates, Richard, 1–4, 10, 15, 16, 19, 21, 25, 38n1

**Z**

Žižek, Slavoj, 118n15

Printed by Books on Demand, Germany